A HISTORY OF GARDENING, 1800-1960

A History of Gardening, 1800-1960

Transforming Gardens Across Two Centuries

Angela Youngman

PEN & SWORD HISTORY

AN IMPRINT OF PEN & SWORD BOOKS LTD.
YORKSHIRE · PHILADELPHIA

First published in Great Britain in 2025 by
Pen & Sword History
An imprint of
Pen & Sword Books Ltd
Yorkshire - Philadelphia

Copyright © Angela Youngman, 2025

ISBN 978 1 39908 089 7

The right of Angela Youngman to be identified as the Author of this work has been asserted by her in accordance with the Copyright, Designs and Patents Act 1988.

A CIP catalogue record for this book is available from the British Library.

All rights reserved. No part of this book may be reproduced, transmitted, downloaded, decompiled or reverse engineered in any form or by any means, electronic or mechanical including photocopying, recording or by any information storage and retrieval system, without permission from the Publisher in writing. NO AI TRAINING: Without in any way limiting the Author's and Publisher's exclusive rights under copyright, any use of this publication to "train" generative artificial intelligence (AI) technologies to generate text is expressly prohibited. The Author and Publisher reserve all rights to license uses of this work for generative AI training and development of machine learning language models.

Typeset in INDIA by IMPEC eSolutions
Printed and bound in UK by CPI Group (UK) Ltd, Croydon, CR0 4YY

The Publisher's authorised representative in the EU for product safety is Authorised Rep Compliance Ltd., Ground Floor, 71 Lower Baggot Street, Dublin D02 P593, Ireland
www.arccompliance.com

For a complete list of Pen & Sword titles please contact

PEN & SWORD BOOKS LIMITED
47 Church Street, Barnsley, South Yorkshire, S70 2AS, England
E-mail: enquiries@pen-and-sword.co.uk
Website: www.pen-and-sword.co.uk

or

PEN AND SWORD BOOKS
1950 Lawrence Rd, Havertown, PA 19083, USA
E-mail: uspen-and-sword@casematepublishers.com
Website: www.penandswordbooks.com

Contents

Introduction		vii
Chapter 1	The Gardeners – Training and Careers	1
Chapter 2	The Head Gardener	18
Chapter 3	The Rise of Female Gardeners	30
Chapter 4	Urban Housing and Gardens	49
Chapter 5	Garden Styles	61
Chapter 6	Transforming Cities and Urban Areas	87
Chapter 7	Horticultural Societies and Shows	97
Chapter 8	Commercialisation	111
Chapter 9	Plant Hunting and its Impact on Gardens	134
Chapter 10	Technological Innovation	146
Chapter 11	Workhouse Gardening	162
Chapter 12	The Allotment Movement	173
Chapter 13	Garden Tourism	183
Chapter 14	The First World War and Its Impact	196
Chapter 15	Between the Wars	201
Chapter 16	The Second World War and a Different Approach	214
Chapter 17	Post-War Gardening and the Arrival of Garden Centres	225
Conclusion		232
Resources		236
Index		238

Introduction

Gardening has always played a major role in human life, with houses frequently possessing an area in which vegetables, herbs and some flowers could be grown. There is evidence of a steady development in gardening since the early seventeenth century, but what made the nineteenth and early twentieth centuries different was the sheer speed and size of the transformation that took place. Cultivating a garden was no longer just for sustenance, but for pleasure, fuelled by the wider changes in society that were taking place such as industrialisation, mechanisation, transport, leisure time and the role of women.

This was a period when the concept of gardening as a leisure activity developed, along with a vast array of changes in garden design, plant breeding, horticultural shows and societies, mass market tourism and even the way in which plants were bought and sold. Higher levels of literacy and disposable income made it possible for people across all sectors of society to benefit. From the royal family to factory workers, a shared interest in gardening became apparent.

For entrepreneurs, it was an ideal opportunity to take advantage of the demand for information, search out exotic plants in far-flung countries, experiment with technology and create major companies whose influence on the sector has been remarkable. Increasing overseas travel by ordinary people led to the arrival of new concepts and exotic landscapes, such as the Biddulph Grange Chinese Garden in Staffordshire, which includes a lake, pavilion and bridge, and Ella Christie's Japanese Garden in Scotland.

For centuries, garden styles had been dominated by what was being undertaken on the big estates, through the activities of landscapers such as Lancelot 'Capability' Brown. Throughout the nineteenth and early twentieth centuries, there was a major change in focus with attention spreading to the needs of smaller gardens, especially in towns and suburbs. This led to the development of new garden styles ranging from carpet bedding to cottage gardens, rockeries, stumperies, greenhouse gardening and allotments. Many of the most well-known and enduring seed varieties were introduced during this period, including frilly-edged sweet peas, purple sprouting broccoli, snowball turnips, 'Painted Lady' runner beans, 'Tom Thumb' lettuce and 'All the Year Round' lettuce.

Innovation and experimentation led to the creation of countless new products such as the arrival of greenhouses and lawnmowers. Considerable fortunes were made by people like Joseph Paxton, who had begun his career as a gardener's apprentice. New standards were established in terms of training, of products, plants and seeds – this was an era of garden transformation on a major scale. Professional training became available in colleges, leading ultimately to the first degree in horticulture. From once being merely servants, gardeners became well-regarded professionals in their own right, able to take advantage of an ever-expanding range of career opportunities from plant-hunting to writing. Magazines appeared in vast numbers, along with books and radio programmes designed to impart knowledge to a continuously growing audience.

This was the era when major brands were created, names that have stood the test of time such as Suttons Seeds, along with a vast heritage of public parks, garden suburbs and garden cities. For women, it was an era of change, offering new opportunities which were eagerly taken up by ladies such as Jane Loudon, Gertrude Jekyll, and Vita Sackville-West. The challenges posed by two world wars brought yet more changes and with the advent of garden centres and containerised plants during the 1950s, the transformation of gardening into a mass market industry was complete.

Chapter 1

The Gardeners – Training and Careers

Working in a garden was generally regarded as a good occupation in the nineteenth and early twentieth centuries, despite the long hours. It offered considerable potential career opportunities, which expanded even further as the nineteenth century progressed.

Demand for suitably skilled staff was high. Wealthy landowners required high quality staff capable of running their estates and kitchen gardens as well as caring for desirable exotic flowers and produce. Equally keen were the ranks of the industrialists and entrepreneurs who were increasingly investing in land and property, while in the cities and towns the burgeoning middle class were keen to create their own gardens. Alongside these were countless nurserymen and seed companies supplying the plants, seeds and sundries essential to any garden. For men such as Joseph Paxton and John Claudius Loudon, it proved to be a very lucrative career in which fortunes could be made.

Sons frequently followed fathers into the profession. It was regarded as a good career option, providing training, steady employment and accommodation. They would have learned basic tasks from a very early age, helping their father with simple jobs like weeding. In addition, jobs were generally obtained via word-of-mouth recommendation, so it would have been much easier for the son of a gardener to start working full time for his father, or employer, especially on big estates where large numbers of staff were needed within the pleasure and kitchen gardens. There was a strict hierarchy within these gardens, with the garden boys at the bottom and the head gardener at the top. In between were the apprentices, the journeymen, and assistant or under gardeners, who were often responsible for a specific function such as the hot houses, tree care, propagation, and vegetables. They were also responsible for providing the house with appropriate flowers, as well as fruit and vegetables for meals.

Whatever the job, working hours were long, often starting at dawn and finishing late at night, six days a week. This did not include the time needed to collect tools or to clean them afterwards. Time keeping was strict – a bell was rung for the start and end of the day, or to announce mealtimes. Staff had thirty minutes for breakfast and one hour for lunch. The cook at the big house normally provided the gardeners with a hot meal for lunch, while in the evening it was the gardeners' responsibility and usually involved a slice of bread and jam; they were not allowed to use produce from the garden. Clothing was simple: boots, thick trousers tied beneath the knee, an apron with pockets, jacket and a hat.

Once a month every gardener was responsible for bothy duty, which involved cleaning, doing the washing up, caring for plants overnight in the greenhouses and gardens and making sure that the correct temperatures were maintained. This might involve stoking boilers, checking pumps, adjusting ventilators or covering plants when temperatures fell too low. Once the day was over, every trainee from garden boy to under gardener was expected to study by candlelight, memorising plants and gardening techniques. There were strict rules to follow: forgetting to wash the greenhouse glass could result in a fine; failing to compete their duties could result in more fines; while at Chatsworth, gardeners were told that 'if anyone gathers any kind of vegetable, fruits, flowers, specimens or cuttings of any plants without permission, he will be fined five shillings. If repeated, discharged.' Being discharged was a serious penalty because it ruined the gardener's reputation and made it extremely difficult to find work elsewhere, since references were always required.

Living and working conditions could be hard. John Clare, the poet, spent some time working as a gardener's apprentice at Burghley House, near Stamford. It was not a pleasant situation, however, as all the staff were unhappy and the head gardener 'foul tempered'. Clare and the foreman eventually fled from the site, escaping out of a window to freedom. A working day could sometimes begin as early as 4am and last until 5 or 6pm, with short breaks for breakfast and lunch. Most had to take turns working on Sundays, ensuring that plant care was uninterrupted. At Kew, gardeners had to pull carts of coke by hand along underground tunnels to reach the Palm House. William Coleman described Rolleston Hall as the 'hardest place I ever lived in', having been employed as a foreman responsible for the hothouses which had to be kept within 1° of a required temperature. Although he had help from a stoker and apprentice during the day, at night he had the sole responsibility for seventeen boilers which had to be kept fuelled, together with ventilators requiring constant closing or opening to maintain the set temperature.

Most garden staff lived on site, in a communal bothy beside the kitchen garden. Such bothies were usually very basic, providing little more than an outside toilet, a bed, table and chairs. In 1830, Daniel Judd worked at Brockett Hall in Hertfordshire. He wrote that the bothy in which he was living was 'a wretched place, situated between and joining two stokeholes...the roof covered with old fashioned pantiles, without any ceiling, so that when there came any drifting snow it found its way to us as we lay in bed.' It was not unknown for gardeners living in the bothy to supplement their bedding with sacks for additional warmth.

Garden boys spent much of their time washing pots and stacking them. It was an essential task since only by having a constant supply of spotlessly clean pots could other gardeners raise the quantity of plants needed around the garden. Other typical daily tasks included priming water pumps to set water flowing, filling water carts and water barrows for use in the greenhouses, teasing apart fibres for making compost, sweeping, raking and sometimes pollinating fruit using a rabbit tail fastened to a cane.

Every garden boy spent approximately three years in the job, before moving to an official three-year apprenticeship aged 14, where they would be given instruction as well as learning on the job. If they were training under a distinguished head gardener, they would also have to pay for such a privilege. Apart from learning all the necessary garden skills, they had to acquire botanical knowledge, an understanding of natural history, chemistry, meteorology, garden machinery and all emerging technology. Each apprentice kept a personal work record and John Loudon quotes typical notes made by J. Gott, an apprentice at Aubrey Hall, Warwickshire, in his *Encyclopaedia of Gardening* (1825). Mr Gott made references to peas being killed by frosts, a cone shaped iron tree being used to grow climbing roses and a fellow gardener being sacked for distilling parsnip whisky in one of the garden sheds. At night, trainees studied the various subjects required by a skilled gardener. They also had to learn correct manners and behaviour. This was regarded as extremely important for their long-term career prospects as they would be expected to come into contact with the gentry and landlords. *The Gardener's Magazine*, the first British periodical devoted to horticulture, contained an editorial from the Squire's gardener in 1869 stating that:

> Modesty is characteristic of superior ability. Neatness in appearance and a prompt and ready address are always pleasing to employers. Snobbishness and foppery are utterly contemptible in the eyes of those whose bread we eat, or who are our superiors in position, and who look at us from an elevated social stand-point.

At the end of an apprenticeship, the newly qualified gardeners were expected to travel around the country, gaining experience as and where they could. John Loudon's *Encyclopaedia of Gardening* indicated that the men should 'move on to a different part of the country…leisurely on foot botanising and collecting insects and minerals and visiting every distinguished garden on his way.'

Regarded as journeymen, their aim was to gain skills in as many different gardening sectors as possible. A typical example was that of William McCulloch, who began his career as a garden boy working on the same estate as his father. Once his apprenticeship was ended, the 18-year-old travelled to Dublin where he went to work in a plant enthusiast's garden. Two years later, he was back in Scotland working in Edinburgh's Royal Botanic Garden, followed by a position designed to gain management experience by working as a foreman on the Duke of Atholl's estate at Dunkeld. His next move was to London to work in a commercial nursery operated by James Grey & Sons and then to the London Horticultural Society's grounds.

Another example is that of William Cresswell. Aged 21, he became a journeyman gardener at Elm Lodge in Streatham, London with sole responsibility for a 3-acre garden and vegetable area. He later moved to work at Carters Seeds, before becoming Second Man in the kitchen garden at Audley End, Essex. Here he supervised junior gardeners and took turns watering, ventilating and heating greenhouses as well as propagating plants. In March 1874, his diary notes that there was snow on the ground but he was potting up pelargonium geraniums: 1,196 Lord Palmerston, 1,719 Christine and 1,154 Vesuvius.

When a journeyman had gained sufficient experience, he could be employed as a foreman or sub gardener, taking responsibility for a specific area of a garden. As Loudon noted, 'In extensive gardens where a number of hands are employed they are commonly grouped or arranged in divisions, and one of the journeymen of the longest standing employed as foreman, or sub-master, to the rest.'

A foreman's role was to supervise the work of journeymen and apprentices, ensuring they started work punctually and maintained the cleanliness of the tools. Depending on their area of employment, the foreman would also be responsible for arranging fruit and flowers for tables and vases within the big house. This could involve several changes of flowers and fruit throughout the day. At Holkham Hall, Norfolk, in the 1830s, table decorations were changed for each meal. The foreman had to pick fruit, arrange it on leaves on dishes or plates and present it with an accompanying label written in perfect copperplate.

They would also be responsible for creating bouquets, corsages, hair adornments and buttonholes required for the countless social engagements undertaken by the landowner and his family. Garden manuals frequently contained extensive instructions on making up the latest styles in 'personal decoration', highlighting flowers that had the staying power to survive crowded rooms. Additional help was provided by ingenious slender, glass tubes that could be filled with water or damp cotton wool to hold the flowers in place and be concealed within a lady's hair style. Gardeners had to be skilled in creating a variety of styles such as wreaths and sprays of flowers capable of being attached to the hair, or pinned-on light trails of foliage wound into the hair at the back. Bouquets required flowers to be bound with damp moss around each stem, involving considerable skill to combine colours, shades and flower types. Advice pages in garden manuals recommended that gardeners could use variegated foliage as an edging because it looked attractive, while very dark flowers with a few bright leaves would go with a dark costume, and that sweet briar and lemon scented verbena were perfect for scent but had to be placed under the frame where they could not be seen since they looked untidy. They were also told that they should use lighter rather than darker shades of blue if matching a dress, but never to use ivy-leaved geraniums as they emitted a sickly smell when torn.

Skilled gardeners were very conscious of their status within the garden hierarchy and were reluctant to undertake lower-skilled tasks such as those of a garden labourer even for a short time. *The Gardeners' Chronicle* reported that on one occasion, a large establishment employing nearly sixty gardeners received news that important visitors were about to arrive, but when the head gardener requested young gardeners from the plant and forcing houses provide assistance to help make the garden tidy, they refused, saying it was 'labourer's work'. When informed that they would lose their jobs if they did not comply, several handed in their notice and sought employment elsewhere.

For many gardeners, the London Horticultural Society (later known as the Royal Horticultural Society) grounds at Chiswick were a highly desirable and prestigious training location. Anyone accepted into the ranks of the London Horticultural Society gardeners had to be able to read detailed, complicated literature, as well as write clearly and concisely. The majority of young men would have had only a limited education at this time, and their training as a gardener would have required them to become very knowledgeable. Once at Chiswick, the next step was usually that of a head gardener, a position generally achieved via recommendations. By this point, gardeners were expected to be extremely proficient in all aspects of their work. Loudon pointed out in his *Encyclopaedia* that:

> The knowledge of languages, history, geography, arts, sciences and literature, which a gardener daily occupied with his profession may acquire, provided he begins at the commencement of his apprenticeship and continues to apply his leisure hours in reading till he is twenty or twenty-five years of age, is by no means inconsiderable.

A few years later, in 1826, Loudon wrote in *The Gardener's Magazine* that:

> As gardening has advanced, and its productions and its province extended, the situation of head gardener has become more and

more important; he has become a more confidential servant, entrusted with more power, and frequently consulted and communicated with by the master and mistress of the family.

Although most gardeners continued to be trained via traditional apprenticeships with head gardeners, demand for professional college-based training resulting in recognised qualifications grew steadily.

In April 1866, the Royal Horticultural Society (RHS), in conjunction with the Royal Society of Arts (RSA), launched a special exam. Participants had to travel to London to take part in an RSA three-hour written exam, followed by a practical test supervised by the RHS. If participants gained enough marks to qualify for a 1st or 2nd class level in either 'the operations of the Fruit and Vegetable Garden' or 'the operation of the Flower-Garden', travelling expenses were refunded and they were given the status of an Associate of the Royal Horticultural Society. The scheme did not prove very popular, however. Few potential participants were prepared to travel to London, employers were uninterested in encouraging their staff to take part and there was an overall lack of incentive for individual gardeners, who gained no real benefits from the scheme.

In 1889, Swanley Horticultural College was launched with the aim of 'training pupils in agriculture and horticulture, and in all matters connected with the cultivation and utilization of land for horticultural farming, grazing, gardening or any other purposes either at home or abroad.' Initially it targeted only male students but soon found women enquiring about admission. The first women were admitted in 1891, living in a special hostel for women students.

A new RHS exam was launched in 1892, which provided additional qualifications for gardeners and could be taken by anyone who paid the required fee of 3 shillings. This exam steadily became increasingly popular, especially with students of the various colleges such as Swanley and Studeley. In 1913, the Royal Horticultural Society

National Diploma was established to provide a formal qualification for gardeners, with the first examination being held the following year. In 1916, the first degree course in horticulture was introduced at Wye College, part of the University of London.

Horticultural societies offered ways for both amateur and professional gardeners to expand their knowledge and gain extra practical skills by attending lectures and talks given by experts and head gardeners, such as the 1864 talk about ferns to the Tower Hamlets Society given by the head gardener at Victoria Park. Two years later, the East Tower Hamlets Society enjoyed talks on grape cultivation and *Lilium auratum* (Golden rayed oriental lily).

Numerous Mechanics and Workmen's Institutes were set up in towns and cities nationwide. These were mainly attended by men, providing instruction, talks and access to books on a wide range of subjects. Gardening, along with topics like botany, was extremely popular, especially since it gave access to knowledge that might not otherwise be available. Most books on botany used large amounts of Latin, which the majority of people could not understand. In 1852, the Clay Cross Workmen's Institute proposed to create its own gardening society on the basis that it would 'promote the cultivation of gardens useful and ornamental, to encourage habits of industry and domestic taste, and to foster a love of home among the working classes.'

Some companies also sought to encourage staff to improve their education. During a visit to the Suttons premises at Reading, a reporter from *The Gardeners' Chronicle* noted:

> They have a library and reading room which adjoins the office on the first floor over the front shop. This is furnished with all the leading periodicals and standard works on gardening, together with the Chamber's Works, the monthly volumes and other books belonging to the Religious Tract Society. One of

the shop men acts as librarian and it is open to all men and boys on the establishment.

A further visit in 1861 revealed that the facilities had been extended as the reading room now included history, travel books and daily newspapers:

These are available at meal times and every evening after business hours. On application to the librarian, books can be borrowed to read at home. One evening recently, a friendly soiree was well attended by about 40 young men and clerks, shop men, warehousemen etc who spent a social evening with the principals of the company.

By 1889, staff could take advantage of opportunities to learn about new technology when Suttons provided a private lecture and exhibition on Edison's Perfected Phonograph. During the evening, participants learned about the history of the phonograph, explored the nature of sound and applications, saw photographical slides using an oxy-hydrogen lantern, as well as an exhibition of records and performances.

Children and Gardening

Children were increasingly encouraged to participate in gardening. It was seen as a healthy activity suitable for all, whether from the working class or royalty. As a child, John Loudon was given a small garden area where he created walls and flower beds. His wife, Jane, later recalled being told that 'so eager was he to obtain seeds to sow in it, that when a jar of tamarinds arrived from an uncle in the West Indies, he gave the other children his share of the fruit, on condition of his having all the seeds.' William Cobbett's children were given flower beds and a vegetable plot to cultivate, while in Ireland, Emily, the Duchess of

Leinster, provided small gardens for children attending her estate school.

Charlotte Brontë's *Jane Eyre* (1847) contains a description of the school at Lowood, where Jane describes the 'scores of little beds' that were 'very bleak in winter'. During the summer, when a typhus epidemic sweeps through the school, these beds were bright with flowers, especially hollyhocks, lilies and daisies, but she regards them as being 'useless for most of the inmates of Lowood, except to furnish now and then a handful of herbs and blossoms to put in a coffin'.

Over at Osborne House, Queen Victoria and Prince Albert's summer retreat in the Isle of Wight, the Prince Consort organised small gardens for the royal children on the estate in a quiet corner surrounding the Swiss Cottage. The two older boys, Bertie and Alfred, helped to build the Swiss Cottage itself, with Queen Victoria writing in her journal that Alfred 'worked as hard and steadily as a regular labourer' and was paid at the same rate by his father. Each child had their own garden plot, and the tools to cultivate it themselves. The under gardener, Mr Warne, assessed all the fruit and vegetables grown by the children, and if he said it was good enough, then Prince Albert paid the market rate for the produce to the child who had grown it.

With the passing of the 1880 Education Act, school attendance became compulsory for 5- to 10-year-olds, and gardening formed part of the curriculum for boys at many schools. John Wright, chief instructor of the County Councils of Kent and Surrey, published *Garden Flowers and Plants: A Primer for Amateurs* in 1895. His introduction stated that 'The importance of domestic gardening is now recognised by the Board of Education as a legitimate subject for teaching in elementary and continuation schools, and a great impetus will thus be given to the work in its various aspects, including floriculture.' Even if there was not much physical space available for vegetable plots, the development of window boxes as a growing method was encouraged. Surrey County Council noted that 'Horticulture is the oldest of the arts, and the foundation of all others… [The council] has made arrangements…not only for gardens in which boys may be taught while they are at school, but for "continuation gardens" in which they may make further instruction, when they have left it.'

By 1908, magazines such as *The Gardener* included gardening columns for children, while seed companies such as Suttons were offering children's flower collections.

Other Career Opportunities

For those gardeners who did not want to become head gardeners, or who failed to complete the full training, or lacked the necessary skills and contacts, there were alternative options available. Some people chose to work for plant nurseries or go on plant hunting expeditions. Others chose to set up small nurseries or market gardens providing a variety of produce. Such entrepreneurs could enjoy a reasonable lifestyle, especially if their location was well chosen. Writing in the *London Labour and the London Poor* (1840), Henry Mayhew estimated that every Saturday morning 2,000 donkey barrows and 3,000 women brought baskets of fruit and flowers for sale in London, together with countless costermongers, porters, salesmen and carters especially in the vicinity of Covent Garden.

Others became involved in seed distribution or surveying. A compendium of traders active in the cities of London and Westminster compiled by R. Campbell contained listings under the term 'gardener' for fruiters and land surveyors 'employed in measuring land, and laying it out in Gardens and other kinds of Policy about Gentlemen's Seats', while:

> The Seed-shopkeeper sells all manner of Garden and Grass Seeds, Gardeners Tools, Matts & Co, and some of them Nursery-men &c, and furnish Gentlemen with young Trees,

both Fruit and Forest, with Flower Roots. It is a very profitable branch and in a few hands, requires no more skill than other Retail Trades if they are not in the Nursery-way, but if they are, they must be compleat [*sic*] Gardeners.

It has been estimated that by 1839 there were nineteen nurseries and eleven seedsmen in London, and 150 elsewhere, reflecting how quickly the trade was growing outside the capital. Chelsea was particularly popular with nurserymen, as the King's Road was seen as being the most fashionable place for nobility and gentry to buy plants for their estates.

Many took up roles as gardeners in small estates such as those owned by members of the gentry, or the newly wealthy industrialists and professionals such as lawyers. These were gardens that could be maintained by just one or two people, although considerable work might still be required. *The Gardeners' Chronicle* magazine noted the experience of one gardener who had just one assistant to help him cultivate and maintain '4,848 yards of kitchen garden, 548 yards of wall trees, 38 yards long range of pines and 1,200 pots of plants, 2 acres of lawn, shrubbery and a coach drive.' As the century progressed, advertisements for gardeners appeared. In 1873, the Suttons catalogue contained an advertisement stating:

STEWARDS, BAILIFFS, AND GARDENERS

We keep a list of Stewards, Bailiffs and Gardeners who are seeking situations, and shall be pleased to render assistance to any of our customers who may require a thoroughly reliable and practical man in either of these capacities.

Self-employed jobbing gardeners and garden labourers often worked on a casual basis, constantly seeking out new customers.

Nurseries might employ such a jobbing gardener to undertake a task for them on a client's garden. They might deal regularly with ten or more gardens during a week, spending a little time at each. Such gardeners owned their own tools, supplied plants and seeds – a fact that sometimes resulted in accusations that they were stealing cuttings or neglecting their employer's plants in order to create a demand for replacements. Garden labourers were the lowest in the gardening hierarchy, being employed to do seasonal jobs such as trenching and digging for short periods.

Other jobbing gardeners worked on short term contracts, usually for a nursery or household. Their task was to create exuberant garden displays for a set period of time, usually up to ten weeks. The gardener would come to the house regularly to undertake maintenance of the display, or to care for plants hired for special events and parties on a short-term basis, which might be as little as two or three days. Incomes could be low, and it could be a precarious existence, with no fall back beyond the workhouse if the gardener had an accident or grew too old for the work.

Assessing the industry in 1822, John Loudon divided gardeners into a total of thirty-four different types. These included 'operators or serving gardeners, dealers in gardening or garden tradesmen, counsellors, professors, artists and patrons'. Pay rates could be low, especially for those towards the bottom of the hierarchy. Writing in *The Gardener's Magazine*, Loudon noted that illiterate bricklayers with little skill in figures who had completed their apprenticeship could expect to earn 5 to 7 shillings per day. Meanwhile, a highly skilled gardener who had completed an apprenticeship and was trained in land surveying, geometry and botany, as well as being well read, could expect a daily income of just 2 shillings or 2 shillings and 6 pence.

The establishment of public parks and botanical gardens offered new types of opportunities for gardeners, since staff were needed to care for the gardens and grow the flowers, as well as maintain order among the visitors. Whatever the type of job on offer, patronage was extremely important. Having the right recommendation could ensure success, especially if it involved a prominent head gardener or well-known gardening personality.

Ultimately, for gardeners who had no other income and no pension, or were seriously injured through their work, the workhouse beckoned. In 1826, *The Gardener's Magazine* published a letter from a Mr Archibald Naughton from Hackney. He wrote, 'I began jobbing on my own account and a poor business I have found it ever since. When I first began, the highest wages were 3s a day, and obliged to find my own tools. I had a good deal of employment at first.' He went onto note that problems occurred when his savings and possessions were stolen. His wife became ill, and they had to move to Hackney for clearer air. He continued 'Where I have been ever since, just being able to gain a livelihood, by laying out the gardens for the new buildings going on in the neighbourhood.' Recognising that his future prospects were bleak and included the likelihood of having to go into the workhouse, he advised other gardeners 'never give up any place whatsoever for the condition of a jobbing gardener, for that is greater slavery than being a common labourer.'

Attempts were made to try to help less fortunate gardeners. In 1838, Joseph Paxton helped to set up the Benevolent Institution for the Relief of Aged and Indigent Gardeners and their Widow (this became a Royal Institution in 1860). By 1832, the Benevolent Institution was paying out over £500 a year, caring for pensioners who had an average age of 77.

Other ex-gardeners sought alternative solutions. In 1852, *The Gardeners' Chronicle* carried a request for help: 'A few friends to the family of Mr James Carton, once Gardener at Syon House, now wholly destitute, having formed a small purse in order that he may emigrate with his family to Australia, solicit some further aid in order to complete their arrangement.'

The 1851 Census referred to three types of paid gardeners: domestic, jobbing and other gardeners and nurserymen resulting in estimates of around 5,000 domestic gardeners, 3,000 nurserymen and approximately 80,000 other gardeners.

For many gardeners, market gardening and seed companies provided a valuable source of employment. In 1842, Suttons Seeds took on James Messenger as an apprentice. The resultant indentures are recorded in Earley History Group's History of Suttons Seeds:

> It is understood and agreed that James Messenger…is not to be provided with any food, drink, lodging wearing apparel or washing by his Master, but these and all other necessaries are to be provided by himself or his friend.

> It is also agreed the wages James Messenger shall receive from Martin Hope Sutton or the Master to whom he is assigned shall be as follows:

> From the first year from the date here of three shillings per week, for the next year four shillings, for the next year five shillings, for the next year six shillings, for the next year nine shillings and for the seventh year the wages to be mutually agreed upon at the expiration of the sixth year if he remains in the service of the same Master.

> The hours of working are to be from six o'clock am to nine o'clock pm in the months of April, May, June, July, August and September; and from seven o'clock am to nine o'clock pm in the months of October, November, December, January, February and March; and the aforesaid James Messenger will have to perform such work as is absolutely necessary for the

preservation of the plants in the Greenhouse Pits from the weather also on Sundays.

Amateur gardeners took advantage of opportunities to gain extra income from gardening. Henry Dearlove, a labourer in Reigate, possessed an allotment of just half an acre. It was very productive as the *Flower, Fruit & Vegetable Magazine* noted in 1898:

> He has 120 feet of glass, and in the houses, he grows strawberries in the spring and tomatoes in the summer. One year he gathered 90lbs of strawberries in eight days from his biggest house, and three years running he has raised more than a ton of tomatoes each season. Out of doors, he grows strawberries, rhubarb and peas and beans for market. The forced strawberries he sends to Covent Garden, and the other produce is disposed of locally. Average net profit £80 per year.

Chapter 2

The Head Gardener

Head gardeners were undoubtedly the leaders of the garden world, and employment was generally the result of word-of-mouth recommendation. Ambitious senior foremen would start highlighting the fact that they were interested in promotion and looking for a position, seeking out any contacts that might help them. As the nineteenth century progressed, advertisements for head gardeners were sometimes placed in garden magazines.

Although exact numbers are unknown, it has been estimated that there were probably over 1,000 active head gardeners in early Victorian times, rising to around 4,000 by 1914. They dominated all aspects of gardening, from choosing plants to judging shows. As Toby Musgrave points out in *The Head Gardeners* (2007), they possessed a status and importance that extended far beyond their own fiefdoms and were on a par with the highest-ranking servants, such as the butler within a grand house. The fame of a head gardener and his expertise reflected favourably on an estate. Competition for the services of a highly regarded head gardener could be intense.

The role of a head gardener encompassed a wide range of functions. They effectively managed large teams of staff and were responsible for thousands of pounds worth of expenditure every year. They were expected to have extensive knowledge about all aspects of horticulture, including forcing techniques, keep updated on all new trends, bring prestige to garden owners, cultivate exotic species and lawns, take responsibility for plant collections, maintain gardens in pristine condition, and oversee table decorations. Head gardeners were occasionally listed in trade directories and were always well known within the industry. For their employees, their word was law. Rules and regulations were strictly enforced. For example, at Bicton in Devon, the head gardener was known to fine employees 3 pence for coming to work in a morning without shoes properly laced or tied.

The head gardener always stood out – he was the only person allowed to wear a bowler hat. He was provided with a house and was expected to be a married man. Sometimes the accommodation was in a large building shared by another senior employee, as can be seen at Stagenhoe Park, where the head gardener, Matthew Ball and his family lived in one half of the Gardener's Lodge. The butler, William Exon, and his family occupied the other half of the building. At Holkham Hall, the head gardener was given a separate house close to the main entrance to the estate, some distance from the walled garden, where the gardeners lived in the bothy.

Head gardeners rarely undertook practical tasks around the garden. Rather, their job was to manage all aspects of the garden operation, possessing considerable power and authority. Depending on the size of the estate, the head gardener could be responsible for up to fifty staff, and could make or break their workers' careers. They controlled budgets, supervised staff, hired and fired where necessary, designed new areas, undertook all decisions on choosing and ordering new plants, and showed visitors round the garden. The landowner had to ask the permission of the head gardener to visit the estate kitchen garden, ringing a bell for admittance. Even Prince Albert was unable to gain admittance to the kitchen garden at Windsor when he wanted to visit. Some head gardeners were so powerful that landowners would not even pick a flower or fruit without first seeking permission.

Even if they had not written a book or article, head gardeners' names added credence to front covers. The head gardener was expected to write articles for magazines, endorse new varieties of vegetables, seeds and fruit. They could explore plant breeding techniques, try to raise new varieties, and devise new ways of presenting plants within the garden. Nurserymen would invite head gardeners to visit plant growing areas and discuss new introductions. The arrival of widespread horticultural shows and professional associations meant that the head gardener of an estate was expected to act as a judge and take part in committees such as the RHS Fruit and Vegetable Committee. James Vert, head gardener at Audley End, Essex, acted as a judge in the inaugural 1912 Chelsea Flower Show. The prestige in which a head gardener was held is reflected in the fact that many new plants were named after head gardeners, including Donald Beaton, a Scottish head gardener who had a version of the flowering current, *Ribes* x *Beatonii* named after him in 1837.

One task that was closely supervised by the head gardener was the packing of fruit to be sent in hampers from an estate to the landowner's home elsewhere in the country. This was an extremely detailed and skilled task. In 1873, the *Journal of Horticulture* highlighted some of the techniques that had to be employed. A soft brush had to be used to clean fruit, and the fruit had to thoroughly dry before packing. Peaches could be packed in layers of bran, making sure that no corner was left unfilled. Cherries had to be washed and brushed, wiped dry and laid between two sheets of tissue paper before being packed in alternate layers of tow.

It was not unknown for a head gardener to be asked to redesign large sections of an estate's garden. This might be from a desire by the landowner for a more fashionable garden incorporating new features, or to make it more practical, and to provide extra facilities such as a conservatory. One such head gardener was Matthew Ball, who was given the role at Stagenhoe Park by landowner Henry Rogers in 1846. To help him, Ball had a team of twenty gardeners. The Garden Museum London contains an archive of the drawings made by Ball detailing the changes and plans he made for Stagenhoe. A new entrance and carriageways were created, together with a large ornamental lake complete with small islands, a fountain and waterfalls. All the soil from the lake excavation was placed in front of the house to create a terrace. He created detailed plans for a geometric, symmetrical parterre with gravel paths separating the flower beds. Accompanying the layout was a list of summer bedding plants such as geraniums, calceolarias, and verbena, together with exact quantities required, and pin pricks identifying where each group was to be planted. Yuccas were positioned at each corner. This drawing would have been presented to the landowner when discussing plans for the garden and would also help to show how the various colours would work together. His garden team would have then grown these plants to order within the estate greenhouses.

For those head gardeners who possessed an entrepreneurial streak, such as Joseph Paxton, business ventures were another way of making extra income.

The story of Joseph Paxton shows how a young man could rise in the world through gardening. Born at Milton Bryant on the Woburn Estate in 1803, his father is believed to have been a farm labourer. Paxton was the seventh son in the family and after attending an estate school at Woburn, he trained as a gardener. In 1821, Paxton was employed as a head gardener to Sir Gregory Osborne Page Turner at the nearby Battlesden Park. Within a couple of years, Sir Gregory was exhibiting signs of insanity, eventually going bankrupt in 1824. Recognising what was happening, Paxton left Sir Gregory's employ some months before bankruptcy proceedings began.

Paxton became one of the first entrants to the Horticultural Society's Chiswick training scheme. Although this represented an initial drop in status, Paxton believed it offered better long-term career potential. His instinct paid off. Initially starting as a gardener in the Ornamental Garden working with new exotic introductions such as verbenas and petunias, he was appointed under gardener in the Arboretum at Chiswick in 1825. While working in the Arboretum, he came into contact with the Duke of Devonshire, who asked him to move to Chatsworth House in Derbyshire with responsibility for its extensive gardens. As part of his new job as head gardener, he was given a horse, house, a salary of £65 per year, plus free fruit and vegetables.

Accepting the job, Paxton lost no time in making an impact. Recalling his first day in his new role, he wrote:

> I left London by the Comet coach for Chesterfield, arrived at Chatsworth at 4.30 am in the morning of the ninth of May 1826. As no person was to be seen at that early hour, I got over the greenhouse gate by the old covered way, explored the pleasure grounds, and looked round the outside of the house. I then went down to the kitchen gardens, scaled the outside wall and saw the whole place, set the men to work there at six o'clock; then returned to Chatsworth and got Thomas Weldon to play me the water works, and afterwards went to breakfast with poor dear Mrs Gregory and her niece. The latter fell in love with me, and I with her, and thus completed my first morning's work at Chatsworth, before nine o'clock.

In 1827, Paxton married Sarah Brown, Mrs Gregory's niece, and remained Chatsworth's head gardener for the next thirty years. Sarah provided invaluable help throughout his career, acting as his proxy whenever he was absent from Chatsworth. He sent letters giving instructions, which were followed exactly, with Sarah managing the foreman and directly instructing all the staff.

Paxton's skill with plants was outstanding. An early success was the Cavendish Banana. Purchased for £10 (approximately £1,200 today), the plant was carefully cultivated by Paxton using 'plenty of water, rich loam soil and well-rotten dung'. In 1835, it flowered for the first time. By May 1836 there were over 100 fruits ripening on the plant.

Ultimately this plant became the ancestor of commercially grown bananas worldwide, with over seven billion Cavendish Bananas now eaten annually in the UK.

Over the years, Paxton extended and transformed the cottage he had originally been given as head gardener. In the 1840 edition of *Adam's Gem of the Peak*, it was described as 'Mr Paxton's elegant cottage' and was soon redeveloped into a 'pretty Anglo-Italian villa' complete with a purpose-built library. An article in Loudon's *Gardener's Magazine* for 1842 refers to the room possessing a marble chimney piece complete with shell-work and oak bookcases. A huge plate glass window allowed him to look into the adjacent 100-foot conservatory. A year later, Paxton and his wife Sarah entertained Queen Victoria, Prince Albert and the Duke of Wellington, with the Queen reported to be 'very pleased with the neatness and order' of his home.

His work at Chatsworth resulted in immense publicity for both Paxton and the Duke of Devonshire, especially with the construction of the Great Stove, the first great greenhouse he created, which later provided the footprint for his Great Exhibition greenhouse-style building (see Chapter 10). Paxton's expertise meant that he was consulted and became involved in numerous endeavours unrelated to Chatsworth, including designing the first People's Park at Birkenhead in 1847, becoming involved in publishing successful garden magazines and various business investments. Ultimately, he gained a house for life from the duke, while his personal investments in products such as greenhouses and railways made him independently wealthy. He was even knighted and became a member of parliament. Paxton recognised that he had been fortunate in his career, commenting that 'I happened to come in the flood time, and by the energies that God had given me, and by the able assistance of many eminent men, I have been enabled to carry out these great works, and to attain the position I now occupy.' At his death in 1865, *The Times* described him as the 'greatest gardener of his time, the founder of a new style of architecture, and a man of genius.'

The role of head gardener was almost entirely dominated by men. Even after female gardeners became a significant force in the industry, they were rarely appointed as head gardeners. An exception was that of Elizabeth Burton, who was head gardener at Mavisbank, Scotland for thirty-eight years. A pioneer in Scottish horticulture, Elizabeth acquired her gardening skills through practical work in the gardens of various relatives and family friends. She also took a series of evening classes at Heriot-Watt College, resulting in being awarded certificates in Advanced Principles of Agriculture. As a result of her work redesigning a garden at Craufurd Bank House, Lasswade, Elizabeth came to the attention of Dr George Wilson, medical superintendent of the Mavisbank Institution for the Nervous, who appointed her head gardener in 1896, with the task of working with female patients in the garden. As the hospital expanded, so did the work of Elizabeth Burton, who took on more responsibilities including overseeing an extended team of employees. Ultimately, she was responsible for 100 acres of hospital grounds, the estate's livestock of hens, sheep and pigs, plus providing all the hospital's vegetables and cut flowers on a daily basis.

Having reached the position of head gardener on a big estate, some people stayed there for the rest of their working lives. Others moved on to a more prestigious estate. At Audley End, Essex, William Harrison was appointed head gardener in 1879, having previously served in a similar position to Admiral Duncombe at Kinwick Percy, Yorkshire, and Sir Richard Brook of Norton Priory, Cheshire. Matthew Ball moved from Stagenhoe Park in 1869 when the estate was sold to the Earl of Caithness, bringing with him his own head gardener from Scotland. Ball and his family moved to Hemel Hempstead where he worked as a gardener, and by 1881 he was working as a cemetery superintendent at Isleworth and living in a lodge at the entrance.

Financially, a head gardener could expect to earn more than just his salary, especially if they developed special skills or achieved a high reputation.

They could take advantage of numerous benefits such as offering skills as a garden designer to other landowners, invest in a nursery, or create innovative products and plants. At Givons, Leatherhead, the head gardener, William Peters, bred a new strawberry variety which he named 'Givons Late Prolific'. It attracted an order for 25,000 runners from Messrs Laxtons, while at Wrest Park, head gardener Seward Snow marketed two vegetables he had developed: Snows Matchless Cos Lettuce and Broccoli Snow's Early White. Silas Cole, head gardener at Althrop, bred a frilly edged sweet pea which he named Countess Spencer. It quickly became popular and led to the creation of a range of wavy 'Spencer' sweet peas that have never gone out of fashion.

Apprentices routinely paid the head gardener a fee for their training. This was usually around £3 to £5 (£360 to £600) but sometimes could be as high as £15 (£1,800), reflecting the head gardener's prestige in allowing him to charge a premium price. In some cases, the head gardener might even apply such training fees to journeymen. Unconfirmed industry reports indicate that one such head gardener required £10 from every journeyman he employed. Alternatively, they would take a weekly deduction from the journeyman's salary. One journeyman was reported to find 1 shilling deducted from his pay packet and was told 'it was a fashion of the place for the gardener to get a shilling a week off his men and those who did not like it could hook it', while another gardener in Preston indicated that his head gardener took a premium of £3, plus a slice of wages from everyone. Outside workers had to pay him 1s 6d a week, while hothouse workers paid 2 shillings.

Some head gardeners were even able to make a profit from produce grown in the kitchen garden, on occasions when surpluses, unwanted by the estate, were sold in local markets. Touring gardens in the west of Scotland, Loudon noted that since the owners were absent, the head gardener was selling all the garden produce.

Taking part in competitions, especially prestigious regional or national ones, could result in large sums of prize money. It became a tradition that prize money belonged to the gardener rather than the owner. The Duke of Devonshire wrote to Joseph Paxton congratulating him on winning a prize in the 1831 Sheffield Horticultural Show. The duke was happy for Paxton to receive all the credit – and the prize money – even though the exhibit had officially belonged to the landowner, and had been grown at his expense. Winning the prize as the duke's head gardener brought prestige to both Paxton and the Duke of Devonshire.

One of the more contentious payments received by head gardeners related to commissions (the gardener's discount) on all orders placed with plant nurseries. Jonathan Denby points out in his dissertation 'As the Houses, So the People' that 'It was almost invariable practice throughout the nineteenth century for head gardeners to be given a percentage of all orders from nurseries and seedsmen. This was called variously a "discount", "privilege", "percentage" or "douceur".' Ordering a new glasshouse could lead to a 25 percent discount. Most plant related companies offered a 5 percent commission, but there are reports that some businesses offered up to 20 percent to attract new clients. Such discounts could result in significant sums of money for the head gardener. Buying plants from a nursery to fill a flower garden could amount to £400 or £500, while there were instances where even higher sums were paid – not always with the landowner's permission. This resulted in a notorious legal case known as Williams v Leslie heard at the High Court in London during 1875.

It all started when a head gardener named Hood was employed at Castle Leslie, County Monaghan. The castle gardens had been personally designed by the landowner, Colonel Charles Leslie, who was a keen gardener. He kept a close watch over the gardens and the work of his head gardener until his death in 1871. The new owner, John Leslie, spent much of his time in London and had less interest in the garden, visiting the estate only for a short time each year. It was a situation that Mr Hood turned to his own monetary advantage. By 1873, John Leslie became worried over the size of the garden-related bills, setting a strict limit of £600 per year. Hood ignored this, and the bills continued to mount. In the autumn of 1874, Leslie accidentally received a receipt from a firm of auctioneers relating to plants that had been sold by Mr Hood. After investigating the situation, it became clear that Mr Hood had been buying plants from a London nurseryman named Williams and then reselling them at auction for cash. Hood was immediately dismissed, and Leslie contested the bills from Williams, stating that Hood had not had the authority to order such a number of plants.

During the trial, it became clear that such over ordering had not been the only way in which Hood had ripped off his employer. He had spent £3,000 with various companies and gained a cash payment worth 5 percent of the value of each order. In addition, Hood had continued the practice set up by Colonel Leslie of exhibiting produce at shows, but had purchased plants from Williams' catalogue and exhibited them under his own name. Some of the plants were quite expensive, such as a *Lapageria Rosea* which cost £22 3s. This enabled him to win a range of cups and cash prizes at the Glasgow International Horticultural Show. Asked to give the cups to his former employer, he refused saying that the cups bore his name, not that of his employer. John Leslie lost the case, and had to pay the full amount to Williams, minus the 5 percent discount Hood had received.

The practice of paying discounts came to an end in 1906, when the Prevention of Corruption Bill made taking of discounts unapproved by the landowner a criminal offence. Seeking legal advice on the changed situation, The Horticultural Trades Association discovered that it was now illegal to receive any commission, even a Christmas box or hospitality. When the provisions of the act were challenged in court four years later, over unmarked cases of whisky being given to head gardeners under the guise of Cutbush's Insecticide, the jury brought in a verdict of not guilty, even though the judge regarded it as corruption under the terms of the Act of Parliament.

Hood was not the only head gardener who found themselves in trouble. Three years after William Baxter became head gardener at Culzean, Scotland, in 1871, he was dismissed for tampering with the books and redirecting the money for his own use. He then fled to Chile to avoid having to be punished or to have to pay back the debt. At Audley End, head gardener William Harrison was dismissed in 1881 because the landowner and land agent felt he had failed to keep the gardens in good order.

On retirement, some head gardeners were given a pension but usually had to find a home elsewhere. If they were lucky, the estate owner might have something available. There are examples of highly regarded head gardeners receiving retirement gifts. Queen Victoria presented Thomas Ingram, head gardener at Frogmore, a retirement purse of £150, a tea and coffee service, a gold watch and a grace and favour home at Upton Lodge, Slough. Robert Thomson received a testimonial worth £400 when he retired from the RHS gardens at Chiswick. Some employers even left legacies for their former head gardeners. The Earl of Leven left £500 to the head gardener at his estate in Roehampton, and £200 to his head gardener at Glenferness. Some head gardeners set up their own businesses. In Derbyshire, John Lamb, head gardener at Mackheaton, resigned his position in 1851 before purchasing a farm and becoming very wealthy. Others lived in poverty and often had to seek help from their contacts within the industry to survive.

As the nineteenth century progressed, there was growing recognition of the problems that could be faced by indigent head gardeners and their staff. In 1865, the Duke of Devonshire became president of the Gardeners' Royal Benevolent Institution, while Joseph Paxton was chairman. The organisation had been set up to help impoverished elderly gardeners and their widows, paying twenty men £16 a year and eleven widows £12 each. Paxton pointed out at the institution's thirteenth anniversary dinner that gardeners' wages were below those of comparable artisans, forcing increasing numbers of gardeners to seek help from the institution.

Chapter 3

The Rise of Female Gardeners

At the beginning of the nineteenth century, the world of gardening was very much dominated by men. Women played a minor role, acting as a quiet presence, and few undertook serious tasks like digging and cultivation. If they did, then it was rarely mentioned. This situation soon changed dramatically. Jane Loudon, wife of John, become a highly successful author of gardening books, as women took on an increasingly active role, with even the young royal princesses being expected to learn to cultivate their own gardens at Osborne House. By the end of the century, women were opting for gardening as a career and attending college, and within years the country was depending on women to grow the produce needed to feed the nation. The activities of women such as Ellen Willmott and Gertrude Jekyll helped transform all aspects of gardening.

Until the late eighteenth century, there had been little documentary evidence of women being actively involved in gardening. Women were generally expected to help with the care of herbs, especially culinary and medicinal ones, and potentially elsewhere if they had the time, as writer Charles Lawrence points out in his book *Practical Directions for the Cultivation of Cottage Gardens* (1831). He suggested that wives should 'have a regular time, every day, allotted for the performance of her various duties, and should so arrange them, as to devote as much time as possible, of the most favourable part of the day, to the garden.' The study of botany was increasingly advocated as a suitable occupation for young women. Even Queen Charlotte, wife of King George III, encouraged her daughters to study botany and gain an understanding of horticulture. In 1796, Miss Priscilla Wakefield wrote *An Introduction to Botany*, deliberately targeting young women – it proved highly popular, remaining in print until 1841. In her introduction she commented that botany could 'become a substitute for some of the trifling, not to say pernicious objects, that too frequently occupy the leisure of young ladies of fashionable manners, and, by employing their faculties, rationally, act as an antidote to levity and idleness.'

Jane Austen's correspondence with her sister Cassandra hints at the level of interest and involvement women had when it came to domestic gardening. In 1807, while living in Southampton, she refers to creating a garden. The Austen family had planted a syringa, and a border under the terrace wall had been filled with currants, gooseberries and raspberries. In another account, her mother, Mrs Austen, noted that 'my flesh is much warmer, my blood freer flows, when I work in the garden with rakes and hoes'. Apparently, Mrs Austen was very good at cultivating potatoes!

Writer Maria Edgeworth had been introduced to gardening as a child and remained a keen gardener all her life, commenting, 'I am very happy building castles of flowers in it…I am now making a spick and span new trellis, digging up, trenching, manuring my garden – a total revolution.' Carnations and camellias were among her favourite flowers and in 1830 she noted that 'my peony tree is the most beautiful thing on earth'.

Women steadily took on more of the tasks around the garden, including digging, as Jane Loudon indicated in her book, *Instructions on Gardening for Ladies* (1834): 'a Lady with a small light spade may, by taking time, succeed in doing all the digging that can be required in a small garden.' Jane Loudon was particularly keen on encouraging women to take up flower gardening since 'that is pre-eminently a woman's kind of garden labour, only indeed to give an interest in its effects.' She became an active proponent in favour of getting more women interested publishing books targeted at a female readership, with titles like *The Lady's Magazine of Gardening* and *Every Lady's Guide to Her Own Greenhouses, Hothouse and Conservatory*. Clothing did create problems, as skirts were not ideal for digging and as Rosa, a contributor to *The Cottage Gardener* magazine pointed out, 'the rose and sweetbriar tear our bonnets and collars to pieces and we tread most vexatiously on our raiment when stopping to avoid them.' As women became more and more involved, so other issues began to surface, especially the effect on hands, leading to recommendations for using Vaseline and that used kidskin gloves were better than any gardening gloves.

Gardens became an integral part of the lives of the gentry and middle-class Victorian women. They acted as a focus for social events and leisure activities, with space being devoted to garden games like croquet and lawn tennis. Flowers were needed for the house and women might spend several hours a day creating appropriate décor. As Roderick Floud points out in his 2019 book *An Economic History of the English Garden*, 'Gardening was a respectable activity for women, an extension of their domestic sphere.' During the London season, gardens became a fashionable location for parties and other social events, and a tradition of holding garden parties emerged. In 1891, the Earl and Countess of Ilchester gave a garden party at Holland House, while in 1896, Lady Ilchester was assisted by the Marchioness of Salisbury and Lady Gwendoline Cecil in receiving over 1,500 guests at a garden party, with newspaper reports referring to the fact that areas such as the Dutch and Italian gardens were at their best. In 1898, *The Times* noted that 'Countess Percy gave the first of a series of garden parties at Syon House, Isleworth, yesterday afternoon', during which 'refreshments were served in an enormous marquee' adorned with flowers. Equally important within the social season were events such as the Kew and RHS horticultural shows and visits to places like Kensington Palace Gardens, Hyde Park Gardens, Royal Surrey

Gardens and Cremorne Gardens. The introduction of new features such as a fernery at the Cremorne Gardens would provide a key element in their social attractiveness. *The Times* noted in 1884 that the Royal Botanic Society exhibitions aroused considerable interest and 'that the numbers of visitors was so great as to make the examination of flowers a task of some difficulty'. Fetes organised at these locations invariably involved payment of an entry fee, which rendered them unsuitable for many potential visitors. At the Cremorne Gardens in Chelsea, visitors paid 1 shilling to enter and enjoy the 14-acre gardens as well as afternoon musical and acrobatic entertainment, while in the evening visitors could dance the night away.

Evidence of the scale of interest being expressed by women is shown in Loudon's comments on their participation in horticultural shows and societies:

> A good many of the prizes are awarded to ladies, and this we are delighted to see, whether their gardeners are named or not. The cares of gardening are worthy of, and suitable for, ladies of every rank, from the cottage to the palace. There is nothing unfeminine in them, and as the resources for the enjoyment of ladies residing in the country is limited compared to men under the same circumstances, we are happy to see that they avail themselves of such as are within their reach.

Many women became familiar participants in exhibitions and competitions, including Mrs Lawrence Dayton Green, who won over fifty prizes in the Horticultural Society and was the first to grow a purple blue climbing nasturtium from Chile. Middle-class women were expected to acquire knowledge of plants whether for gardening or by expanding their interest into illustration, flower arranging and related craft work. Women had long been recognised the artistic potential of flowers, gaining considerable renown such as Dutch artist

Rachel Ruysch. Another flower painter, Mary Moser, was paid £900 to illustrate a room at Frogmore for Queen Charlotte. Their skills could be of a very high standard, as can be seen in the detailed water colour illustrations of plant life created by Beatrix Potter, whose academic study of spore germination of rare forms of fungi was rejected by the Linnean Society simply because she was a woman. As the century progressed, educational establishments such as the Royal Holloway College for Women at Egham, Surrey provided training in botanical study, based on the botanical garden created in the college grounds by lecturer Margaret Benson.

Flower arranging became a highly important skill from the nineteenth century onwards and was regarded as a key female responsibility. It was not just regarding the provision of flowers for vases to be placed in rooms, but also table decorations, posies and flowers for the hair, resulting in long discussions with the head gardener. The impetus for this development of flower arranging began as a result of changes in dining styles. Traditionally, people had dined in the French style, with all the courses being placed on the table at the same time, as diners helped themselves to whatever food they desired. Thus, food became part of the table decoration. Following the introduction of Russian-style dining, servants began bringing food in course by course. Elaborate flower arrangements were therefore used to fill in the gaps on the table. Flowers were also seen as essential accompaniments for outfits worn by women attending social engagements. No young lady would attend a ball without some flowers in her hair or wearing a small corsage at her breast. In upper-class houses, a gardener would be given the task of completing such arrangements, but in all other houses, such as those of the gentry and middle classes, it became the responsibility of wives and daughters. This led to a massive development in literature such as *Vases for the Breakfast Table*, which were designed to provide ideas and instruction. Even Mrs Beeton offered advice on the subject. A fashion also developed involving developing displays that could act as a form of communication using a language of flowers. Young ladies using this language needed to make their choices very carefully and possess a detailed botanical knowledge since it was easy to make mistakes: a single pink meant pure love whereas a variegated pink meant rejection!

Women took control of gardens attached to their homes, developing and transforming them. Mrs Charlotte Marryat created a 100-acre garden at Wimbledon House, which included all the ingredients deemed essential to nineteenth-century gardens: shrubberies, a summer house, grotto, rocky cascade, a lake complete with islands, conservatory, orangery, and hot houses for tropical plants. Over in Ealing, Louisa Lawrence organised six gardeners to develop a 28-acre garden containing over 4,000 different species including 500 varieties of roses and 277 varieties of stove orchids. The resultant design attracted considerable acclaim from gardening writers, as well as fifty-three medals within a three-year period at Horticultural Society shows. According to the 1842 *Ladies Magazine of Gardening*, her skills in growing orchids were extraordinary, and the writer exclaimed how her orchid house contained:

Gigantic specimens of papyrus... Widely spreading ferns, a splendid specimen of *Nepenthes distillaria*... Such a collection of those plants which only exist in shade, heat and moisture, as is rarely seen. It was not, however, only with the beauty of the plants that I was delighted: it was the admirable arrangement of the house itself, and the effect produced by the deep shade thrown upon it by the gigantic leaves of the tropical plants while the ear was soothed by the murmuring sound of dropping water. The contrast afforded by this house to the scene presented by the adjoining flower-garden, bright with scarlet verbenas, salvia patens, fuschia fulgans, and all the vivid colours of modern flowers was very striking.

At Waddesdon Manor, Buckinghamshire Alice de Rothschild took an active role in organising the family gardens, as well as the nearby Eyethrope Gardens, which acted as her daytime house. As she had suffered from rheumatic fever, Alice de Rothschild had to avoid being near water at night, so always slept at Waddesdon. The two sites required the services of 160 gardeners. Not content with this, she also took on Villa Victoria, a 333-acre estate near Grasse in France. According to the Rothschild archives, this was 'possibly one of the most ostentatious and extravagant gardens ever seen' and was visited frequently by Queen Victoria. With over 100 gardeners, the maintenance costs were over £500,000 annually, and involved the planting of 55,000 daisies, 25,000 pansies, 10,000 wallflowers, 5,000 forget-me-nots, 23,000 bulbs and narcissi.

Another prominent Victorian female gardener was Ellen Willmott. A passionate plant collector, she owned plant-filled properties in Italy and the South of France, as well as an extensive garden at Warley Place, Essex containing over 600 narcissi varieties as well as a vast rockery complete with a glass-roofed cave known as the Filmy Fern Grotto filled with varieties from Britain and New Zealand. On one occasion she undertook an experiment to find the best potato by growing every type available. People could always tell when she had been visiting the gardens of friends and acquaintances, since she sprinkled seeds of one of her favourite flowers around – the Sea Holly *Eryngium Gigantum* which became known as Miss Willmott's Ghost. Plants and gardening were her passion. In 1906 she wrote to Professor Sarjent at the Arnold Arboretum Harvard admitting 'my plants and my gardens come before anything in life for me and all my time is given up to working in one garden or another, and when it is too dark to see the plants themselves, I read or write about them.' It was a passion that eventually bankrupted her, resulting in the sale of her overseas properties while Warley Place gardens had fallen into neglect.

By far the most well-known of all Victorian women gardeners was Gertrude Jekyll, and her impact on the sector was dramatic, especially in terms of garden design. Until this point, it was unusual for 'well brought up' girls to create careers of this kind. As Catherine Horwood points out in *Gardening Women* (2010), 'She was making it acceptable for respectable women to become professional by earning money, not just by writing about gardens or illustrating plants but also by designing beds and borders and whole garden schemes.'

Jekyll had an artist's eye for plants and design, and rather than organising garden transformations, she became known for creating designs. She never charged for the designs, instead focusing on supplying all the plants required to fulfil a design via her own nursery at Munstead. The number of plants supplied could be extensive. In 1910 she is known to have sent over 1,200 plants to Sir George Sitwell, and the following year supplied 600 plants to Roger Fry. The key feature of her designs involved creating relaxed environments, with drifts of scent and colour flowing into and blending with each other.

During her lifetime, Jekyll worked jointly with architect Edwin Lutyens on 112 gardens, plus hundreds more on her own. Although she was particularly interested in garden design and in almost all cases worked remotely, Jekyll was no armchair gardener. She wrote over 2,000 articles and ten books within nine years, and was also a skilled metalworker, silversmith and painter. She believed strongly in the need to combine art and gardening, writing in her book *Wood and Garden* (1899), 'For planting ground is painting a landscape with living things and I hold that good gardening takes rank with the bounds of the fine arts, so I hold that to plant well needs an artist of no mean capacity.'

Another famous female gardener was Mary Elizabeth Burton, who became Scotland's first female head gardener. Dr Joseph Bell and Dr George W. Balfour had set up a private mental hospital in Lasswade, and knowing of Burton's interest in gardening, asked her to try to interest the female patients in gardening as a cure. She became so successful at her task that she was appointed head gardener in 1897. One of her specialities was potato cultivation, and this ultimately led her becoming the first female president of the Scottish Horticultural Association and the first British woman to be made an Associate Honour of the Royal Horticultural Society.

Only a few women were employed in the big estate kitchen gardens. These were the weeding women, who were paid little more than a garden boy no matter how much experience they possessed. The weeding woman spent much of their time weeding areas of the kitchen garden, primarily paths. At Holkham Hall, weeding women spent all their time removing every single weed, no matter how tiny, from the gravel paths around the walled kitchen garden. The paths had to be kept completely clean, so each weed was picked out by hand. They might also be asked to do other finicky tasks like picking caterpillars off produce or following a gardener to drop potatoes into pre-dug holes.

For working-class women, the development of specialist seed companies and nurseries offered new opportunities. Instead of having to go into service, or work in factories, they could seek work in propagating houses, taking on routine tasks like pricking out, potting on, sorting and packing seeds.

One working-class girl made a significant impact on gardening purely by accident. Mary Anne Brailsford lived with her parents in a cottage in the village of Southwell, Nottinghamshire. In 1809, she was helping her mother in the kitchen when she decided to plant some pips from an apple that she was using for cooking. One of the pips germinated, and Mary eventually planted it in the garden. She later married and moved away, but the tree continued to thrive. After her parents' death, Mary sold the cottage to a local butcher named Matthew Bramley. By this point, the tree was becoming well known in the area for its superb fruit. A local nurseryman asked if he could propagate it and it soon became very popular. In 1883 the Bramley

Apple gained a First Class certificate at the RHS and is now grown in many countries around the world.

Following the rise in interest in gardening among middle-class women who could afford to pay the fees, attention began to focus on the value of professional training. In 1881, Fanny Wilkinson became the first female pupil at the School of Gardening established at Crystal Palace, Sydenham when special arrangements were made to admit 'lady students' due to the sheer number of female applications being received. Within three years Wilkinson had been appointed honorary landscape gardener to the Metropolitan Public Gardens Association (MPGA) and was responsible for designing gardens like Myatts Field Park, Camberwell. Her initial design successes led her to start charging the MPGA, thus giving her the status of one of the earliest professional female gardeners. Fanny Wilkinson actually listed herself in trade directories as a landscape gardener and later became a leading campaigner for women's education and training.

In 1891, the Swanley Horticultural College began admitting women, initially in mixed classes, when five female students joined the college. A special 'supervisor of ladies' was appointed to chaperone the female students and accompany them to lectures. The girls lived in a separate house from their male colleagues but were able to join in all the activities. Numbers rose quickly and by 1895 there were thirty-four female students. They took all the required elements in the syllabus, including zoology, horticulture, meteorology, book-keeping, surveying, the law as it related to horticulture, dairy work, poultry and bee keeping. At the end of the course, they had to achieve a First Class pass in the RHS exam in order to gain a Swanley College certificate. As part of the exam, the students had to spent two days undertaking practical assignments at Wisley. A typical task involved being given a variety of unlabelled composts, boxes and pots, plus six anonymous plants. Each student was expected to identify each plant, choose appropriate compost and plant it up before labelling it and explaining their choices. One of the first female students, Annie Glover, gained the highest marks of all the students, male and female, on her course, winning a silver gilt medal after achieving 260 points out of a possible 300. By 1901, Swanley decided to stop training men and focus purely on women. The standard of training provided at Swanley was high, but the costs were equally so; annual fees amounted to £80 a year, making it accessible only to those who could afford it, such as upper middle-class, educated women.

Kew Gardens began training women in 1895. Former Swanley students Annie Glover and Alice Hutchings were appointed as 'improvers' and paid a weekly wage of 10 shillings. Just like any other recruit, they started work in the horticultural pits, taking cuttings and potting on young plants. Within six months, their wages had risen to 14 shillings a week and by April 1898, Alice had become the sub foreman in the herb department. Other women who had also trained at Swanley soon joined them and their presence as working gardeners soon began to attract attention. When they were appointed, consideration was given to the type of clothing they had to wear. Long skirts and petticoats were deemed inappropriate when undertaking practical tasks like digging, climbing ladders, dealing with trees or moving between valuable potted plants in crowded greenhouses. As a result, it was decided that female gardeners should wear brown bloomers, woollen stockings, boots, jackets, waistcoats, ties and caps. When travelling to and from work, their bloomers were to be covered with a long mackintosh. The sight of these female gardeners at Kew aroused considerable interest, culminating in a 'Kewriosity' poem published in *Fun Magazine* in 1900. It read:

> A rumour went forth, and the town was aglow
> From Greenwich to Richmond, from Peckham to Bow –
> And the man-in-the-street made a fine how-de-do,
> When he heard of the ladies who gardened at Kew.

They gardened in bloomers, the newspapers said;
So to Kew without warning all Londoners sped:
From the roofs of the buses they had a fine view
Of the ladies in bloomers who gardened at Kew.

The orchids were slighted, the lilies were scorned,
The dahlias were flouted till botanists mourned,
But the Londoners shouted, 'What ho, there, Go to;
Who wants to see blooms now you've bloomers at Kew.'

So the botanists held a big meeting and said:
'This won't do, all London has gone off its head,
This costume we find is too painfully "new",
It is making a side-show of beautiful Kew.

'These ladies in bloomers are treated as freaks,
In future they'd all better garden in breeks.'
Now they look so like men no rushes to view,
And a pastoral quiet has settled on Kew.

Other colleges were set up specifically for women. In 1898, Lady Warwick – herself a keen gardener – advertised in *Country Life* magazine for trainees to attend a new college at the Lady Warwick Hostel in Reading. She was deliberately targeting well-educated middle-class girls, and it was a venture which proved very successful. Numbers increased rapidly and soon outgrew the original premises, resulting in a move for the hostel – now renamed Lady Warwick College – to Studley Castle, Warwickshire. The students took courses based on the curriculum at Reading University and in 1916, its exams were granted RHS accreditation.

In 1902, Frances Garnet Wolseley established the Glynde College for Lady Gardeners, supported by high-profile patrons like Gertrude

Jekyll and William Robinson. Wolseley believed it would be a good way of helping women find work, having identified a problem when her mother hired a female gardener with children who had been deserted by her husband. She commented that it could be hard to get women to think of gardening as a suitable profession: 'We do not get the right women. If only the daughters of country squires, Army and Navy…some of whom have but limited income and are obliged to earn their living, would come to us for training, good remuneration in an intensely interesting life would be theirs.' Students set out to create a professional image from the beginning, wearing practical clothing such as short skirts, leggings, boots, a khaki coat or oilskins when digging in the rain.

Similar training schools appeared at Elmwood Nurseries, Cosham and Aldersley Hall, Chester, set up by the Misses Cornelius Wheeler. Regimes were strict and focused on the acquisition of practical skills rather than academic ones. Students were expected to do everything around a garden, including nighttime duties like stoking furnaces or covering cold frames when temperatures suddenly dropped.

Female gardeners encountered considerable criticism. Many opponents of women as gardeners felt that the tasks would make them too muscular and lose their feminine shapes. Others said that they were simply not strong enough to undertake heavy gardening tasks or did not possess the supervisory skills necessary to organise large gardens. Even Jane Loudon initially commented that using a mowing machine might be too much for women, before admitting that it could be 'excellent exercise to the arms and every part of the body'.

Despite this, the number of female gardeners, both amateur and professional, increased steadily. In 1899, the first professional organisation for female gardeners was formed under the aegis of the Women's Agricultural and Horticultural Union. Traveller Ella Christie became enamoured of Japanese garden styles and in 1908 set out to recreate the concept at her home in Cowden Castle, Perthshire.

She sought the help of a female Japanese designer, Taki Handa, who had trained at the Nagoya Royal School of Garden Design, who was at that time studying at Studley College. Taki Handa accepted the challenge, travelling to Scotland to take up her new position, becoming the only woman to be credited with the design of this type of garden. Considerable landscaping had to be undertaken before construction could begin. The 7-acre site was a marshy field, and a ditch had to be dammed in order to create the required lake. The aim was to create Shā Raku En, 'the place of pleasure and delight'. Mounds were created giving areas such as the Flat Gardens and the Slopes of Mount Fuji, with the perfect stones being imported to create the right effect. Professor Suzuki, 18th Hereditary Head of the Soami School of Imperial Garden Design at Nagoya, visited the garden regularly over the next few years to prune the various shrubs and trees. It has been described as 'the most important Japanese garden in the Western World'.

Some women even set up their own businesses, as an announcement in the *Hampstead Garden Suburb Town Crier* newspaper indicated in 1912. It stated that Miss Bevett and Miss Garlick were willing to provide householders with gardening work 'by day or week for long or short periods'.

It was not just practical gardening in which women made their mark during this period. They were also active writers. Indeed, Jane Loudon became the most influential of all female horticultural writers during the nineteenth century. She developed a love of gardening after her marriage and took up the pen to provide women with a detailed source of information. Her first books set out to provide a guide to British wildflowers and an easy-to-understand introduction to botany for ladies.

Published in 1846, her *Ladies' Companion to the Flower Garden* quickly sold more than 20,000 copies and stayed in print for over thirty years. Initially published in monthly issues costing 2s 6d each, it was eventually sold in bound volumes. Her target market was clearly identified: ladies who lived in the new suburban villas and houses being constructed on the outskirts of towns and cities. She wrote how, 'A lady, with the assistance of a common labourer to level and prepare the ground, may turn a barren waste into a flower garden with her own hands.' After her *Ladies' Companion*, Louden then averaged one book a year for the next fifteen years.

Anne Pratt chose to focus on education-based garden publishing. Over a thirteen-year period she created seventeen books, all of which were purchased by Queen Victoria for her children. A skilled writer and artist, her book *The Field, The Garden and the Woodland* (1846) went through three editions in less than a decade. Her next five-volume series, *The Flowering Plants and Ferns of Great Britain* (1855) proved to be the most popular standard work of the period. Another series, *The Flowering Plants of Great Britain* (1855) was sold as a volume set of five books, or as a weekly part work costing 1 shilling per issue. In addition, sheets from the book were printed separately and sold to provide a pictorial resource for teachers, which could be hung on classroom walls. She told her readers that 'one of the chief objects is to aid those who have not hitherto studied Botany', while in the introduction to her book *Flowers and their Associations* (1840), Pratt wrote it 'was intended chiefly for the information and amusement of those who, while fond of flowers have not made them the source of their study.' Her influence in terms of education and general interest was such that she has been credited with generating considerable interest in British flora by combining science and flowers. In 1853, Queen Victoria gave her a grant from the Civil List, recognising her role in spreading knowledge and information about plants.

The work of Alicia Amherst reflects just how far women had progressed in terms of the garden sector. She was interested in studying the history of gardening, and despite having no academic training undertook innovative research into archive material in

Cambridge, the Public Record Office, and the British Library. Her resultant book *A History of Gardening in England* (1896) gained her the honorary freedom of the Worshipful Company of Gardeners and the Freedom of the City of London in 1896.

Although many of these gardening women are believed to have had considerable sympathy for the aims of the Suffragettes, there was little support when, in 1913, Suffragettes Olive Wharry and Lilian Lenton attacked the Kew Glasshouses and burnt the Tea Pavilion to the ground in a publicity stunt. A contemporary record in the *Journal of Horticulture* noted how 'they smashed a quantity of glass in the orchid house, and in a manner that one can scarcely accredit to sane adults, wantonly tried to destroy the plants. Rare and delicate plants, under bell-glasses, attracted the special venom of these feminists.'

Following the First World War, the number of women taking up gardening as a career increased still further. This was a period characterised by 'surplus women', women whose fiancées had been killed in the war, and with a shortage of men had far less chance of finding a husband. Other women wanted to strike out on their own, having experienced the freedom and gained skills during wartime, especially through serving in the Land Army. Gardening offered potential opportunities to develop careers as working gardeners and designers. Norah Lindsay was one of the many women who took this path. Her marriage had ended by 1918 and given her precarious financial situation, she offered her skills as a garden designer to her many society friends. Working on a retainer basis, she used public transport to travel nationwide to work on sites including Blickling Hall, Cliveden and Mottisfont. She advocated a relaxed style of gardening, noting that 'in a garden where labour is scarce and the soil is beneficent, all manner of tiny seedlings get overlooked till, lo and behold! A handsome clump has established in the most unlikely position claiming squatter's rights, and in nine cases out of ten, succeeding in establishing its claim.'

The existing Women's Agricultural and Horticultural International Union changed its name to the Women's Farm and Garden Association, focusing on the need to organise apprenticeships for these new women gardeners. More and more girls sought professional training, mainly at Swanley, and although some scholarships were available, almost all students came from upper-class backgrounds. Fees were high, and there were also the high costs relating to clothing and accommodation. Uniforms had to be purchased from specific stores like Harrods, while during the winter, students were required to wear a tunic made from Swanley Tweed. Tunics had to possess three pleats front and back and be sufficiently long enough to touch the ground when the student was kneeling down. In addition, students had to acquire a Boy Scouts belt from Messrs. Gamages in London, blouses each costing 27s 6d, white or brown jerseys, extra-long stockings and regulation knickers – specified as being '15 inches from waist to crotch, then 10¼ inches long'. To complete the outfit, girls wore a brown felt hat, a mackintosh, coloured silk handkerchief, blue serge apron, strong gardening gloves, clogs, gumboots and strong boots. Summer uniforms were slightly different and involved green tunics made from material available only from Harrods, blouses, a plain straw hat, extra-long summer weight stockings obtainable from Bond Street-based London Glove Company. Each student also had to bring with them their own personal linen in the form of two pairs of sheets, two pillowcases, four towels and four dinner napkins, all of which had to be carefully labelled. The training was arduous, but students left with a highly regarded qualification. Brenda Colvin was one such student. She joined Swanley just after the end of the First World War and by 1922 had set up a business as a landscape architect designing all manner of projects from window boxes to school grounds. Over the next two decades, Colvin was involved in over 300 projects, including an addition to the Archduke Charles Albert Hapsburg's garden at Zywiec in Poland.

The activities of these women designers and gardeners introduced new stylistic concepts and ideas. At Sissinghurst, Vita Sackville-West created a fashion for pastels and purples, including a legendary White Garden about which she wrote 'There will be white pansies, and white peonies and white irises with their grey leaves... All the same I cannot help hoping that the great ghostly barn-owl will sweep silently across a pale garden, next summer, in the twilight – the plate garden that I am now planning under the first flakes of snow.' Over at Bodnant in Wales, Lady Aberconway developed spectacular semi-formal borders and terraces focusing on native plants, roses, paeonies and herbaceous perennials. In 1931 her skills were recognised when the RHS granted her the highly prestigious Victoria medal.

A revival in herb gardening soon began, led by two women Hilda Layel and Maud Grieve. Demand for culinary and medicinal herbs had increased during the First World War and in 1937, Hilda Layel wrote a book entitled *The Magic of Herbs: A Modern Book of Secrets*, aiming to highlight both the history and use of herbs in medicine and pharmacy. She also set up the first Culpeper's store in Baker Street, London and established the Society of Herbalists (which later became the Herb Society). Maud Grieve had also had a long interest in herbalism, albeit from a cultivation standpoint, having set up an Association of Herb Growers prior to the start of the First World War thanks to her 'Vegetable Drug Farm and Medicinal Herb Nursery' at her home in Buckinghamshire. Layel and Grieve had both worked together to create a definitive herb guide known as *A Modern Herbal*. Published in 1931, it was the first such guide to be published for over a hundred years. As Hilda Layel pointed out, 'Surely it makes a garden more romantic and wonderful to know that wallflowers, irises, lupins, delphiniums, columbines, dahlias and chrysanthemums, every flower in the garden from the first Snowdrop to the Christmas Rose are not only there for man's pleasure but have their compassionate use in his pain.'

Culpeper's went on to set up a factory in Gloucestershire to provide herbal products for their shops. It proved be extremely successful and during the Second World War provided a range of medicines, drugs and health food for the RAF using locally grown fruit, vegetables and herbs such as coltsfoot, comfrey, cowslip, garlic, horsetail, nettle, parsley, watercress, leek and dandelions.

In 1941, Hilda Layel led the way in combating the government's proposed Pharmacy and Medicines Bill, which would seek to restrict all sales of medicines and herbs to pharmacies, thus preventing herbalists from prescribing and selling dried herbs. Hilda's staunch opposition, combined with that of her allies like Viscount Plummer, who had benefited from herbal remedies during the First World War, resulted in crucial amendments being incorporated.

The ending of the Second World War brought yet more change to the status and training of female gardeners. Although the return of soldiers from the armed services did mean that many found themselves replaced by men, there was a steady move towards greater long-term opportunities for women, with the recognition that women could play an important role in the labour force. Women sought appropriate training in the world of gardening: by 1948 there were over 2,000 students registered at Studley. However, the government's decision to move towards co-educational schools led to the closing of colleges like Studley, while Swanley College was simply amalgamated into the South Eastern Agricultural College at Wye, then into Imperial College, London.

Chapter 4

Urban Housing and Gardens

The late eighteenth and nineteenth centuries witnessed a major change in the way in which people viewed housing and gardens. Large landowners enclosed their lands under the terms of the Enclosure Acts, thus making it harder for the rural poor to make a living in the countryside as they could no longer farm or place animals on common land. In addition, the vogue for Capability Brown and Humphrey Repton-style landscapes surrounding their great houses meant that villages were often deliberately moved to create scenic views. In Jane Austen's *Mansfield Park* (1814), improvements to the fictional Sotherton Court are discussed with the owner, Mr Rushworth, commenting that Sotherton looked like a 'dismal old prison':

'Oh! For shame!' cried Mrs Norris. 'A prison indeed! Sotherton Court is the noblest old place in the world.'

'It wants improvement, ma'am, beyond anything. I never saw a place that wanted so much improvement in my life; and it is so forlorn that I do not know what can be done with it... I hope I shall have some good friend to help me.'

'Your best friend upon such an occasion,' said Miss Bertram, calmly, 'would be Mr Repton, I imagine.'

'That is what I was thinking of. As he has done so well by Smith, I think I had better have him at once. His terms are five guineas a day.'

At Holkham Hall, the construction of a new house set in landscaped grounds led to the village being steadily moved further away from its original site through the construction of new houses closer to the coast. The original village houses were destroyed and the stone used elsewhere, thus providing a better view for the hall itself. Over at Blaise Castle, near Bristol, the Quaker banker John Scandrett Harford commissioned John Nash to build a village around a village green complete with small gardens hidden behind hedges to create a picturesque image of the castle itself. Other landowners in search of the picturesque added towers, follies and arches, reflecting the popularity of Gothic horror in literature.

Many industrialists and merchants and their families moved away from towns, building houses and establishing large gardens in more desirable areas. A typical example was the physician Robert Darwin and his wife Susannah (daughter of pottery magnate Josiah Wedgewood), who left the Potteries and built a house named The Mount on 7 acres of land near Shrewsbury. The garden they created became well known for the quality of its flowers, trees, hot houses and terraces.

Poet William Wordsworth encouraged the idea of gardening as a retreat, a place of relaxation. In a letter to Lady Beaumont in 1807, he recommended construction of a trellised bower in which the flower borders would be 'edged with boxwood, its paths paved with different coloured pebbles, with a mossed seat and some table and a hedge of eglantine and bay.' To make the perfect scene, there should also be a stone fountain and an 'ivied cottage surrounded by English shrubs and flowers.'

Within towns, the gentry and emerging middle classes occupied houses with varying amounts of garden. In 1838 John Loudon published *The Suburban Gardener and Villa Companion*, the first time anyone had focused on such gardens. It divided houses and gardens into categories ranging from first- to fourth-rate depending on their size, focusing attention primarily on the final three groups. The first category of houses referred to parks and farms of up to 100 acres or more. Houses falling into the second category possessed between 2 to 10 acres of garden and were occupied by professionals and wealthy tradesmen. Third-rate houses were typically those to be found in suburbs like Chiswick and possessed long narrow gardens targeting smaller businessmen. By far the largest group was destined for mechanics, clerks and artisans, and these fourth-rate houses offered a small frontage of just 14 feet, and a small back garden.

Loudon's book set out to give ideas on how to maximise gardens in these spaces, providing templates such as the 'gardenesque' which was regarded as 'more suitable for those persons who are botanists, rather than admirers of scenery because it is best calculated for displaying the individual beauty of trees and plants.' These gardens would be planted and maintained by private gardeners such as Cuthbert Embleton, who worked as a gardener in Brixton. Living separately from his employer, he travelled each day to do the garden. Loudon's ideal style was romantic, with lots of climbers, while windows would open out onto an urn-filled terrace leading to a feature like a pool, and beyond this would be a kitchen garden. Above all, it was a way in which the gardeners could maximise all aspects of their garden by growing as many species as possible. The simplest of Loudon's garden templates involved two rectangular grass sections in the front garden, divided by a path. A large shrub was to be planted in the centre of each section, with smaller ones at each corner. The back garden was to be 'planted with four rows of low trees, two near each walk…leaving a broad space in the middle about 100ft in length, well adapted for a party walking backwards and forward in the summer season, or a dance, or for placing a tent on, for sitting under at the farther end.' Such a garden would cost up to £40 to plant and landscape, with paved walkways, 6-feet-tall trees, a refuse pit and a fixing posts for a clothes line. He believed it would be ideal for 'an occupier who had no time to spare for its culture, and who did not wish for flowers. It would not suit a lady who was fond of gardening, but for one who was not, or had no time to attend to it, and who had several children, this garden could be very suitable.'

Alternatively, he believed that this size of garden could provide a good supply of food with nasturtiums, herbs and dwarf fruit trees growing in the front beds. At the back of the house, there would be enough space for gooseberries, marrows, asparagus, sea kale, artichokes, cabbages, peas, turnips, carrots, leeks, garlic, lettuce, chicory, celery, mustard, cress and radishes, all involving two hours' work each day between April to September in addition to help from a manservant or the householder's wife. He believed that it was not worth employing a gardener since 'for the £15 or £20 a year which he must pay a hired gardener he might purchase as much fruit and vegetables as he could grow.'

Householders wanting a garden suitable for 'exercise and recreation' involving a range of plants would need a total of 1,800 plants for front and back, including alpines in pots and a lawn and payment of £10 for a jobbing gardener to maintain it. Loudon's own garden was somewhat larger, costing £100 to plant and £300 for greenhouses with eighty-two planters containing 'all the orders and tribes of hot house plants in cultivation in Britain', plus 600 alpine species in the garden.

For many people, especially among landowners, gardens became something of a status symbol in which they competed to create the most extravagant bedding displays, or to have the earliest fruit. There were reports that bedding plant lists were used to demonstrate wealth: 10,000 plants for a squire, 20,000 for a baronet, 30,000 for an earl and 50,000 for a duke. In 1856, Shrubland Park's head gardener proudly indicated that he used 100,000 plants to create the estate's floral displays.

Throughout the nineteenth century, towns and cities expanded dramatically, with over 800,000 men, women and children moving from the countryside to seek work. Houses were frequently quickly constructed and consisted of back-to-back terraced houses in narrow alleys and courts, where there was no scope for gardens. Quite apart from the pollution created following the rise of industrialisation, the air and soil was contaminated by soot. Coal was the main fuel used for heating, and this produced vast quantities of soot, especially in the winter. Pea souper fogs were common, especially in London, when people found it extremely hard to find their way around streets due to the dense fog. In *Bleak House* (1852), *Little Dorrit* (1857), and *Our Mutual Friend* (1865), Charles Dickens highlighted the sheer quantities of soot, dirt and dust that were present with references to dirty air, gardens full of dust, dust mountains, stagnant pools outside brickmakers houses and even a 'golden dustman' who made a fortune from dust. Streets were incredibly dirty, with boys acting as street sweepers creating paths for people to cross the road. Dust yards emerged, in which vast quantities of dust were collected up before being eventually transported by barge to be recycled on agricultural land.

In this atmosphere, establishing gardens in towns could be very hard. Shirley Hibberd commented in his 1923 book *The Town Garden* that 'It is generally thought that a city garden is an impossibility! That vegetation cannot be reconciled to the close air, the darkness, and the smoke of towns; and that all attempts to mingle the rural with the rural with the urban must…turn out failures.' Meanwhile, Charles Dickens refers to the roof garden created by Mr Riah, a Jewish moneylender in *Our Mutual Friend*, as being 'a blackened chimney-stack over which some humble creeper had been trained…a few boxes of humble flowers and ever-greens completed the garden; and the encompassing wilderness of dowager old chimneys twirled their cowls and fluttered their smoke.'

In some towns like Preston, Lancashire, the level of smoke pollution was so high that soot had to be regularly removed from the surface of the soil. Consequently, garden magazines increasingly provided advice as to the type of plants that could survive these conditions.

Although the environment was not ideal for plants and gardening, demand for plants and greenery was high. For those who could afford it, one option was to lease plants by the day, week, or month. During the Regency period, nurserymen like James Cochran created profitable businesses fulfilling the requirements of the 'Beau monde', the upper-class ladies and gentlemen visiting London for the Season. At society events such as receptions, balls, and even afternoon visits, people wanted flowers to decorate rooms, frequently trying to outdo each other in terms of displays. At a ball, for example, there would be potted plants and floral arrangements on the floor, on side tables, in front of mirrors and on dining tables. Typical flowers could include heartsease, dianthus, mignonette, stocks, and roses, all placed in a variety of pots and containers including special Wedgewood pots. There were even occasions when pots of fruit-bearing trees would be placed at the sides of a dining room, with guests picking their own fruit to eat at the end of the meal. This was a very lucrative business for nurserymen like James Cochran, who in 1816 supplied the Duke of Grafton with '104 plants for the night, kept a week' at a cost of £7 6s, while flowers for Mrs Baring's party involved considerable expense. Here, Cochran had to provide 1,004 plants together with 'the use of 27 green baskets, moss, twine, wire, nails, sticks etc to 5 men 2 days (£2.10.0) horse and cart 2 days (£1.10s) a large quantity of laurel and evergreens, cut flowers for china jars for tables, horse, cart and men clearing away', leading to a total cost of £65 15s. In June 1818, Mr Cockrel spent £62 on 1,240 plants and paid £1 10s for delivery, setting them in place and then collecting them the following day.

Equally popular was the concept of hiring plants to decorate the outside of a building. London nurseryman James Mangles issued a floral calendar in 1839 indicating that the only way for families 'to maintain a gay display in their windows' since 'no skill or art... No assiduity or care – will protect plants from the destructive infection of the pernicious "blacks",' was to take out a contract covering the supply and replacement of plants on a regular basis. He offered contracts by the year, quarter, month, week or just for the summer. Demand ranged from hiring a few plants for window boxes such as migonnettes at 6 shillings per dozen, or a minimum of seventy plants for use on balconies, in dining rooms, gardens or greenhouse pots.

Despite the dirt and contamination, many gardeners tried hard to grow their own flowers and create some kind of garden, often via window boxes and allotments, or rented garden space on the outskirts of an urban area. In Durham, for example, around 2,000 gardens are known to have existed around the edge of the city, which were rented at a cost of £16 per acre, with occupants ranging from grocers to labourers. William Howitt's 1844 *Rural Life in England* commented, 'There are, in the outskirts of Nottingham, upwards of 5,000 gardens, the bulk of which are occupied by the working class... In winter, they have rather desolate aspects... In spring and summer, they look exceedingly well.'

Howitt went on to say that:

Early in Spring – as soon, in fact, as the days begin to lengthen – you see them digging into their gardens, clearing away the dead stalks of last year's growth, and digging up the soil; but especially on fine days in February and March are they busy. Trees are pruned, beds are dug, walks cleaned, and all the refuse and decayed vegetation piled up, in heaps; the smoke of the fires in which it is burnt, rolling up from many a garden, and sending its pungent odour to meet you afar off. It is pleasant to see, as the season advances, how busy their occupants become, bustling there with their busses in the hands and their tools on their shoulders, wheeling in manure; and cleaning out their summer-house; and what an air of daily increasing neatness they assume, till they are one wide expanse of blossomed fruit-trees and flowering fragrance.

People tried very hard to cultivate what space they had available, utilising innovative ways of helping plants survive such as growing standard roses under umbrellas to shade them from the soot. In *Great Expectations* (1861), Dickens described an attempt to create an oasis of greenery in very small areas, when John Wemmick, clerk to the lawyer Mr Jaggers, lived in a house with mock Gothic windows and takes Pip on a tour around the garden, which included:

> A bower about a dozen yards off, but which was approached by such ingenious twists of path that it took quite a long time to get at. Our punch was cooling in an ornamental lake, on whose margin the bower was raised. This piece of water (with an island in the middle that might have been our salad for supper) was of a circular form, and he had constructed a little fountain in it, which, when you set a little mill going and a cork out of a pipe, played to that powerful extent that it made the back of your hand quite wet.

Even in London, gardens could be discovered in the most surprising of places. Elizabeth Kent's family had a rooftop garden near St Paul's Churchyard. Hector Gavin was a physician living in the East End of London and his book *Sanitary Ramblings* (1848) highlighted some of the unexpected scenes he discovered while strolling around Hackney. In Whiskers Gardens he was surprised to find:

> A very extensive piece of ground, which is laid out in neat plots as gardens. The choicest flowers are frequently raised here, and great taste and considerable refinement are evidently possessed by those who cultivate them…the weary artisan, and the toil worn weaver here dedicate their spare hours…to the cultivation of beautiful flowers.

Industrial and urban areas often provided the biggest number of enthusiasts judging by the number of specialist florists' associations, including the Sheffield Cutlers, who became highly skilled in growing and breeding varieties of auriculas.

Gardening increasingly became regarded as a way of keeping working men busy, happy and less inclined to become involved in politics or criminal activity. According to Loudon, 'flower-gardening had emerged as a means by which humble men could prove their respectability. Gardening, it was believed, had a civilising effect upon the poor.'

In 1820, John Moggridge built some experimental villages in Monmouthshire, Wales. Each house had its own small garden and was leased out for the period of 'four lives or ninety-nine years, if the latter exceeded the former'. This created a sense of security among the tenants, who now had an added reason for developing gardens and keeping their houses in good condition. Prizes were given for the best gardens, as well as the best fruit, vegetables and flowers. During a miners' strike in 1827, Moggridge stated that those miners who had gardens were the most peaceful and self-reliant.

Ten years later, speaking at the South Devon and East Cornwall and Horticultural Society meeting, Dr Hamilton commented that:

> By promoting the innocent and salutary effects of gardening among their poorer tenantry, by contributing in the names of the most deserving to the cottager's fund, and stimulating them to become competitors for the cottager's prizes, gentlemen will not only promote the welfare of their tenantry, but by awakening a taste for the innocent and healthful recreations of gardening among the neighbouring peasantry, reform their habits, elevate their morals, and improve their condition; teaching them to become independent of the soul-debasing, spirit-breaking aid

of parochial charity, and thus relieve our parishes of one of their most oppressive burdens, the poor's rate.

In 1866, Lord Leicester, owner of Holkham Hall, stated that it was beneficial for a landowner to provide good quality housing for his estate workers. The majority of his workers occupied the 521 cottages on his estate, whereas those workers who lived elsewhere had 3 or 4 miles to walk each day and paid high rents to live in poor accommodation. The provision of good accommodation was therefore beneficial for everyone.

Commercial companies also recognised the advantages of providing decent accommodation, since it would encourage staff to stay with them rather than moving on. In 1873, Veitch and Sons moved thirty of their male employees into a large house near the nursery. Bedrooms were placed on the upper floors, and on the ground floor were a library, newsroom, smoking room and dining room. An adjacent field was converted into a recreation area. Contemporary reports noted 'no expense has been saved to procure for them homely and country-like privileges, a boon which young men unaccustomed to town life cannot fail to appreciate.'

Availability of garden space changed over the century, reflecting the continued expansion of urban areas. This was partly the result of initiatives by various manufacturers and industrialists, who long recognised the need to provide a healthier environment for their workforce. In the late eighteenth century, Richard Crawshay established an ironworks in Merthyr Tydfil, complete with houses with gardens for his employees.

At Leadhills, Stirlingshire, James Stirling was appointed manager of the local mine company with orders to improve profitability. He did so by improving miners' living conditions by building stone cottages with gardens, thus encouraging them to take up gardening as well as offering a health insurance scheme and education for the children. Other mining companies followed suit. None of the houses was large and they were generally terraced in style. Examples of typical Victorian miners' housing of the period can be seen at Beamish Museum, near Durham, which has set up a Victorian town containing houses that were originally built for the Hetton Coal Company in a bid to recruit miners. The terraced houses are small but have simple a garden front and back, complete with cinder paths.

In 1878, Robert Dent's *Old and New Birmingham* spoke about:

> Little plots of ground let for a guinea per annum, laid out with flowers, or planted with vegetables, currents and gooseberry bushes, strawberries and other useful 'garden stuff' becoming increasingly scarce due to the spread of housing resulting in shabby suburbs which have long since covered the pleasant artisan gardens of seventy years ago.

Despite this, in Birmingham and most other big cities, most people did not lease or rent gardens.

Improvements in health came to be closely linked with gardening. Encouraging people to participate in outdoor tasks within the garden were increasingly recognised as being health giving. This is clearly illustrated in Frances Hodgson Burnett's 1911 children's novel, *The Secret Garden*, which starts in a garden of death, and ends in a garden of rebirth. It features a young girl who discovers a walled garden that has been locked away at her new home and who becomes friendly with the gardener. She regains her strength by being outside in the gardens and learning about plants. In due course she uses the garden to help her cousin recover from an illness that had left him confined to a wheelchair, restoring both his physical and mental health. The story reflects Frances Hodgson Burnett's love affair with gardens that began as a child living in a Manchester terrace, which backed onto fields. She recalled that those fields were the 'back garden of Eden', a place of perpetual summer and flowers, in light and air. For Burnett, gardens were always a place of healing and resurrection, commenting that 'As long as one has a garden one has a future, and as long as one has a future one is alive.'

Chapter 5

Garden Styles

As the nineteenth century dawned, gardening styles were beginning to move on from the Capability Brown landscapes surrounding great houses, with picturesque styles complete with hermits in caves and grottos declining in popularity. In *Sense and Sensibility* (1811), Jane Austen mocked this style by having Edward Ferrar comment that he prefers 'Tall straight trees rather than short, blasted ones' and that he disliked 'nettles or thistles, or heath blossoms.'

The gentry were paying more attention to their gardens, creating 'wildernesses' full of shrubs and paths along with areas for cut flowers to adorn their houses. These were places to walk in, especially when entertaining visitors. In Jane Austen's *Pride and Prejudice* (1813), Lady Catherine de Bourgh requests that Elizabeth Bennet walks with her along the 'prettyish kind of little wilderness on one side of your lawn'. Herbs were widely grown in the gardens along with common flowers like hollyhocks, roses, honeysuckle, larkspur, tulips and pinks. In due course, it was not unusual to find several styles working alongside each other, with house owners having a long list of desirable features ranging from rock gardens to orchards that they tried to incorporate even into the smallest area.

Criticism began to appear about the way householders were combining styles. Shirley Hibberd, author of *The Town Garden* (1855), encouraged his readers to accept gardening to match locations with 'no piles of stone by hall doors to act as rockeries' or 'winding paths, to make butchers boys giddy and perplex the stranger'. Instead, they should focus on creating harmonious greenery without the garishness of carpet bedding.

Many of the dominant garden trends that have become commonplace in modern gardens owe their origins to the styles that emerged during the nineteenth and first half of the twentieth century.

Kitchen and Walled Gardens

These formed an essential element in almost every garden from town gardens to workhouses, and the grand walled gardens of the great estates. This was a period when the range of flowers, vegetables and similar produce being cultivated expanded rapidly, with new introductions due to nursery breeding programmes or as exotic introductions from overseas. Such gardens were expected to provide all the produce necessary for use in the kitchen and around the house. The head gardener would inform the cook what was available, and it would then be harvested to suit requirements. This could be very specific, such as forty beetroots, all of which had to be exactly the same size, resulting in nearly twice the amount being harvested in order to match demand.

Kitchen gardens were generally placed out of sight, hidden behind walls or bushes depending on available space. Planting was in straight rows, divided by paths. The concept of rotation cropping became normal practice, allowing the soil to recover nutrients and benefit from different types of crops.

Almost every large estate had its own walled garden. Mrs Jennings in *Sense and Sensibility* describes such a garden as having 'great garden walls that are covered with the very best fruit trees in the country, and such a mulberry tree in one corner! Then there is a dovecote, some delightful stewponds and a very pretty canal; and everything in short that one could wish for.'

The walled garden was designed with two purposes in mind: to provide food for the house and to be an area where the house owner could bring guests to view exotic produce and desirable plants. The size of a walled garden varied between half an acre to several. A common feature of walled gardens was their distance from the main house – they provided a function that had to be hidden from general view. At Windsor, the walled kitchen garden was located 1.5 miles from the castle. A special gravel drive was installed so that Queen Victoria did not have to walk very far, instead riding in a pony and trap. When the landowner appeared with guests, it was expected that apprentices and under gardeners would keep out of sight, moving away from whatever area of the garden they were working in. Only the head gardener would deal with these guests.

At Holkham Hall, the walled garden is located some distance from the main house. Occupying 6 acres, it is completely enclosed by 14-feet-tall brick walls, which include a large gardener's bothy that provided accommodation for garden boys, apprentices, journeymen and foremen. The head gardener had a separate house just beyond the entrance to the main house. On entering the garden, the house owner or visitor would ring a bell at the entrance. This would summon the head gardener, who would then take them on a tour of the first part of the garden, an area visible from the entrance. This area acted as an exhibition space where guests could view choice plants, and the house owner could show off his gardener's skills. Among the choice plants grown in this area were pineapples, bananas, melons and vines. The layout was simple: wide, gravelled paths provided clean, easy access for guests to explore the extensive display beds containing both produce and flowers, a decorative stone watering pool and a series of hot houses leaning against a tall, brick wall running the entire width of the walled garden. Doorways in the central wall provided access for the gardeners to the working area beyond – an area that was out of bounds to visitors.

Building walled gardens offered considerable advantages to estate gardeners. The tall walls created an interior micro-climate making it easier to grow a wide range of plants, especially exotics, as well as protection against rabbits and deer living in the adjacent parkland. Trees such as apricots could be trained against the walls, helping to encourage greater fruiting. Cold frames incorporated bevelled glass allowing water to run down the centre panes into channels and be captured for later use, while sunken pit houses were designed to allow warm air generated by stoves to circulate. Similar hot pipes led through all the greenhouses and hot houses. During the winter, it was the task of the gardeners to tend the boilers all night, monitoring heat levels, while during the summer they had to constantly check levels of ventilation, making adjustments where necessary. Between 800 to 1,000 tonnes of coal were needed every year to provide the necessary heating fuel.

Some walled gardens incorporated serpentine or crinkle-crankle walls rather than straight ones. Apart from their decorative qualities, the curves in the walls could act as sun traps and provide greater protection for delicate plants.

The costs of creating a walled garden could be high. The Royal Palaces originally had kitchen gardens attached to each one, but in the mid nineteenth century it was decided that it would make better financial sense to have one very large garden. The closure of the other kitchen gardens, such as that at Kensington Palace, would result in funds to spend on the new one at Frogmore (Windsor), although costs soon outweighed advantages. In August 1941, *The Times* described what went into creating the new royal kitchen garden:

> Garden walls, forcing houses, Conservatories, Pine, Melon and other pits, Mushroom houses, Gardeners and Under Garden Houses and Shed Buildings. A brick wall, 12 feet high, and nearly 2,000 yards in length, has just been contracted by the

(office of) Woods and Forests to be erected by Mr Chadwick. A handsome terrace, with a wall in front, 800 feet long, will be constructed in the gardens (for the Promenade of the Royal Family) extending nearly the length of one side, with several flights of stone steps leading from the gardens.

As construction progressed, Queen Victoria and Prince Albert made many requests for various alterations, thus increasing the overall cost. These requests included Prince Albert's decision to order extra rooms in one of the gardener's houses and a water closet purely for the use of royal attendants. The eventual cost of £44,962 6s was nearly twice the original estimate.

- Once constructed, the new walled kitchen garden included: 840 feet of hothouses, plus growing pits 1,665 feet long providing a range of early asparagus, cucumbers, melons, pineapples, French beans and grapes.
- 13 acres of vegetables which were, in due course, extended to 21 acres and were screened by fruit trees.
- Houses for the head gardener and his deputy.
- A fountain measuring 30 feet in diameter made from polished granite.
- Two reception rooms in a gardener's house for use by the Queen and Prince when visiting the gardens.

Even royalty had to seek permission to enter the walled garden, as *The Times* reported:

The Bells required at the Entrances for the convenience of the workman and others generally as well as to prevent injury to the doors from persons kicking violently against them… beside which the want of them has recently been complained of by Prince Albert also with Her Majesty frequently visits the Gardens without any previous notice: Upon a late occasion His Royal Highness was obliged to return being unable to get into the gardens and having no means of making his attention known to enter.

Glasshouses

Glasshouses were nothing new, with variations on glasshouses existing as long ago as Roman times, when gardeners had to find a daily way of supplying specific fruit required by Emperor Tiberius, resulting in the creation of growing carts on wheels covered by an opaque material. In 1577, Thomas Hill wrote in his book *The Gardener's Labyrinth* that:

> The young plants may be defended from cold and boisterous windes, yea, frosts, the cold aire, and hot Sunne, if Glasses made for the onely purpose, be set over them, which on such wise bestowed on the beds, yielded in a manner to Tiberius Caesar, Cucumbers all the year, in which he took great delight…

Large estates frequently incorporated glasshouses within their kitchen gardens, using underfloor pipes heated by charcoal stoves. The creation of these glasshouses was expensive, and possession of a glasshouse reflected the power and prestige of the landowner. The cost of the glass, let alone the heating, was extremely high. Removal of taxes on windows and glass in 1851, along with technological improvements in glass production, led to a massive growth in demand.

By the mid nineteenth century, the use of glasshouses to grow elaborate displays of exotic plants and palms and produce was widespread. No longer confined to the great estates, glasshouses were appearing in even the smallest gardens, although the major cost was providing the fuel to keep them heated during winter. Coal-burning boilers were the most common option, although some glasshouse owners did experiment with alternatives, particularly animal manure. There are records of an Essex farmer named Mr Joseph French forcing vines and nectarines by creating 6-feet-wide piles of cow dung along the interior sides of his vinery. Fresh dung was constantly added to cover the old dung, and as it decomposed, it gave off heat levels that were said to reach around 18-21°C (65-70°F).

All kinds of glasshouses were created including display houses, alpine houses, ferneries, orangeries, mushroom houses, conservatories and greenhouses. Each had a slightly different function, designed to grow specific types of produce and/or act as a way of showing off collections of plants. Considerable innovation went into the creation of these buildings such as Quarry Bank's combination of vineries flanking a show house that incorporated an early example of a rounded, curved iron frame. Meanwhile, at Cragside, in Northumberland, the orchard house possessed turntables on which were placed potted plants, allowing them to be easily moved throughout the day, thus ensuring the plants received even lighting in order to achieve consistent growth.

Apart from being used to grow exotic plants, glasshouses were invaluable in enabling gardeners to grow the vast quantities of annuals required to create displays of carpet bedding during the summer season.

Cottage Gardening

Cottage gardening was a popular style throughout the nineteenth century. This was the age-old garden style that could be found surrounding cottages in rural areas, which by the mid-1800s had become repositories of plants that had vanished from fashionable gardens, such as auriculas, pinks and tulips. Loudon pointed out that tradesmen and workers often had 'the best cottage-gardens, and many of them, especially at Norwich, Manchester and Paisley, excel in the culture of florists' flowers.' John Clare's poem 'The Shepherd's Calendar' describes the general image of a typical cottage garden:

> But such as every farmer's garden yield
> Fine cabbage roses painted like her face
> And shining pansys trimmed in golden lace
> And tall tuft larkheels feathered wi flowers
> And woodbines climbing o'er the door in bowers
> And London tufts of many a mottl'd hue
> And pale pink pea and monkshood darkly blue
> And white and purple jilliflowers that stay
> Lingering in blossom summer half away

Less effusive were more practical descriptions of gardens linked to the homes of farm labourers, which focused on growing food such as fruiting trees, current and gooseberry bushes, and vegetables. Surplus produce was taken to market. In 1848, George William Johnson founded an inexpensive magazine, *The Cottage Gardener*, which was dedicated to this form of gardening. By 1854, it was selling 6,000 copies weekly, thus reflecting the demand for suitable information.

The rise of the Arts and Crafts movement, which encouraged a more romantic, informal planting style, fitted in perfectly with the cottage garden concept promoted by Gertrude Jekyll and William Robinson. William Morris criticised carpet bedding as being 'an aberration of the human mind', a view shared by Robinson, while Jekyll used ideas from Morris' textile designs within her garden. Cottage gardens by comparison were places that could act as a retreat from the world. Writing about the construction of his new garden at Red House, William Morris stated: 'Large or small, it should look both orderly and rich... It should by no means imitate either the wilfulness or the wildness of Nature, but should look like a thing never to be seen except near a house. It should, in fact, look like a part of the house.' His architect, Philip Webb, issued orders that the builders were not to remove any trees or bushes without his express permission, and gave instructions for the type of plants and climbers to be used when the house was completed. The result was a garden full of relaxed herbaceous borders and fragrant hedges, which ultimately helped make cottage gardening fashionable not just in Britain, but also in America.

Both Jekyll and Robinson recognised the way decorative cottage gardens could be created using English wildflowers alongside plants derived from other temperate climates. Robinson pointed out the advantages of this style:

English cottage gardens first, are never bare and seldom ugly... cottage gardeners are good in their plots, and in the course of years they make them fertile, and the shelter of the little house and hedge favours the flowers...it is the absence of any pretentious plan which lets the flowers tell their story to the heart. They often teach lessons that 'great' gardeners should learn, and are pretty from Violet and Snowdrop time till the Fuchsia bushes bloom nearly into winter.

Nearly all are fragrant, as in roses, the annual and biennial flowers of our gardens are rich in fragrance – stocks, mignonettes, sweet peas, sweet sultan, wallflowers, double rockets, sweet scabious, and many others. These, among the easily raised of plants, may be enjoyed by the poorest cottage gardeners.

Blending traditional flowers with appropriate new introductions could add extra interest, such as planting blue Apennine Anemones in an English wood so that they flower before the bluebells, thus giving a much longer period of colour.

Cottage gardening provided a more harmonious, romantic style that avoided the brash colours of conventional bedding schemes. These were the gardens beloved of Victorian artists in search of romantic images, many of whom were heavily influenced by the Arts and Crafts movement, including Helen Allingham. Her paintings of cottages complete with exuberant planting, often with cottagers standing at the door or gate, became highly sought after. One of her contemporaries, Myles Birket Foster, painted similar scenes that often appeared on Cadbury's chocolate boxes of the period.

As Margaret Willes points out in *The Gardens of the British Working Class* (2015), the rise of the cottage garden concept meant that 'The working-class rural gardener had become a hero', with plants being sought out in their gardens by plant breeders. A typical example is the discovery of a pretty, shell-pink sweet pea possessing waved petals in the garden of a grocer in Histon, Cambridgeshire. Developed by a plant breeder, it became the well-known Gladys sweetpea, leading to the creation of Unwins Seeds, which is still renowned for its sweet pea breeding programmes.

Carpet Bedding

The use of carpet bedding dominated the Victorian period. Cut into shapes within lawns, these were flower beds that were designed to be seen from all sides. It was a concept that attracted some criticism from writers, who described them as 'unmeaning flower beds' that resembled 'kidneys, and tadpoles, and sausages, and leeches, and commas'.

Gardeners spent much of the winter and early spring growing plants from thousands of cuttings in greenhouses ready to be taken out and planted in mass colour schemes at the start of the summer. The quantities of flowers required were enormous. John Robson, head gardener to Viscount Holmesdale at Linton Park, Kent, had to fill flower beds plus two ribbon borders measuring 593 by 10 feet, an area reckoned to be the equivalent of 150 circular beds 10 feet in diameter.

Writing in *The Victorian Flower Garden* (1991), Jennifer Davies noted that:

> A lack of proper facilities to cope with bedding plants bedevilled most establishments. The problem was attributed to owners, who on seeing the great bedding displays in their neighbours' gardens, expected their head gardeners to produce the same but without giving them proper houses or additional help. Gardeners complained of the weeks spent watering and moving plants and in some cases, of having to trust candlelight to 'master the potting shed'. Some men, having potted until after midnight, never went to bed at all for fear they would be late at their post in the morning.

Combining colours and laying out the blocks of colour was a time-consuming exercise. The aim was to create a 'harmonious whole', with the emphasis on the use of geometrical shapes. Numerous instructions were devised to help gardeners design their chosen carpet bedding. Writing in her *Ladies' Companion to the Flower Garden*, Jane Loudon recommended using paper covered in squares. In 1861, the *Journal of Horticulture and Cottage Garden* noted that one gardener found it so difficult to cut three perfectly proportioned oval beds in a lawn that the local schoolmaster was asked to mark out the beds. Adjusting colour schemes could be equally difficult. *The Irish Farmer's Digest* provided its readers with a diagram of linked circles identifying harmonious colours such as yellow, yellow green, green and purple, red, red purple, russet and dark blue.

Bright colours dominated these flower beds, with large blocks of often contrasting colours such as blues, oranges, yellows, whites, and scarlets, which were of similar heights but put together in large blocks. Typical plants used in these bedding arrangements included geraniums, snapdragons, verbenas, African marigolds, alyssums, nasturtiums and penstemons. The result was the creation of bright, long-lasting colourful beds. Plant breeders devoted considerable time to creating dwarf varieties, and geraniums with variegated leaves.

1868 marked the arrival of a new style of carpet bedding. Rather than just using blocks of colour, it involved creating a special design in the form of a motto. Devised by head gardener John Fleming at Cliveden, Buckinghamshire, this new innovation immediately attracted the attention of *The Gardeners' Chronicle*. Fleming had used an arrangement of low-growing foliage plants and succulents to create the monogram of the Countess of Sutherland. This idea quickly caught the imagination of gardeners throughout the country, resulting in a wide range of designs, some of which were very elaborate pictures or complex monograms. Typical mottos often included the name of a place, or the words 'God Save the Queen'.

Sometimes also described as Cockney Carpet bedding, it was a style that became very popular in public parks and civic displays and can still be seen today in many seaside towns, where flower beds often include mottos or clocks. This style of planting requires a vast number of plants, which tend to be placed close together in blocks to create maximum visual impact while conveying the desired image. Victoria Park, Hackney incorporated such flower beds in large numbers soon after its opening in 1845. About 200,000 plants were bedded out each year in designs that often involved borders of flat rosettes of cacti, agaves in the centre of the bed to give height and the remainder filled with numerous fuchsias, geraniums, asters and verbenas. Neat labels identified the different type of plants so that people could reproduce designs or grow similar plants at home. Almost all the plants were grown from cuttings within the onsite nurseries every year. It was a design style which meant that beds had to be cleared and totally replaced with a new design. The majority of the plants were simply placed on compost heaps. In 1860, the government decreed that at the end of each season, Victoria Park should distribute the exhausted plants free of charge to local poor people; a decision that was extremely popular. Illustrations from the time show people taking home large sacks and even filling wheelbarrows with plants to take to the nearest workhouses.

Rose Gardens

Rose gardens became increasingly common both in private and public gardens. New varieties appeared following the arrival of new breeding stock such as the China roses and the Bourbon roses, allowing plant breeders to develop repeat flowering bushes. In France, the Empress Josephine created the spectacular rose garden at Malmaison containing roses such as the Souvenir de Malmaison, which influenced garden designers and rose breeders across Europe. Victorians became extremely fond of strongly scented, repeat flowering roses like the Madame Isaac Periere, Roseraie de l'Hay and Blanche Double de Coubert. Gardeners frequently placed roses in a sunken garden as it helped to trap and hold the scent of the flowers.

A typical Victorian rose garden was constructed at Tyntesfield, Bristol, in the 1860s. Built on a layered terrace, the rose garden is surrounded by a shrubbery and edged by rocks. At the front of the garden is a formal retaining wall, complete with a carved balustrade and a series of stone steps marked by two stone lions. Visitors strolled through a metal framed arbour covered in fragrant roses and explored paths leading through rose beds.

In 1912, artist Sir Hubert Van Herkomer commissioned Thomas Mawson to design a sunken rose garden for his home at Bushey. Mawson noted that 'The garden was to be separated from the kitchen garden by a brick-built pergola, with a handsome garden pavilion at one end. The centre of the panel rose garden was to be sunk two feet, with a fountain in the centre.'

In 1932, a major new public garden opened in Regent's Park known as Queen Mary's Rose Garden. Finally completed two years later, it became London's largest collection of roses possessing over 12,000 bushes. The rose garden soon became one of the most popular corners of Regent's Park, appealing to visitors seeking a place of relaxation.

Window Box Gardening

Window boxes were especially popular in industrial areas, providing a small space where plants could be grown even within tenements and multi-occupancy buildings possessing little natural light. Schools often sought to encourage interest in gardening by promoting window-box gardens, or miniature gardens as they were sometimes known, since these could be easily grown by children. Gertrude Jekyll records being contacted by a young boy who wanted someone to help him and provide advice on creating a window box. She decided to assist him and began writing a series of letters providing advice, as well as sending him a box measuring 3x10 inches, plus some small bulbs, mosses, saxifrage and a few tiny stones to put into it. Some schools even held special shows, such as a board school in Leeds where children created flower boxes from soap and powder boxes and filled them with small plants before displaying them to everyone. Catherine Buckton, a wool merchant's wife in Leeds, referred to the sheer amount of work that many children put into creating window boxes. One child reared tiny fuchsia cuttings in his bedroom and had to keep the window spotlessly clean to provide enough light – not an easy task given the amount of soot and dirt that was present in towns. In addition, the child also reared Virginia Stock, French marigolds, nasturtiums and pansies.

Garden shows focusing on window-box gardening became popular, especially shows targeting the poor. In 1860, Reverend Samuel Hadden

Parkes, curate of St George's in Bloomsbury, organised a show in the Bible Mission Rooms. Shelves were set up around the room covered in green tissue paper, upon which a number of window-box gardens were placed. Many were housed not in conventional boxes, but in broken teapots and jugs. All the gardens had been made by poor people within the parish, encouraged by the possibility of winning a cash prize. There were three classes: fathers and mothers (who were not flower dealers), flower dealers and children. Fuchsias, geraniums and annuals formed the majority of flowers used in the displays. Entrance to the show cost just 1d for adults and half a penny for children. At the second show a year later, extra categories were added such as domestic servants. The standard was high, with judges commenting that 'some of the plants would have done credit to any green-house'.

In 1863, a larger show was held in Russell Square, Bloomsbury. Proving successful, it resulted in a second show the following year, which was attended by Charles Dickens. Housed in a large marquee, exhibitors included schools. There was a wide range of flowers on display as well as mini trees grown from pips and stones such as lemon, walnut, oak, locust and date. Among the servant category was a fish basket turned into an annuals' garden edged by stonecrop, made by a poor, army tailor. Afternoon attendance was mainly from middle-class people who paid 1s for entry. Exhibitors had free entry both afternoon and evening, and poorer people could come in for free during the evening. Over 3,000 people attended the show in total.

By the latter part of the nineteenth century, the popularity of window gardening in all its forms – from plants growing up and around walls and windows, on window sills to window boxes and hanging baskets – was so great that Gertrude Jekyll commented that 'there is scarcely a cottage without some plants in the window, indeed the windows are often so much filled with them that the light is too much obscured.'

The Fern Craze and Stumperies

Victorians were very keen on the concept of the 'picturesque', utilising jagged rocks and stumps to make rustic structures described as 'rooteries'. One of the earliest such references was made by Jane Loudon in *The Ladies' Companion to the Flower Garden*, where she refers to 'root-work' saying that:

> Two or three large stools of trees grouped together on a lawn with mould and plants placed in their interstices, form a striking contrast to the smoothness and high art displayed on the general surface of the lawn. The plants placed among the roots, whether in pots concealed by mosses, stones, or mould, or planted in soil, should never be of indigenous kinds common in the locality... But of exotic kinds.

The concept of a rooterie soon changed dramatically when Victorians discovered ferns. Intrigued by them, they went out collecting native species as well as importing new and exotic varieties in massive numbers. This mania for ferns virtually stripped the countryside. Having collected the plants, Victorians sought creative ways of displaying them so that everyone could admire them. Upended tree stumps became the most common method, since the roots could act almost like a rockery, providing moist planting areas shaded by the various roots.

The concept of a stumpery was first introduced at Biddulph Grange, Staffordshire. Designed by artist and gardener Edward William Cooke for the landowner, James Bateman, it involved piling up tree roots to turn them into a fern loving, garden area. Many of the roots were used to frame a garden path, creating a 10-feet-high wall on either side. October 1856 saw *The Gardeners' Chronicle* note that a 'rustic root garden' had been created at Biddulph Grange. Two months later, the same publication wrote a full description of this new style of gardening, using the term 'stumpery' for the first time.

> The root garden, or as it is here called, for want of a better term, 'the Stumpery,' consists of a very picturesque assemblage of old roots or rugged stems and stumps of trees – chiefly the latter – piled to a height of 8 or 10 feet on either side of a winding and rapidly descending walk. They are so irregularly arranged as to jut forward in the boldest prominence, and even to be united into a rustic arch in some parts; while in others they recede far enough to allow room at their base for little gatherings of choice herbaceous plants, bulbs or miniature shrubs.
>
> Mr Bateman, has been singularly fortunate in procuring a quantity of the most gnarled, contorted and varied masses of wood imaginable for this purpose, and they are joined together and disposed with consummate art. The blocks being all of Oak too, they are likely to be very durable. Over considerable portions of the whole, masses of Ivy, Virginian Creeper, Cotoneaster and other trailing plants scramble about in the wildest manner. And the interstices, as well as the open spaces now and then occurring at the base, are all used for the reception of some characteristic and interesting plant or group. For example, near the entrance to this region, the Hellebores, which are among the earliest of the winter-flowering plants, are clustered in great variety. Then follow the Anemones, Epimediums, Scillas, Dog tooth Violets, Lilies of the Valley, each kind receiving the precise amount of sunlight or shade which is desirable for it, and all being intermingled with Gaultherias, Pernettyas, Cotoneasters, Savins and such other dwarf evergreens as serve to produce a sufficiency of green clothing at all seasons of the year. Even the

rarer hardy Orchises and the Cypripediums, have an appropriate corner assigned to them, and seem quite at home in it.

News of the stumpery immediately aroused considerable interest among other fern-loving gardeners. Within a short time, a nearby household, Arley Hall in Cheshire, had created its own version. Named 'The Root Tree', the Arley Hall stumpery was said to resemble a miniature mountain landscape complete with stumps, grotto and pools, all planted up with a large collection of ferns. Many others were created elsewhere including at Ickworth in Suffolk, but as fashions changed, the majority of stumperies disappeared over the years, naturally decomposing into the ground.

The Pre-Raphaelites and William Morris

Artist, designer, environmentalist, poet, William Morris played a major role in the development of garden themes during the latter part of the nineteenth and early twentieth centuries. He was a leading participant in the Arts and Crafts and Pre-Raphaelite movements, which sought to create beauty using the natural world as its base, underpinned by the countryside and the 'simple life' of the Middle Ages. Morris wrote that 'if the earth nourish us all alike, if the sun shines for all of us alike, if to one and all of us the glorious drama of the earth, day and night, summer and winter – can be presented as a thing to understand and love.'

Morris was a co-founder of one of first conservation organisations, the Commons Preservation Society (now known as the Open Spaces Society). When designing his Red House in 1860, he had a clear vision in which the gardens would link seamlessly into the house, creating a series of 'garden rooms' enclosed by wattle fencing, complete with trellises filled with traditional fragrant garden flowers like jasmine, wild rose, and honeysuckle.

Some years later, Morris lived at Kelmscott Manor in the Cotswolds. An old Elizabethan manor house, he was responsible for developing its gardens and receipts from the period show that many plants and trees were acquired at this time. In 1871 Morris wrote, 'the garden is quite unaffected and very pleasant, and looks in fact as though it were a part of the house; at least the clothes of it which I think ought to be the aim of the layer-out of a garden.' During an 1879 lecture focusing on 'Making the Best of It', indicating the best ways of organising a 'smoke-drenched scrap of ground among the bricks', Morris stressed that nature should be allowed to 'do the desired complexity', although fencing should be orderly. Planting should be naturalistic, avoiding tropical plants which nature 'meant to be grotesque' left to botanical gardens. The rose, meanwhile, was seen as the 'queen of flowers'. Some of the designs and plants he advocated were best in gardens were incorporated into his well-known wallpaper designs, such as Trellis, while another design, Strawberry Thief, records the moment Morris caught a thrush stealing strawberries in his garden at Kelmscott. In total, Morris created over fifty wallpapers inspired by wild, naturalistic gardens using acorns, blackthorn, poppies, pimpernel, dog roses, daisies and tulips.

His love of gardening and plants proved extremely influential with the concept of garden rooms, and the link between a house and garden became a common trend among many garden designers over the following decades. These ideas influenced Gertrude Jekyll, William Robinson and can be seen in the vast range of herbaceous borders they created.

Rockeries

Evolving from the numerous grottos incorporated into the landscape garden concepts of the eighteenth century, rockeries became extremely popular. There are unsubstantiated reports that a rock garden was built in Orford, Suffolk in 1767, but most authorities believe that the Chelsea Physic Garden constructed the first such area specifically for growing alpine plants in 1774. Rock gardens of varying sizes soon became a decorative and very desirable feature nationwide.

The ending of the Napoleonic Wars resulted in greater travel overseas and travellers to Switzerland and other mountainous regions became enamoured with the rocky landscape and its alpine plants. It was a concept that was soon being recreated within Britain, with plant hunters bringing back alpine plants suitable for growing in these areas.

One of the first people to grow alpines outdoors in a rock garden was Lady Broughton, at Hoole House, Chester. After visiting, Jane Loudon wrote that it formed 'a miniature copy of the Swiss glaciers, with a valley between, into which the mountain scenery projects and retires, forming several beautiful and picturesque openings, which are diversified... By mountain trees and shrubs, and other plants.' Unfortunately, this rock garden no longer exists.

Many of the rockeries used chunks of rock transported from elsewhere in Britain, but many others utilised a variety of materials. Reports from the period include references to rockery creators using 'fused masses of brick' obtained from brick kilns, rubble and other coarse material, which was then formed into rugged structures, covered with cement and then formed into crags and recesses. Once dry, the construction was 'painted with oil paint to represent veined or stratified granite'. The invention of Pulhamite by James Pulham provided relatively inexpensive sources of rock that were used extensively in places such as Sandringham and Dewstow.

Some of the resultant rockeries were outlandish. At Friar Park, Henley-on-Thames, the eccentric landowner Sir Frank Crisp set out to create a mini Matterhorn, complete with tin mountain goats. The resultant construction was nearly 40 feet high and constructed from over 7,000 tonnes of Yorkshire millstone grit. Some of the rocks were massive, weighing around 6–7 tonnes each. Contemporary accounts published in *The Gardeners' Chronicle* and *The Garden* indicate that:

> An immense excavation was necessary to form a veritable valley whose sides were destined to be walled in and diversified on natural lines... Over and over again these unwieldy masses had to be shifted and rearranged to satisfy the fastidious taste of the owner...it was not a mere question of picturesque massing, but also of contriving the myriad congenial nooks, recesses, pockets and tiny platforms, in and on which alpine plants could thrive, and make themselves truly at home.

As regards its design, readers were informed that:

> There are represented in it mountains of greater and lesser height, valleys, mountain passes, Alpine bridges, overlooking quite formidable precipices; a waterfall commences at the highest point in the rockery, and after winding and twisting in innumerable corrections, for the moment conspicuous, then hidden for a time, at last runs into a small pool surrounded by a little greensward at the lowest point.

Other features included ravines and a glacier with an 'ice grotto' based on the ice caves at Grindelwald, 2,500 plant varieties were grown on the mountain and water turtles and tree frogs had colonised ponds. It was said that the noise of the frogs was often mistaken for nightingales during the summer. Some of the caves were definitely unusual. The Vine Cave contained glass bunches of grapes attached to the roof holding electric lamps and was lined with mirrors offering optical illusions such as 'withered and chained up hands', while the Skeleton Cave contained a skeleton, distorting mirrors and fungi growing on the walls.

A miniature Swiss chalet was constructed at the base of the mountain in which 'one may sit and enjoy the scene, comparing all the main features with a little bronze model of the Matterhorn which Sir Frank had made for the entertainment of his guests'.

According to *The Gardeners' Chronicle*, Sir Frank was never satisfied with the results and was 'ever making such alterations and additions as shall render it ever more interesting and beautiful,' but that visitors could 'hardly fail to be astounded at the natural result'.

Another rock garden specialist, Reginald Farrer, gained the unofficial title 'Prince of Alpine Gardeners'. An eccentric plant hunter, gardener and writer, Farrer was fascinated by rock gardens and alpine plants. Living in Clapham, North Yorkshire he was surrounded by a natural rocky landscape and planted up a limestone 'cliff' beside the banks of a lake at his home using every possible potential alpine plant. On one occasion, he loaded a shotgun with seeds collected on his travels and fired them into the cliff. It was reported that the resulting display of alpine plants was stunning. It was at this site that he trialled countless ideas about rock garden creation such as the use of below-ground irrigation systems and naturalistic 'moraine-gardens' (planted scree). He wrote extensively on the subject and his work eventually led to the formation of the Alpine Garden Society. In 1932, nurseryman Walter Ingwerson wrote that Farrer's book *My Rock Garden* 'has made more converts to the charms of alpine plants and their cultivation in our gardens than any other book ever written. Farrer's infectious enthusiasm spread like wildfire among the gardening public and we should owe him an enormous debt if he had never written another line on this subject.'

Perhaps the most quirky and unusual aspect of the rise of rock gardens during this period was the arrival of garden gnomes. Although gnomes have long formed part of folklore, the idea of having models in gardens had been non-existent. Until 1874, garden gnomes were unknown in Britain, and we owe their arrival to a Victorian, Sir Charles Isham.

The story begins some years earlier in 1846, when Sir Charles inherited Lamport Hall, Northamptonshire. He decided to create a vast rockery 90 feet long, 47 feet wide and 24 feet high facing towards the hall so that he could see it from his bedroom window. Despite its closeness to the house, many visitors to the main garden did not realise the rockery was there until entering it. His aim was to develop a miniature alpine world, resembling a rocky crag or an 'imitation of beautiful unstratified rocks in miniature form', complete with countless crevices, chasms and caves. A waterfall and stone bridge acted as an aqueduct carrying water pumped from the river. Unusually, however, the rockery did not contain a large collection of alpine plants. According to Sir Charles, it was instead made to look 'pleasing and picturesque', and that the plants were selected to 'clothe' the rockery. It contained many dwarf conifers, including pigmy spruce firs, pigmy cedars, a small cedar that Sir Charles found thrown out from a Northamptonshire nursery with the aim of making it resemble a miniature German pine forest. Some of the conifers were over 70 years old, possessing a maximum height of 3 feet. Sir Charles took an active role in the construction of the rockery, helping to carefully place each rock himself. He chiselled holes in many of the rocks for plants to grow inside so that it looked like they were growing through them. An article in the *Journal of Horticulture and Cottage Gardener* from 1872 indicates 'the whole affair is not only the design of the Baronet but almost every stone, large as many of them are, was put in place by his own hands' and that 'the whole is his own handywork and has occupied a period of two and twenty years to bring to its present high perfection.'

No one knows exactly when Sir Charles decided to add gnomes to his rockery, or the company from which he acquired them, but what is certain is that he brought over a selection of gnome models from Germany. Made from plaster and wood, the colourful gnomes took up residence all over the rockery and adjoining garden. The tiny gnomes, measuring just 2-6 inches tall, could be seen emerging from caverns or climbing walls, with some even holding banners demanding decent wages and benevolent employers. Also on the rockery was a life-like terracotta model of a young girl reading a book, with a watering can by her side.

As an avid folklorist, Sir Charles had collected stories of gnomes and mine fairies from across the Peak District, Wales and Central Europe. He believed gnomes to be real and wrote a book entitled *Notes on Gnomes* (1889), which included reported sightings by other people such as a Mr Smith, who saw one near Mold, North Wales. The notebook states 'Presently he perceived a little mine fairy ascend the ladder step by step, it was dressed like a miner, it carried a small pick-axe over its should and was supplied with other mining implements.'

Elsewhere in the book, he referred to the Lamport Rockery stating:

The most characteristic feature of the Rockery is its miniature population. To some it is the chief attraction, who have perhaps never before been introduced into a European garden. The late J.C. Loudon having been impressed with the value of such an adjunct when tastefully introduced, idealised in a wood cut in one of his volumes a group of children under some specimens of Pinus Nanus, with appropriate remarks on the charm such treatment might impart to miniature gardens. What delight would the realisation of this idea have afforded him, especially the gnomes, as it would also their German manufacturers to see the right thing in the right place rather than on a drawing room table, bearing a match box ill adapted for its purpose, now removed.

Had gnomes been but imaginary creations, they would never have been admitted into the Lamport Rockery. But as there is any amount of evidence that they not only have been frequently heard, but also that they have been occasionally seen about certain mines, and in the cottages of miners, some accounts of them are here given... Although we know nothing of the nature of gnomes, this like other transcendental experiences is receiving attention throughout the world. Seeing such things is no longer indicative of mental delusion, but rather EXTENSION OF FACULTY.

The rockery at Lamport proved to be a sensation, attracting considerable attention. It was opened to the public on several occasions, with thousands coming to explore the rockery and gardens when a fete was held in aid of a local orphanage. Magazines included many references to Lamport. In 1888, the *Cosmopolitan Journal* wrote:

The last and most pronounced feature of the Rockery is the miniature population of gnomes, three inches high, at work amongst the stones, as also a group of 'men on strike' at the pit's mouth... Although gnomes and other species of fairies are usually supposed to be but creatures of imagination, their existence is maintained in various parts of the world.

It added that 'there is probably no other piece of ground of such limited dimensions anywhere to be found which has received so much minute and constant culture for over a period of forty years.'

Ten years later, *Country Life* noted, 'The Rockery is a centre of interest. It presents features that will never fade from memory. We have seen nothing more strange, and in a way fascinating, than this miniature rock garden, clothed with small flowers that perfume the small caves, and send their roots into the crevices.' While in 1900, *The Strand Magazine* indicated that 'It is open to question whether any other garden the world over contains features of such peculiar interest as the one that for more than half a century has been the loving care of Sir Charles Isham.'

Not everyone liked the gnomes – Sir Charles Isham's daughters hated them. On his death in 1903, they apparently went round the rockery with air rifles using the gnomes for target practice. Other reports indicate that they held shooting parties targeting them. It was believed that all the gnomes had been destroyed until late in the twentieth century, when one was discovered hidden in a crevice. 'Lampy' is now kept under lock and key at Lamport Hall and is insured for over £1m. He is believed to be oldest garden gnome in the world.

The concept caught the attention of other rockery owners, especially Sir Frank Crisp, who introduced around 100 gnomes into his extensive rockery at Friar Park. By the 1920s, interest in garden gnomes had abated in upper-class gardens due to anti-German feelings following the First World War. Instead, gnomes migrated into middle- and working-class gardens, taking up residence alongside ponds happily fishing, standing on lawns chatting or among trees and bushes. The arrival of Disney's *Snow White and the Seven Dwarfs* animation in 1937 added to their popularity, resulting in their ubiquitous appearance in gardens ever since.

The rise in gardening within towns and cities, especially on the new council house estates and suburban sites following the First World War, saw a diverse range of garden styles being followed. Some were very simple, with lawns divided by a central path, a flowerbed in the centre of each lawn, while back gardens were dominated by vegetable growing and a children's play area. Other gardeners tried to include as many features as they could including fountains, rockeries, rose borders, pergolas and arches. Interestingly, *Hints for the Town Gardener*, published by the London Gardens Society advised that a simple style could be pleasant, saying 'cut out all affectations, such as small bridges…dwarf human figures, china animals, glass ornaments, model houses, windmills etc.'

Chapter 6

Transforming Cities and Urban Areas

With less work available in rural areas as the nineteenth century progressed, people increasingly moved to towns and cities in search of employment. For the majority of people this meant taking low-paying work as servants, factory workers and shops. Many scratched a living hawking food, drink, used clothing, sorting rubbish, cleaning chimneys and similar tasks. It was a hard life and often a visit to the pub was their only respite. The standard of housing was poor, with several families sharing just one house. Leisure time was minimal, if it existed at all. There was no space for gardens. These were unhealthy, crowded tenements in dark streets, often filled with sewage, where disease was rife. Developers were intent on building as much as possible within small areas, with the aim of gaining the highest profits possible.

It was a situation that was untenable in the long term. Poor health and living conditions ultimately impacted on the profitability of industry and businesses, as well as the physical strength of newly recruited soldiers and sailors potentially rendering the country's military services less effective. It also bred discontent, with calls for political change and a wider franchise relating to the 1832 Reform Bill and the rise of Chartism. A further problem was the fact that the closely packed slums encouraged criminal activity. Some areas such as Seven Dials or around the River Fleet in London became notorious as almost no-go places for any forces of law and order.

Most town and city dwellers lacked any access to green spaces or gardens. In London, the Royal Parks of St James', Hyde Park and

Green Park were opened to the public during the seventeenth century, with similar open access later being granted to Kensington Gardens and Regent's Park, but pleasure gardens such as Vauxhall required payment for entry and were very much the preserve of the wealthy, providing a place for the London Season. Demand for green spaces in towns and cities began to gain momentum.

In February 1833, a select committee of the House of Commons began to consider 'the best means of securing Open Spaces in the vicinity of populous towns as Public Walks and Places of Exercise, calculated to promote the Health and Comfort of the Inhabitants'. They came to the conclusion that providing open spaces 'reserved for the amusement of the humbler classes would assist to wean them from low and debasing pleasures…drinking-houses, dog fights and boxing matches'. It was felt that if people were given space for recreation, they would be less likely to become involved in riotous behaviour. Going to the park would provide 'improving' things to do, by learning to appreciate plants and beauty.

Alongside this argument was an awareness that towns had become extremely insanitary, with epidemics such as cholera becoming common. Sanitary reformer William Farr noted in 1839 that 'a park in the East End of London would probably diminish the annual deaths by several thousands'. Such messages were not ignored by civic and political organisations. As Margaret Willes points out in her book *The Gardens of the British Working Class*, 'The Parliamentary Select Committee on the Health of Towns reported in 1840 that the improvement in the provision of parks was essential not only for the welfare of the poor, but also for the safety of property and security of the rich'.

From the 1830s onwards, public parks began to appear nationwide. Initially these were privately financed by groups of local people such as the Victoria (later Royal Victoria) Park in Bath. Although a private park, entry was free to the walking public 'of decent appearance and good behaviour'. Visitors on horseback or in carriages, however, paid a subscription, and donations were sought to undertake regular maintenance.

Municipal authorities and philanthropists became key advocates of the development of public parks. In 1840, the city of Derby launched an arboretum designed by John Loudon. The land had been donated by a local manufacturer, Joseph Strutt, on condition that artisans had to be given free access two days a week as this would allow them to 'enjoy a rare opportunity of expanding their minds by the contemplation of nature'.

Seven years later, the first truly municipal park providing completely free access every day was opened in Birkenhead, requiring users to abstain from swearing, drinking and gambling while visiting. Known as the People's Park, it was designed by Joseph Paxton and incorporated existing features such as gravel pits. Paxton divided the park into two halves, allowing the existing pits to be turned into lakes so that each section could incorporate an irregular-shaped lake with its own island. The remainder of the land was carefully landscaped to provide a series of scenic views using shrubberies, flower beds and rockeries. Instantly popular, it was a style that was quickly copied in other towns across the country as symbols of civic pride. Common ingredients of public parks included lakes, bandstands, flower beds, drinking fountains and shrubberies. The invention of Pulhamite artificial rock meant that it became cost effective to include rockeries and features such as picturesque bridges and rocky streams into public parks. This resulted in projects like the Madeira Walk at Ramsgate Park in Kent, which included waterfalls, pools and tunnels, while at Folkstone, a zig zag path down a cliff added extra interest. Sports facilities were also added to encourage exercise.

One of the biggest such parks was Victoria Park, Hackney. With over 400,000 people living in the area, it was densely populated with narrow streets and virtually no greenery. Disease and criminality were all too common. Led initially by local dignitaries, the campaign for the creation of a public park became very vociferous. There were public meetings and appeals, and eventually a petition containing 30,000 signatures was sent to Queen Victoria, gaining her sympathy and support. She ordered that a house in St James' Palace owned by her bankrupt uncle, the Duke of York, should be sold and the money used to pay for a park to be created in Hackney. The chosen location had been previously used for market gardens, grazing and gravel extraction, thus providing pits that could be transformed into lakes. James Pennethorne landscaped the new park with numerous trees and scented shrubs such as lilac, tamarisk and guilder rose. It proved to be a sensation – and not just with local people.

In 1846, the *Illustrated London News* reported that 'On Sunday and for many weeks past the visitors have exceeded 10,000 and amongst them were many from the West End, upwards of thirty carriages being outside the principal lodge entrance on Sunday between four and six o'clock.' *Lloyds Weekly*, meanwhile, noted that at Victoria Park, '20,000 men, women and children enjoy themselves on a summer's evening and appear to hold the floral beauties sacred.'

Victoria Park became a place of recreation, with bathing and boating in the lakes, frequent concerts and refreshment areas providing simple catering. It was also used for rallies of all kinds – George Bernard Shaw was one of the many speakers who visited Victoria Park for this purpose. He recalled his visit, describing it as:

> A park of 217 acres, fenced in not by railings but by a wooden paling, and containing plenty of greensward, trees, a lake for bathers, flower beds which are triumphs of the admired cockney art of carpet bedding, and a sandpit, originally imported from the sea-side for the delight of children, but speedily deserted on its becoming a natural vermin preserve for all the petty fauna of Kingsland, Hackney and Hoxton. A bandstand, an unfurnished

forum for religious, anti-religious and political orators, cricket pitches, a gymnasium and an old-fashioned stone kiosk among its attractions.

By 1892, glasshouses had been erected to provide a wide selection of exotic plants. These proved to be particularly popular during wintertime as they provided a way for people to achieve some exercise indoors.

The arrival of a miniature Japanese garden in 1910 aroused considerable interest. This miniature garden had been constructed in Japan by the Yokohama Nursery for display at Japanese-British exhibition held at Shepherds Bush, London. At the end of the exhibition, the Mayor of Yokohama gave the garden to Victoria Park. The garden was then housed in one of the greenhouses and mounted on a wheeled trolley allowing it to be placed outside in good weather. Measuring just 9x4 feet, this bonsai garden comprised a typical Japanese style design complete with tiny trees over 100 years old.

It was not just large public areas that could be used to provide much needed green spaces. Smaller areas were also identified. In 1882, the charitable Metropolitan Public Gardens Association (MPGA) was founded in London with the aim 'to give people gardens and to the children playgrounds'. One of its most innovatory moves was to successfully promote an Act of Parliament to open up churchyards and burial grounds as public parks and green spaces. This released a considerable amount of land within urban areas for public use, such as the Victoria Park Cemetery in Tower Hamlets. Occupying an 11-acre site, it was renamed Meath Gardens and transformed into a pretty park by the MPGA's landscape designer Fanny Wilkinson in 1894.

Society ladies took prominent roles at opening ceremonies of these revamped burial grounds, hosting special opening ceremonies. Princess Frederica of Hanover opened the disused burial ground of St Martin's-in-the-Fields as a public garden, while the Countess of

Roseberry opened the grounds of St Martin's in St Pancras. Among other actions taken by the MPGA to open green spaces involved existing garden squares, often areas that were at risk of being developed. Public appeals were launched resulting various squares being improved and laid out properly as gardens, including De Beauvoir Square in Islington and Red Lion Square in Holborn.

Another development encouraging the creation of green spaces was the concept of botanical gardens. These were set up in cities and towns including Birmingham, Sheffield and Cambridge. Initially access was limited to subscribers, but as the years passed, access steadily widened.

The problems posed by the type of accommodation available in cities did not go unnoticed by philanthropists such as Octavia Hill, who had been brought up in a Christian Socialist tradition. Encouraged by a painting by Ford Madox Brown entitled 'Work', which was subtitled 'the ragged wretch on the left is carrying wild seeds and singular plants gathered from the countryside before dawn, and has been saved from a life of idleness by his love of nature', Octavia Hill set out to provide practical help by seeking to buy land for use by the urban poor. In 1864, her first purchases were three houses in Marylebone Place using money lent by John Ruskin. Each property had to pay its own way, and their success led to other similar purchases.

It was a situation that did not go unnoticed, especially by enlightened industrialists like William Lever, George Cadbury and Joseph Rowntree, who developed their villages for their workforce. This meant that employees would have good accommodation, resulting ultimately in a healthier workforce that would contribute to the success of their businesses.

In 1888, the Lever Brothers soap manufacturers launched their new premises at Port Sunlight, near Liverpool. As William Lever explained to his workforce, this would be more than just a factory since they were launching a new village as well. He stated: 'It is my and my brother's hope someday to build houses in which our work people will be able to live and be comfortable – semi-detached houses with gardens back and front in which they will be able to know more about the science of life than they can in a back-to-back slum.'

A few years later, in 1894, chocolate manufacturer George Cadbury started work on a housing development at Bournville, near Birmingham. Although Bournville employees occupied most of the houses, there were other occupants who were not employed by the company. Cadbury had a very clear view of what he wanted from the houses, believing that garden provision was just as important as the building itself. Each house was to have a lawn close to the building, with broad straight paths measuring 3-4 feet wide, constructed of 6 inches of ash and 3 inches of gravel. A path would lead down the garden beside the lawn, and at the end of the lawn turn to the side giving access to an orchard and a vegetable area with peas, beans and raspberry canes planted facing north and south in order to maximise available sunlight. A slight adjustment was made for south-facing houses, where the path had to continue down the side along the edge of the hedge.

Once laid out, each garden was to be supplied with specific plants:

> Eight apple and pear trees, assorted according to the nature of the soil, which in addition to bearing fruit forms a desirable screen between the houses which are back to back; 12 gooseberry, 1 Victoria Plum, 6 creepers for the house including Gloire de Dijon and William Allen Richardson roses, wisteria, white and yellow jasmine etc according to the aspect, as well as one or two forest trees, so placed to frame the building. Hedges of thorn divide the houses, and from road boundaries. The choice of trees and creepers is determined not only by the suitability of the soil or aspect, but also by the general effect gained.

Further north in York, Joseph Rowntree, another Quaker chocolate producer, began work on a model village at New Earswick in 1902.

Gardens were regarded as more important than roads within the development, as well as play areas for the children. Most of the houses were built in a cul-de-sac layout, with each house having space for lawns and growing areas. The buildings were simple and basic, built in terraces with white-washed walls and red-tiled roofs.

Attitudes to towards urban housing were now changing dramatically, moving away from the tenements that had previously been so common. Over the years, increasing publicity surrounding tenements including novels by Charles Dickens, Charles Booth's 'London Poverty Maps' and similar surveys carried out elsewhere had raised awareness of the problems. New developments were now increasingly focused on the need to provide not just better housing, but essential garden space as well.

Entrepreneur Ebenezer Howard sought to create brand new cities offering ideal living conditions. Howard had spent many years working in Chicago, where he had witnessed how the city was rebuilt following a major fire. The town planners had opted for a design comprising housing with gardens located in suburbs along with large public parks. Returning to England, Howard believed that this idea would prove a viable alternative to the accommodation available in the overcrowded, unhealthy cities. In 1899, he launched the Garden City Association with the aim of creating cities that would combine access to green spaces with residential and industrial areas. Each city would be limited in size, creating a cluster of garden cities each containing about 32,000 people. There would be one central city with a population of no more than 58,000. All the cities would be linked by public transport and surrounded by rural countryside. The cities would be owned by a private corporation and governed by the residents themselves.

His suggestions met with considerable interest, including prominent writers like George Bernard Shaw. By 1902, there was sufficient financial support available to launch a Garden City Pioneer Company. Land for the first city was purchased in Letchworth, followed by another in Welwyn in 1919. Despite the initial optimism, development was slow, partly due to availability of land, the outbreak of the First World War and the subsequent economic problems. By 1917, Letchworth had just 10,000 occupants, rising to 20,000 in 1951. A similar slow growth pattern was experienced at Welwyn, which had only 10,000 occupants by 1931.

Other projects took place within existing urban areas, all of which were deliberately designed to provide householders with garden space. The idea of a garden suburb was launched in north London, when Henrietta Barnett, the wife of the founder of Toynbee Hall, Canon Samuel Barnett, came up with the idea of establishing a trust to obtain 80 acres of land around Golders Green and East Finchley. The aim was to provide 243 acres of specially designed residential development together with an 80-acre extension to Hampstead Heath. Work began on site in 1907, building eight homes per acre in a variety of sizes within a cul-de-sac design complete with courts and closes. It was stated that the larger gardens of richer occupants would help 'keep the air pure, and the sky more liberal, the cottage gardens adding that cosy, generous element which ever follows the spade'. All the richer houses would be located in the south, with flats for artisans in the north and villas for the middle class in the centre of the development.

In 1909, the First Housing and Town Planning Act stressed the need for gardens and 'on separation, on space rather than on what filled it, on trees, grass and gardens more than on shops, factories and pavements'. This approach reflected the way in which town planning was being affected by proponents of the 'Garden City' and 'Garden Suburb' concepts, as well as the practical evidence of the success of such approaches provided by Bournville and New Earswick. According to the *Municipal Journal*:

> The average size of the gardens is 350 square yards – a size determined upon careful consideration of the amount a man

can easily and profitably work by spade cultivation in his leisure time. The gardens have provided a great source of health and enjoyment to the villagers. Prizes are awarded in competition for the best-kept gardens, and we find many well-cultivated fruit, vegetable and flower gardens.

Chapter 7

Horticultural Societies and Shows

Landowners, politicians and the clergy were very much in favour of encouraging people to take up gardening. It was seen as a wholesome pursuit, which would encourage sobriety, family life and discourage dissent. By encouraging people to grow food, it would keep men away from pubs and inspire other members of the family to help out. Such attitudes reflected the Victorian concept of benevolence, of encouraging people to help themselves. Although unstated, the fact that people could grow some of their own food meant that it could reduce their need to claim help from the parish, thus in turn helping to minimise or even reduce the poor rates paid by landowners.

Margaret Willes stresses the prevalence of such attitudes in *The Gardens of the British Working Class*. Referring to the activities of Reverend Samuel Parkes in Bloomsbury, who encouraged gardening activities among his poor parishioners, Willes says he was, 'determined to make these desperately poor people into urban gardeners. His determination was, of course, inspired by Victorian evangelism…he believed horticulture would hold off the debasing influences of the music hall, the gin shop and the beer house, uniting the family by giving the man a recreation.'

Providing advice was an essential part of encouraging people to grow their own food. This was a role increasingly taken up by the development of horticultural societies on a national, regional and local level. By the end of the nineteenth century, most villages and towns had their own local horticultural society, holding regular shows where people could show off their produce and potentially gain money or goods by taking part in competitions. Such competitions – especially at local level – invariably involved head gardeners and landowners. In Holkham, for example Lord Leicester helped judge the Holkham village horticultural show.

The concept of horticultural societies originated in the florists' associations – sometimes also referred to as florist societies – which became widespread throughout Britain during the eighteenth century. These associations focused on the breeding and exhibiting of specific types of plants and varied from area to area. Auriculas were most popular in the northern counties of Yorkshire, Cheshire and Lancashire, especially among groups of weavers and cutlers. Suffolk, London and Lancashire were keen on tulips, while in Paisley, Scotland, laced pinks attracted considerable attention. Members often had to abide by elaborate rules and regulations designed to ensure that all members shared potential benefits. The Paisley Florist's Society's book included requirements for group purchases of flower shoots that would be 'equally distributed among members' no matter how much they could pay. It also stated that the book, *The Florist's Directory*, should be available for all members to borrow on a weekly basis.

Founded in April 1768, the Ancient Society of York Florists holds the record for the 'world's longest running horticultural show'. It is also the only society which retains the word 'florists' in its title and still uses a Royal Coat of Arms granted to them by Queen Anne on its documents. The York shows became extremely popular, both in terms of membership and attendance. As the years passed, the York Florists steadily increased the range of flowers exhibited, ultimately including chrysanthemums, which were popular with gardeners on allotments in the Bootham Stray area of the city.

Competitions held by the various florist groups were generally located at public houses and formed part of a dinner event. The flowers were brought to the venue and carefully placed on display so that everyone could see them. Considerable prestige could be gained from success in these competitions, with prize winner's names being listed in local newspapers, as well as publications like *An Account of the Different Flower Shows*, which listed categories and prize winners for shows held in 1826, including the Carnation Show, held at the Angel Inn, Rotherham, which offered prizes for scarlet Picotees, Sir Isaac Newton, Scarlet Flakes, Purple Flakes and Crimson Bizards. Prizes were awarded, generally silverware, with prize money replacing this in the nineteenth century. Such prizes could be valuable – the Manchester Floral and Horticultural Society often gave away between £500 and £600 pounds each year in prizes. Offering monetary prizes did attract criticism, however, with the Norwich Horticultural Society deciding to offer medals due to a growing belief that many competitors were being motivated only by the thought of money.

Unlike the florist groups, the rise in horticultural societies was very much led by the gentry, landowners and industrialists such as Josiah Wedgewood and Sir Joseph Banks, who had a deep interest in the subject. The Horticultural Society of London was launched in 1804, with the aim of encouraging the 'improvement of horticulture', and was followed by the Caledonian Society in 1809. Initially, the London Horticultural Society focused on provision of meetings and discussions, but by 1817, the decision was made to develop an experimental garden. The first such garden was located in Kensington, but it soon became clear that the site was too small and so an alternative location was acquired in Chiswick. It was here that the idea of horticultural fetes began as opposed to an exhibition of flowers held in one room.

Greater attention was also being paid from the 1820s onwards to the need to co-ordinate shows and competitions, publishing records of prize winners. The sheer number of shows being held reflected the massive interest in such activities. In 1821, for example, there were no less than forty-two auricula and polyanthus shows nationwide, as well as twenty-one tulip shows, five ranunculus shows and sixty-nine carnation and pink shows. Frequently, these shows occurred as part of a dinner event, with diners able to see the exhibits on show, or even pass round examples to study. Not everyone left their produce on show, as can be seen from a complaint relating to an 1830 show held by the Ipswich Horticultural Society, where some participants were said to have 'ostentatiously exhibited their fruit, and then selfishly ordered it return back to their own homes, instead of leaving it to promote the general enjoyment of the dinner party of subscribers.'

Horticultural shows and societies were as well organised as those by the florists' associations. They had strict regulations as regards membership, payments that had to be made and participation in the various activities and shows. The requirements of a typical florists' association are highlighted in Thomas Hogg's *Concise and Practical Treatise on the Growth and Culture of the Carnation* (1820). It included references to his local society requiring members to pay a yearly subscription of £1 11s 6d, which was divided between three shows: auricular, pinks, and carnations. In order to take part, members had to pay a dinner ticket to each show. All flowers for exhibiting had to arrive by 1pm, with exhibitors confirming that they had owned each plant being submitted for the previous four months. Judges had to state that they had not been involved in the growing of any of the exhibits.

The Norfolk and Norwich Horticultural Society was set up in 1829, with 200 prospectuses circulated among interested parties, and a public meeting held at the Old Library Room. Fifty gentlemen attended the meeting, and it was resolved to set up a horticultural society. Each member had to pay an annual subscription of 5 shillings, and there were to be six general meetings held every year, providing an opportunity to exhibit fruits, flowers, vegetables and receive prizes. A key reason for establishing the society was described as being 'the encouragement it will only afford to Cottagers, by the distribution of small prizes, to make the most of the little plots of ground which they may chance to occupy' and that 'an interest in the occupation may thus be awakened and he that take an interest in his garden has the temptation weakened to resort to a public house for amusement and there waste his time, his health, and his money, the magnet which attracts him is where it ought to be – at home.' Having said that, most entries tended to come from gentlemen and local clergy.

The first meeting included members bringing along a variety of species such as a Pineoly from America, complete with edible nuts, while Reverand Howman sent 'a Mangel Wurzel of great size and weight'. Later meetings included references to the society's vice president's interest in vines. Records refer to Mr Crawshaw growing Black Homburgs, Black Prince and White Muscat of Alexandria 'grown in greatest abundance and perfection', as well as bringing 'sixty-four bunches of Black Homburgs weighing 70lbs, which were so arranged as to form one magnificent cluster which, surrounded by a profusion of leaves and tendrils of the vine, hanging in bacchanalian glory from the centre of the hall.'

The Hibernian Society was founded in 1830, with the Metropolitan Society of Florists and Amateurs in 1832. Similar societies were soon being set up around the country such as the Cornwall Garden Society. Held in May 1832, the inaugural meeting of the Royal Horticultural Society of Cornwall had the support of King William IV, who donated an annual sum of £10 10s for its activities. The main function of the society was set out as being 'to hold two or three exhibitions of fruit, flowers and vegetables each year to bring the beauty of the Duchy's large gardens and estates to the public notice.'

The minutes of the Norfolk and Norwich Horticultural Society contain a description of the society's exhibition in 1832. The meeting was held at the New Corn Exchange and the records stated that:

> The tables are disposed in the shape of a lozenge, leaving an open area in the centre of the Hall for the company, the right

and left hand tables at the lower end of the Hall for the company, and the corresponding ones at the upper end for flowers, a cross table at the top extends the entire width of the room, and this is generally covered with greenhouse plants and exotics. The Cottagers vegetable and fruit table occupies the lower end, and the sideboards are fitting up for the reception of their flowers. The whole extent of tables when all spread, occupies 749 feet, every inch of which has been frequently covered, and exposed to the admiring gaze of more than a thousand persons.

The London Horticultural Society began holding flower shows in their garden at Chiswick from 1833. Visitors had to pay a fee to visit the Chiswick Gardens and see the various prize-winning plants. It was a move which allowed visitors to explore the whole garden including the hot house, arboretum and orchard.

In addition to society meetings and exhibitions, the Norfolk and Norwich Horticultural Society also held 'dejeuners'. These were much more of a social activity for wealthier participants and were designed to raise funds for the society. Each dejeuner was said to have provided 'covers for around 400 at dinner', followed by a ball, where waltzes and quadrilles could be enjoyed. A typical dejeuner raised over £150.

Membership of the society rose rapidly, and by 1839 it had 404 members. Additional funds were being raised from dinner costs, which could also total around £150. On top of this, entry fees for the various shows, for example the show of 31 May 1848, attracted 900 people, with £14 5s being taken at the door in entrance fees.

For most gardeners, especially amateurs, jobbing gardeners and enthusiasts, attendance at a local flower show or local horticultural society meeting played an important role in their lives. Such activities provided a way in which they could listen to talks by experts, share information, socialise, obtain flowers and seeds cheaply and take part in competitions. Many of these societies met in local pubs, for example, the first annual dinner of the Tower Hamlets Chrysanthemum Society was held at the Eagle Tavern in Mile End, London. The impact horticultural shows and societies had on society was noted by the curators at Sheffield's Botanical Garden, who reported that 'Horticultural and Floricultural Exhibitions have within these few years been working a change in the tastes and recreational pursuits of the inhabitants of this densely populated island.' They also noted how the study and practice of gardening was replacing 'bear baiting, a cockfight, a dog fight or mayhap two animals in human form similarly engaged.'

In 1861, Samuel Broome, head gardener at the Inner Temple, noted in the *Penny Illustrated* newspaper that:

> The working classes are getting passionately fond of flowers, and those among them who enjoy the advantage of a sunny spot of ground out of town cultivate them in their leisure hours on summer evenings as an amusement. They form themselves into little societies. They exhibit their productions in friendly rivalry with one another, and those who are successful go away highly delighted with their prizes.

Children were encouraged to participate. The East End Amateur Horticultural Society often gave fuchsia cuttings to school children so that they could grow them on and exhibit at the summer show.

The range of competitions at shows could be quite extensive, including not just the best vegetables or flowers, but also the best miniature gardens, the best allotments, the best back gardens, the best floral decorations or school gardens. As the nineteenth century progressed, specialist flowers and fruits like potatoes, pansies, dahlias and chrysanthemums were exhibited within stand-alone shows or as part of a wider show. The first show devoted purely to chrysanthemums was held in Norwich in 1843, while a florists' society focused on growing and exhibiting this species was formed three years later in Stoke Newington, London.

Larger competitions and shows such as the Crystal Palace Show often led to participation from seed and garden product companies. By 1857, Suttons was exhibiting at shows like the East Berkshire Agricultural Show and the Birmingham Show, while in 1872 it exhibited at the Vienna Show. Such exhibition stands could be very large – at the Crystal Palace Show in 1887, the Suttons stand showed over twenty varieties of tomatoes.

Prizes varied considerably from show to show and increased in both prestige and value as the century progressed. The 1832 Sheffield Show offered prizes totalling £150, with silver cups valued at £5, £10 and £15 as well as numerous smaller money prizes. At the Norfolk and Norwich Horticultural Society, prize medals in silver and bronze were given out. Each medal was engraved with details of the name of the society, the show, and the date of the society, all surrounded by wreaths of laurel. By 1832 there were suggestions that household items could be given as prizes. Reverend Buckle supported giving silver spoons as 'gardeners would have an opportunity of possessing a testimonial to his skill, but likewise of converting it to a valuable and useful appendage to his household cupboard or his wife's tea-boards'. After some discussion the proposal was accepted, and it was decided that gardeners winning first prize should have the option of choosing a large silver medal, a silver tablespoon or 16 shillings. The winner of the second prize in each category would receive a Crawshaw silver medal, a silver dessert spoon or sugar tongs or 5 shillings, while third place winners attracted a bronze medal, silver teaspoon or 5 shillings.

By 1848, cottagers were proving very successful in their exhibits at the show, with the *Norfolk Chronicle* of that year commenting that the 'cottagers table exhibited some excellent specimens of flowers, in the cultivation of which, as in their vegetables, they must have taken great care. £8 4s 6d was distributed as prizes among them'.

Cash prizes were particularly common in the local shows, or in competitions sponsored by seed companies like Daniels of Norwich, while larger shows often used items that could be used around the house. *The Gardener's Magazine* noted that the East End Amateur Horticultural Society offered both cash and items such as 'a handsome timepiece and tea and coffee services and a pair of lustres, a chased cup, and a cruet stand.'

The cost of prizes, especially at regional and national shows, came under criticism by the 1870s. In 1873, the Bath Exhibition gave prizes worth £1,800, while the 1874 Midland Counties Show awarded prizes of £1,210. The following year, the RHS found itself unable to meet the costs of prize money, leading the treasurer to declare, 'We owe for prizes £1,400 and, if I were to pay these rabid prize-men, we should come to a dead stand. I would rather cut my hand off than sign a cheque to pay these prizes.' In this case, rabid prize-men referred to the head gardeners! Despite his comments, the costs of prize giving continued to rise, resulting the Manchester Horticultural Society paying out £2,000 in prizes in 1881.

In many areas, the content of horticultural shows branched out to attract a much wider audience, often resulting in massive attendance numbers. The Bishop Auckland Floral Exhibition in County Durham became one of the largest in the country, attracting over 25,000 people, with many travelling on special cheap excursion trains from Stockton on Tees, Barnard Castle, Durham and Sunderland. Exhibitors even came from as far afield as Salisbury and Saffron Walden. Located in the extensive grounds of the Bishop's Palace, the show steadily extended into the streets of the town. Contemporary reports in the *Durham County Advertiser* indicate that:

Many of the windows of the shops and places of business displayed a considerable amount of bunting and flags bearing various mottos and devices. The marketplace, in which were stationed various menagerie, thespian booths and exhibitions naturally attracted on occasions of this character, presented a most animated appearance.

Meanwhile, reporters from the *Newcastle Daily Chronicle* commented that the show 'exhibited wonders of all kinds, from the performing elephant to those anomalies – the fat Scotchman and a learned pig.'

By the late 1860s, specialist shows were facing greater competition in terms of demands on available leisure time, resulting from the emergence of new activities in which people could use their free time, such as sports. Football matches could attract vast crowds and by 1871, the creation of the Football Association resulted in the development of league team competitions. Railways were offering cheap day excursions and greater literacy meant that many people were taking advantage of greater educational opportunities to attend talks, visit museums and galleries.

Despite such competition, interest in the activities of various horticultural shows and societies continued. Prince Albert had granted the London Horticultural Society a charter, turning it into the prestigious Royal Horticultural Society. The first RHS show (the forerunner of the current Chelsea Flower Show) was held at the RHS garden at Kensington in 1862, while Kew Gardens organised a prestigious Royal Botanic Show within Regent's Park. Shows of this kind increasingly formed part of the social season. In addition, many shows were becoming much more varied and included some form of entertainment, although the weather could cause problems. The Norfolk and Norwich Horticultural Society recorded that its 1879 exhibition included entertainment from the band of the Scots Guards, but that 'the pleasure and enjoyment of the whole were marred by the persistent weather'. Some years later, at the society's Rose Show in 1886, 'a gale of wind wrought much havoc among the tents, the fruit tent collapsing altogether'. In 1889 the Rose Show proved more successful, attracting several thousand people resulting in gate receipts of £114. The 20th Hussars Band was in attendance, and as night fell, the participants were able to see the grounds illuminated.

Many enthusiasts began to focus on involvement in national societies such as the National Rose Show, the National Chrysanthemum Society (which developed out of the Stoke Newington Society), while the Hammersmith Heartsease Society transformed into the National Pansy and Viola Society. Many competitions could be highly prestigious and involved not just a judging period but a social event as well. In November 1890, *The Gardeners' Chronicle* recorded details of the Ancient Society of York Florists' chrysanthemum show. It noted that the event 'was arranged in the spacious Exhibition building. Groups were arranged both in circles and semi-circles affording a pleasing change from the usual style. The list of prize winners showed that most awards went to gardeners of titled and landed gentry from many parts of the country.' Six years later, the society's chrysanthemum show involved an 'orchestra tastefully adorned with palms and shrubs and presented a picturesque appearance'.

Some seed companies worked with horticultural societies to provide prizes for competitions or even held their own. This was a good way of gaining publicity for their merchandise, as well encouraging gardeners to strive to grow better plants. Suttons Seeds announced:

> Having taken great interest in the encouragement of Cottagers in industrious habits, we have been for many years in the practice of supplying to Clergymen and others, seeds for distribution to Cottagers at greatly reduced prices. We wish it to be understood also, that for the establishment of new Cottagers Shows, and certain other cases in which it may be inconvenient to expend

money in the purchase of seeds, we're often willing to supply them gratis for free distribution.

Another company that was actively involved was Daniels Bros. of Norwich. In its 1901 *Spring Illustrated Guide for Amateur Gardeners*, it revealed a range of prize competitions available to customers, stating that:

> As we believe that the stimulus, which these competitions give to higher cultivation, is of much practical value, we have this year devoted a further £20 to these prizes, increasing the number offered for each subject, so that a larger number of our clients may have a chance of gaining a prize.

Daniels Bros. offered a total of £125 in cash prizes throughout the year for its own completion and was quick to confirm that its involvement with horticultural society competitions would also continue, saying, 'these prizes are quite apart from the very large number we are this season, as usual, offering in connection with the many Horticultural societies throughout the country.'

In order to take part in one of Daniels' seasonal competitions held in July, August and October, gardeners were expected to buy specific types of Daniels seeds. The company stressed that all entries must be grown from seeds 'procured direct from us by the competitor during the present year'. These seeds had to be grown on, and the resultant plants sent by road or by post 'prepaid and accompanied by the packet or label which accompanied the seeds from which the exhibit is grown'. If competitors wanted their produce returned, then return postage had to be provided in advance.

Upon entering one of Daniels' competitions, competitors had the chance of winning one of ten prizes per category. For example, the participants in the Pea Daniels Honeydew competition had to provide eighteen pods, but were rewarded with a first prize of £2, with the prize money decreasing depending on position, giving just 5s for tenth place. A competition for Nine Fruits had a first prize of £3, and 7s 6d for tenth place.

As well as competitions organised by seed companies and horticultural societies, many organisations and businesses used competitions as a way of encouraging pride in their workplace, or among local people. Railway companies were particularly effective at this, since they often encouraged station masters to grow plants using company colours to adorn local railway stations, and held competitions for the best station gardens. There were local competitions, too, designed to raise money for charities, such as the Nailsea Show, which sought to raise money for the Crimean War Wounded, or the Ipswich Cucumber Society, which focused on the length of cucumbers.

Newspapers began holding competitions for keen gardeners. Following King George V's coronation in 1911, the *Daily Mail* launched a nationwide competition for amateur gardeners who employed no more than one gardener. Focusing on sweet peas, the newspaper wrote that it was the 'most English of flowers' and 'the most decorative and most democratic, the one by every condition best suited to become the prevalent ornament of Coronation Year'. The competition attracted a massive response from keen gardeners and over 38,000 bunches of sweet peas were sent to Crystal Palace for judging. The winner was Mrs Fraser, the wife of a Scottish church minister, whose husband won third prize.

Participation in shows and competitions could be keen and were often linked into larger shows. In 1910, the *Book of the Flower Show* by Charles Curtis indicated that there were over 1,000 societies nationwide holding at least one show each year. Numbers continued to increase slowly, with new societies formed for specific purposes, such as the North of England Horticultural Society established in 1911. It had a clear purpose – to provide a high-quality showcase highlighting plants and produce that could be grown in a colder northern climate.

The First World War interrupted proceedings, resulting in its first show being held in 1920 at the Old Winter Gardens in Harrogate.

Similar problems were encountered by the Norfolk and Norwich Horticultural Society, which had discontinued its shows during the war. On deciding to resume the shows, the members decided that it would also 'provide classes for allotment holders and small gardeners and in this way, hoped to add to their numbers and enhance greatly the usefulness of the society in promoting horticulture in all its branches and thereby materially add to the home production of foodstuffs.' Despite this, the main focus remained on the activities of the middle- and upper-class members.

Interest in horticultural societies and horticultural competitions continued throughout the twentieth century, although during the Second World War many of the large shows were suspended. Instead, the activities of horticultural societies became focused on promoting 'Dig for Victory' activities. Normal events and activities were quickly resumed after 1945.

Chapter 8

Commercialisation

For nurseries and growers, the increased interest in gardening offered major opportunities to develop new markets, but this came at a cost. Gardeners were keen to obtain new varieties and new species to show off in their gardens. Many nurserymen and growers would visit shows and society exhibitions in the hope of finding the perfect plant for breeding purposes.

There was massive competition for the new varieties being discovered by plant hunters overseas. Initial prices for such new varieties could be very high but dropped equally quickly as soon as they became more widely available. In his book *An Economic History of the English Garden*, Roderick Floud points out that John Telford, nurseryman of York, sold a rhododendron for 15s in 1775 – a figure Floud estimates as being around £1,142 in today's currency. Two years later, William and John Perfect of Pontefract sold a Cape Jasmine for 10s 6d.

Breeding plants could provide useful income for working men, showing plants within florists' association displays or at horticultural shows. In 1777, nurseries were selling auriculas, polyanthuses and carnations at prices ranging from 1s to £2. That same year, Joseph Partington, a member of a florist association in Eccles, won 21 shillings for a first prize-winning auricula. In 1829, Loudon noted that it was not unusual 'for a working man who earns, perhaps, from eighteen shillings to thirty shillings per week, to give two guineas for a new variety of auricular, with a view to crossing it with some other, and raising seedlings of new properties.'

Some enthusiasts turned their hobby into successful businesses. Oldham-based enthusiast John Mellor has been described as the 'father of working men botanists of Lancashire'. Initially a handloom weaver and cotton spinner, his skill at raising plants led to the creation of four nursery gardens and the post of president of the Roynton Botanical Society – a title he held for thirty years.

The expansion of new techniques also encouraged the development of significant nursery businesses. Thomas Rivers was one such entrepreneur. Born at Sawbridgeworth in Hertfordshire in 1798 into a family of nurserymen trading in cabbage plants, flowers and fruit trees, he succeeded his father in the business in 1827. He later took advantage of changing trends to develop a lucrative business budding roses onto native wild dog roses and by publishing a *Catalogue of Roses*, which was described by John Loudon as 'the most useful catalogue of roses in the English language'. Rivers then used similar techniques to revolutionise the fruit tree industry, together with the development of orchard houses able to shelter plants from the cold and encourage longer fruiting periods. Within a short time, he was noting that 'orchard houses are now familiar things, hundreds are now rising up all over the face of the country; no garden structures have ever so rapidly advanced in popularity.'

Many other nurserymen and traders were quick to take advantage of the numerous business opportunities appearing in all sectors of the industry from high streets to cultivation. By the early nineteenth century almost every provincial town and city included nursery and seed businesses. Many of these companies bought and sold produce around the country, such as William Caldwell of Knutsworth in Cheshire. In 1805 he spent £203 buying seeds and bulbs from London, plus another £120 buying plants. Ten years later, James Cochran of London acquired plants and seeds worth £20,544 from suppliers in London, Colchester and Pontefract, plus an additional £737-worth of hyacinths from a Dutch supplier.

Such entrepreneurs maximised every potential opportunity. James Barron of Sheffield operated both a nursery and a shop selling everything needed by gardeners and farmers. He also offered a range of garden services whereby gentlemen could hire his gardeners 'by the day or week'. Placing an advertisement in the local paper, he invited potential customers to explore his stockholding, which included machinery from Scotland such as turnip sowing machines and potato shovels. Meanwhile, 'in the Horticultural Department, J.B.'s seeds are carefully selected from the best markets, he has also a superior collection of Dahlias, Auriculas, Calceolorias, Greenhouse plants and Co.' Another advert a few years later highlighted another buying expedition:

> J.B. having just returned from London, where he has purchased a large stock of the Best Horticultural and Agricultural Productions, the superior excellence of which induces him to solicit the attention of his Friends and Neighbours and hopes they will honour him with an early call, so they may examine, judge and select for themselves. He has all the usual kinds of Forest Trees, Evergreen and Flowering Shrubs, Roses in great variety, standard and trained Fruit, currant bushes & co, with a selection of the most recent introduced plants from all parts of the country, in excellent condition, and for sale at moderate prices.

Further north, in Bishop Auckland, nurseryman Thomas Sibbald set up a shop in the marketplace which proved very popular, but encountered problems when the land used for his nursery stock was required by the North Eastern Railway in 1865. Much of his stock was moved, but he still needed to hold an auction to reduce the overall stockholding. The sheer number of plants sold in the resulting auction reflected the scale of plant demand in the area:

About 32,000 Fruit and Forest Trees, Ornamental shrubs &c &c, two greenhouses, stove and propagating house. The stock comprises choice and well grown varieties of Peaches, Apricots, Cherries, Plums, Pears, Apples and other Fruit trees. The Forest trees consist of Larch, Spruce, Fir, Lime, Beech, Poplar, Oak, Chestnut &c, &c. Amongst the Pines are fine specimens of Wellingtonia Picea Excelsa, Cedrus Atlantica &c. Amongst the shrubs are Abor Vitaes, Yew, Hollies, Rhododendrons, Junipers, Laurels, Heaths, Roses &c &c. The whole of the stock is in fine healthy condition and will be sold without reserve, as the ground must be cleared. The sale affords an excellent opportunity for Noblemen, Gentlemen, Nurserymen, Gardeners and Amateurs.

Demand for seeds and plants grew extensively throughout the nineteenth century in line with the trend for formal planting and carpet bedding. It was a situation ripe for exploitation by innovative seed companies, some of which have since become extremely well known. Suttons Seeds is one such business.

Brothers James Sutton (a miller) and John Sutton (a corn dealer) traded in Reading, and it was John's second son, Martin Hope Sutton, who became the founder of the seeds business. Having read widely in botany and other gardening topics, Martin developed an experimental garden company selling seeds against his father's wishes when he was just 13 years old. Having created a list of seeds in 1832, he advertised them in the *Reading Mercury* under his father's name. It proved very successful and the resultant business grew fast. In 1833, seeds and bulbous flower roots accounted for just 2 percent of stock, but one year later it accounted for 42 percent of the whole business. By 1849, Suttons was experiencing annual sales of £4,700, creating profits of £1,240.

Suttons continued to expand its activities by developing new and better seeds, experimenting with breeding and development techniques for all types of seeds, root crops, grasses, vegetables and flowers, as well as establishing a nursery growing fruit trees, roses and American tree species. In 1851, Suttons exhibited at the Great Exhibition in Hyde Park, London. The company premises at Reading employed over 100 people during the main distribution periods. Occupying over 6 acres of ground, the building was extensive, covering all aspects of seed distribution including stores, grass and root seed, despatch office, farm orders, pea packing, bulb orders and a post office. Visiting Suttons in 1867, *The Gardeners' Chronicle* was clearly impressed, noting that 'on approaching the company in the market place at Reading, one sees an unostentatious building, but on entering it is obviously one of the most unique, but also one of the most extensive and best managed seed stores in the kingdom'. The magazine went on to say that:

> An additional house recently erected, and heated with hot water, expressly for the purpose of testing the germinating power of new seeds, immediately they are received from the contract Growers employed by Messrs Sutton. We are informed upwards of 8,000 acres are in this way occupied every year with seeds for the great Reading firm, their practice being to select roots perfectly true to their type, from which the seed is saved. This choice seed is subsequently distributed among the growers employed by them to grow the required quantities.

By 1875, Martin Sutton and his brother Alfred had developed Suttons Seeds into the biggest retail business within the British seed trade, and in Europe, when measured by turnover and customer numbers.

Not all entrepreneurs were as successful as Suttons. James Cochran of London was outwardly successful, experiencing a constant demand for his company's services, but actual profits were harder to maintain. Clients did not pay their bills and Cochran's ledgers reveal sizeable debts, including those by Lord Dillan, who had fled to France leaving Cochran with an unpaid bill of £12 4s. Meanwhile, Dr Symons of Chiswick owed £20 6s 11d. In May 1816, Cochran had 138 unpaid bills totalling £424. Debts steadily mounted up and by the time of his death, Cochran was in severe financial difficulties. His wife and daughters were left impoverished and although his nephew tried to save the business, he failed and eventually became a beadle at Paddington Workhouse.

Much depended on a mixture of luck, cashflow and the weather. In 1834, nurserymen George and John Harrison of Downham Market had to sell their business due to financial problems. The *Norfolk Chronicle* recorded that they had 'Assigned all their personal Estate and effects to trustees for the equal benefit of such of their creditors as should execute the same indenture within two calendar months.' This announcement was accompanied by an advertisement dealing with their stock:

> To Nurserymen. To be sold by private contract. All that valuable assortment of Nursery trees, late the property of Messrs John and George Harrison in the Nursery grounds at Dereham Market and Stow Bardolph in the County of Norfolk. The above consists of several thousand Oak, Ash, Beech, Fir, Elm and other plants in a most flourishing state. A lease of the Nursery ground for any length of time may be had.

Another failed nurseryman was Sheffield-based James Barrow. Initially very successful, he seems to have overreached himself, incurring high expenses though his purchasing trips to Scotland and London at a time when competition for sales was becoming more intense. His attempts to sell his shop and stockholding in 1839 were unsuccessful and by 1842, he had been committed to Sheffield Gaol due to his unpaid debts. It took several years for the debts to be slowly cleared, mainly through sales of his plants and merchandise. By 1851, he was working as a gardener for hire on a short-term basis.

By the mid nineteenth century, retailers, seed companies and nurserymen were finding life much harder. It was becoming a crowded marketplace and the constant demand for new varieties could make trading predictions difficult. Companies could easily find themselves with lots of obsolete stock. The cost of creating new varieties was not cheap, as breeding just one new plant required thousands of pollination crosses, with often only one or two proving potentially viable. It took time to build up stock levels ready for purchase by consumers. Bedding plants were particularly vulnerable to these problems since they were designed for a short season covering June to September. Fashions in colour and style could change very quickly, meaning cashflow problems could easily arise.

Where newspapers had previously contained various advertisements from nurserymen and seedsmen promoting their wares, in the 1720s Kensington-based nurseryman Robert Furber adopted an innovative marketing approach focusing on distributing catalogues, becoming the first person in England to use colourful plant illustrations within advertising material. One of his most famous catalogues was the *Twelve Months of Flowers* (1730), identifying all the plants Furber grew month by month, while another was *The Flower Garden Displayed* (1732), containing 400 images of fashionable plants.

Nurserymen and seed companies became increasingly dependent on such promotional material. Catalogues became a crucial element in the way plants were sold. To sell new varieties and new species, potential customers needed to be able to imagine what the plants would be like. In addition, new plant introductions would be heavily advertised in plant magazines and newspapers. To make them more memorable, growers usually added their names to that of the plant. Harrison's Nursery in Downham Market, for example, specialised in dahlias, resulting in introductions like Harrison's Gem and Harrison's

Don Jon. By 1830, Loddiges of London were offering 12,000 types of plants, including 1,470 roses within its catalogue. Initially seed and plant prices were inked in by hand, reflecting yearly variations, but Suttons became the first company to print prices in its catalogues, as well as providing printed advice on growing and cooking unusual vegetables.

Even the smallest of companies would have their own catalogues to distribute to customers. R&A Taylor were seed merchants who moved to King's Lynn, Norfolk in 1800, where they opened a store. Supplies of seeds were ordered from nurserymen in Bedfordshire and sent by barge to King's Lynn, where they were unloaded at the back entrance of the shop on Purfleet Creek. By 1849, the Taylor family were paying an annual rent of £66 (estimated to be around £6,000 in modern currency). The shop became extremely profitable. Most of their wares were sold locally, ordered through the company's annual catalogue, which incorporated intricate, detailed hand-drawn illustrations of the various plants. The quantities being ordered could be high, as can be seen from an 1849 shop ledger which noted that Mr Coxall, a market gardener in nearby Wiggenhall St Germans, had ordered four bushels of Windsor broad bean seeds and 1,500 Savoy cabbage plants. The Union Workhouse purchased cabbage, onion and turnip seeds, while the Reverend Bransby purchased artichokes, peas, beans, radishes, celery, endive, cabbage, Brussels sprouts, cucumbers and potatoes. Within a few years, R&A Taylor had gained a prestigious customer when they began selling fruit, seeds and plants to the Prince of Wales at his new home at nearby Sandringham. The list of seeds provided included mustard, cucumber, spinach, sea kale and mignonette. Fulfilling orders like this was time consuming and required considerable care. A shop assistant had to carefully weigh out all the required quantities and fill individual packets with the seeds.

Developing a market beyond the immediate locality of a seed company or shop become easier to achieve following the launch of the

Uniform Penny Post in 1840. Sending small items, letters and orders around the country became a fast, reliable way of trading, especially since it was accompanied by the introduction of money orders, thus creating a safe way to pay by cash. Post Office money orders involved low fees, which made it easier for members of the public to send small sums. The arrival of the railways provided a further impetus to rapid ordering, payment and fulfilment, increasing the speed with which orders could be sent anywhere in the country. Earley Local History Group's history of Suttons Seeds notes how entrepreneurial companies quickly took advantage of its potential: 'Martin Hope Sutton was at Reading Station on 30 March 1840, to see the first train depart for London, and took advantage of the crowds to sell flower seed to spectators and passers-by.'

Seed companies like Suttons, Carters and Daniels expanded their activities rapidly. Considerable attention was focused on advertising and marketing methods to help maximise sales. Suttons became a pioneer in such activity, introducing activities that have remained a feature of the industry ever since and ensuring the company became one of the first mail-order companies worldwide. As Earley Local History Group points out, 'Martin Hope's marketing strategy seems to have been to create a marketing edge by offering a more customer-focused business service than his competitors, and to be the first to understand the business value of the new technologies.' By 1863, Suttons were participating in British agricultural and horticultural shows, while the following year saw catalogues being distributed on the Continent and throughout the Empire. Advertising was regarded as extremely important, and considerable sums were spent promoting the company: 'In one year alone (1868-69) he spent £2,300 on advertising in journals and at agricultural shows, and £2,200 on printing catalogues.'

Trains and the postal service offered fast distribution methods. As soon as the Penny Post was launched in January 1840, Suttons started distributing free broadsheets to its customers, while trains delivered goods efficiently.

Earley Local History Group note that:

> By 1856, the company had illustrated seed catalogues giving not only the full range of seeds available, but sowing and growing hints, as well as testimonials from satisfied customers. These became so useful to gardeners that they quickly became known as Amateurs Guides rather than catalogues once the farm seeds had been separated into a separate catalogue. For those customers requiring larger quantities of seeds, bulbs or sundries, they instigated another first; the sending of goods free of charge, delivered to the nearest railway station.

The combination of this efficient, inexpensive mail service combined with the advent of faster travel through the rail networks and shipping facilities overseas meant companies like Suttons and Carters expanded their activities rapidly. Suttons were soon supplying seeds around the world, including to places as far away as Japan, the USA, South Africa, Australia and New Zealand. It even set up a branch in Calcutta, India enabling it to serve the expatriate market as well as sourcing seeds to be sold back into Britain. By the 1850s Suttons had begun selling its seeds in labelled packets bearing its own name, thus helping the company to create a specific, recognised brand.

Other seed companies took similar action, albeit mainly on a national basis. A typical advertisement placed in garden magazines highlighting extensive distribution facilities is that of Great Yarmouth-based Youell & Company, which read: 'Communications by steamer and railway to all parts of England, Ireland and Scotland, as well as to the Continent. All orders of £2 upwards delivered free to London, Newcastle and Hull, as well as any railway station within 150 miles of the nurseries.'

The gardeners' bothy at Holkam Hall, Norfolk, where the apprentices and under gardeners would have lived in Victorian times. (*Karis Youngman*)

Right: Door dividing the area visitors were allowed into from that of the working gardeners at Holkham walled garden. (*Karis Youngman*)

Below: Gravel paths that would have been hand weeded by the weeding women. (*Karis Youngman*)

Victorian bevelled glass in use in Holkham walled garden. (*Karis Youngman*)

Left: Victorian Hothouse in Holkham walled garden. (*Karis Youngman*)

Below: Map showing layout of Holkham walled garden. (*Karis Youngman*)

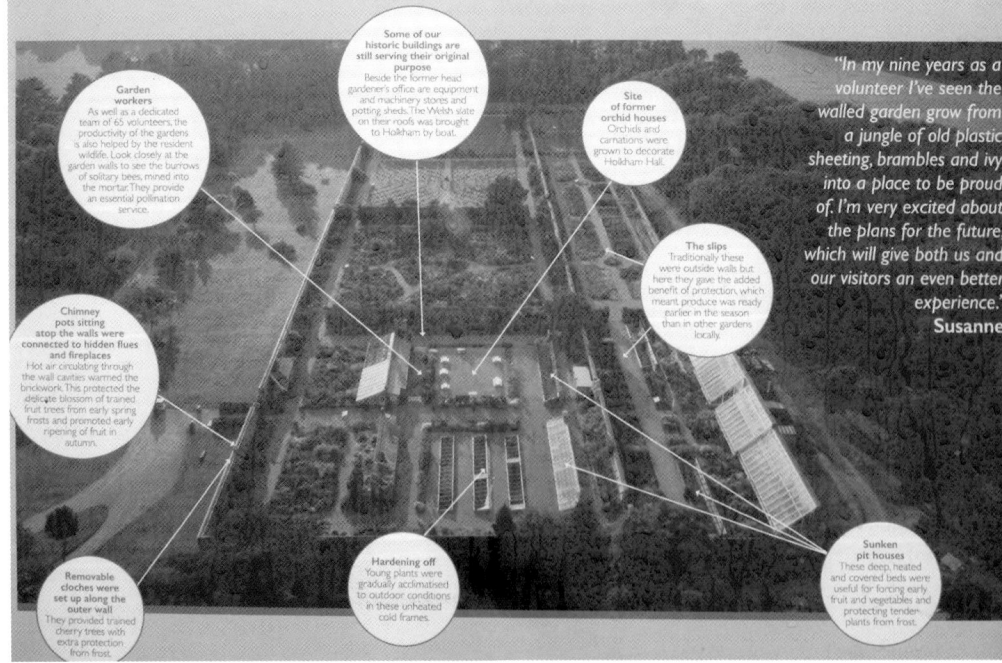

Above: Alms houses built for servants just outside the gates of Holkham. (*Karis Youngman*)

Right: A formal garden at Cliveden, Buckinghamshire, with lawned walks. (*Angela Youngman*)

Sunken rose garden at Belvoir Castle, Leicestershire. (*Angela Youngman*)

Above: Sir Charles Isham seated on his rockery at Lamport Hall, Northamptonshire. (*Lamport Hall*)

Left: Lampy, the last remaining gnome from Sir Charles Isham's rockery at Lamport Hall.

A scene on the rockery at Lamport Hall. (*Lamport Hall*)

Chatsworth House, Derbyshire, and its landscaped gardens. (*Angela Youngman*)

The search for picturesque vistas at Cliveden. (*Angela Youngman*)

Carpet bedding. (*Angela Youngman*)

Left: Gardening on an air raid shelter. (*Angela Youngman*)

Below: Notcutts' tent and display in Woodbridge, 1880. (*Nottcuts*)

Right: The site of what would be Britain's first garden centre. (*Stewarts*)

Below: An artist's impression of Britain's first garden centre. (*Stewarts*)

Bottom: Notcutts' first garden centre, 1958. (*Nottcuts*)

Above: Stewarts Garden Centre in the early 1960s, with eager gardeners buying the new containerised trees and plants. (*Stewarts*)

Left: Recycling within Sophie Godber's display garden at RHS Flower Show Tatton Court, 2024. (*Sophie Godber*)

Below: Tomies Cuisine the Nobonsai Garden at RHS Chelsea Flower Show, 2024. (*Tomies*)

Established in 1844, the Norwich-based Daniels Bros. seed catalogues proudly indicated that the company grew its own seeds and that some were even grown especially for royalty, such as the 'Sandringham Dwarf White Celery as grown for the Prince of Wales'. The amount of information varies from catalogue to catalogue, marking its increasing business success. Initial catalogues offered limited information and a few drawings, whereas later versions were much more expansive. The company's spring 1871 catalogue and Amateur Guide contains only one hand-drawn illustration and very little background information beyond a page of growing advice. Flower seeds such as Clarkia Elegans and Double Viscaria Oculata are identified by their name and nothing else. There are no indications as to colour, size or even how many seeds are in the packet. It also offered flower seeds in penny packets 'for the convenience of those having but small gardens'. Anyone ordering fewer than twelve packets were requested to provide an extra stamp for postage when making their order.

When dealing with vegetable seeds, Daniels Bros. become a little more expansive, with added comments such as 'Wormwood: exceedingly bitter', while scurvy grass could be used like water cress. The range of vegetable seeds was comprehensive. Gardeners had a wide choice, for example, Chinese mustard, Coxes Golden Gem Melon, garnishing parsley, three varieties of tomato, asparagus, five varieties of beet, six varieties of broad beans, nine of dwarf or kidney beans, four types of runner beans, seven of kale, seventeen types of broccoli, three Brussels sprouts, ten cabbage, three Savoy cabbage, four capsicum, five carrot, four cauliflower, four celery, three leek, eight types of melon, two types of mustard, eleven of onions, two of parsley, two parsnip, twenty two varieties of peas, twelve of radish, nine of turnip, eight tomato, three spinach and just one each of Salisfy and Scorzonera.

Given that interest in gardening had become prevalent throughout all groups of society, it is no surprise that royalty was involved, led primarily by the activities of Prince Albert. In the 1850s, Suttons began supplying seeds to Queen Victoria's household, and in 1871 gained a Royal Warrant from the Prince of Wales (later King Edward VII), and Queen Victoria in 1884. Other seed companies followed suit and by 1879, Daniels was proudly highlighting its royal patrons: HM The Queen and HRH The Prince of Wales, placing their royal crests prominently on the cover of its catalogues. These covers had become quite ornate, involving much more colour, a decorative black border and pale green covers complete with ornate hand-drawn pictures. Inside, the large A4-sized catalogue contained botanically correct illustrations, growing advice, plus a vast array of fruit trees, roses and plants of all kinds including a specialist selection of hyacinths, plus a collection of florists' tulips helpfully commenting that these had become scarce.

In its spring 1879 *Illustrated Guide for Amateur Gardeners*, Daniels provided not just information but atmosphere, with numerous black and white images, plus idealistic drawings such as a horse and cart piled with hay, surrounded by women sheaving and piling it up. Daniels sought to make life easier for gardeners by creating collections of vegetable seeds available at set prices. The No. 3 collection price of 31 shillings and 6 pence was clearly aimed at allotment holders or people with large vegetable gardens since it included:

15 pints peas
4 pints beans
3 pints French beans
2 packets beets
2 packets borecole
1 packet Brussels sprouts
3 packets broccoli
3 packets cabbage
½ ounce Savoy

3 ounces carrots
2 packets cauliflower
2 celery
1 packet Couve Tronchuda cabbage
4 ounces + 1 packet cress
2 packets cucumber
1 packet endive
1 packet gourd (Pumpkin)
1 ounce leek
3 sorts of lettuce
6 ounces mustard
1 packet melon
4 ounces onions
1 ounce parsley
2 ounces radish
1 pint spinach
1 packet salsify
1 packet scorzonera
4 ounces turnip
2 packets vegetable marrow
4 packets herbs
1 packet rampion (a useful salad)
1 packet tomato
1 capsicum

Colour became an increasingly important element. By 1891, its *Illustrated Guide for Amateur Gardeners* had expanded to 128 pages, stressing the company's royal links and coloured pages listing 'our new coloured illustrations' alongside variety and price. Customers were required to pay 1 shilling for the booklet. Even more varieties were now on offer such as sixty-one varieties of early and late potatoes, sixty types of peas, ten varieties of broccoli and seven varieties of Brussels sprouts, together with more types of flowers. Hyacinths were in demand, and Daniels were providing background information on their cultivation in Holland. Seed collections had clearly proved popular as Daniels increased the number of collections, but customers needed to take a leap of faith as to what was included. Very little information was provided – a No. 7 complete collection costing 12s 6d provided the best kinds of seeds for succession in a small garden; an unspecified selection of thirty varieties cost 5s for a Cottager's Garden; and just sixteen varieties in a Cottager's Packet cost 2s 9d. Interestingly, the company were now offering herbs in cultivation, seeds for song birds (especially canaries), and a vast array of pruning and other gardening sundries.

Around 1899, Daniels expanded into a shop in the Royal Arcade, Norwich, and had seed grounds along the Ipswich Road, as well as a nursery in Town Close, Newmarket Road. Its *Illustrated Guide for Amateur Gardeners* had increased in size to 160 pages, but still cost 1 shilling. It had become even more aspirational, using black and white photographic images showing people playing cricket, as well as croquet players in action on a large lawn. Adjacent images focused on the availability of high-quality lawn grass seed while elsewhere in the guide were images of desirable prize growing plants such as 'A Grand New Potato Daniels Sensation', described as 'one of the heaviest cropping and best varieties we have ever grown', which offered 'capital disease-resistance'. Separate catalogues such as *Bulbs, Roses, Fruit Trees & Co.* highlighted their specialist ranges such as collections of the twelve finest exhibition hyacinths costing 8s 6d, and Dutch crocus described as cheap, showy varieties 'splendidly effective when planted in lines or large masses of distinct colours'. Other varieties on offer were numerous perennials, hybrid perpetual roses, fruit trees, approximately 100 varieties of apples including unusual ones such as Yorkshire Greening, the Sandringham, Jolly Beggar and Col Harbord's Pippin. Gardeners could buy plants specifically for fencing such as privet, laurel and box green; greenhouse and stove plants, plus grapevines, cherries, gooseberries and plums.

The use of catalogues as a promotional method also led companies like Daniels to highlight the way in which the company encouraged gardeners to choose its seeds rather than those of any other businesses. Prize competitions totalling £125 were being held focusing purely on specific Daniels seeds. The company stated: 'As we believe that the stimulus, which these competitions give to higher cultivation, is of much practical value, we have this year devoted a further £20 to these prizes, increasing the number offered for each subject, so that a larger number of our clients may have a chance of gaining a prize,' adding that 'these prizes are quite apart from the very large number we are this season, as usual, offering in connection with the many Horticultural societies throughout the country.'

The increasing commercialisation of seed sales through catalogues and shops created both problems and opportunities for suppliers and workforces. There were problems of quality control ensuring that every packet of seeds was high quality. Adulteration was common, and it could often be hard for gardeners to tell whether seeds were the named variety or mixed with cheaper options such as mustard.

Supplying wide varieties of seed did require a large workforce, a task which increasingly provided opportunities for women. In 1870, *The Gardener's Magazine* noted that Carters Seeds used women sorters based at their premises in Holborn:

> The sorters are placed beside great benches, on which the seed is poured out in quantities. At the end of the bench is a small slit, and beneath the slit hangs a great bag. The sorter draws forward the seed and rolls it through the slit into the bag every grain that is the proper size and shape and colour, but quickly detects and throws out every seed that is small or misshapen or badly coloured or in any way wrong.

Apart from buying direct from the seed companies, people had access to a wide network of methods to acquire seeds, young plants and garden equipment, such as greengrocers, corn chandlers and hardware stores. In his book *London Labour and the London Poor*, Henry Mayhew noted that 'root sellers' (plant sellers) traded from stalls in streets during May, June and July. Their stalls were extremely colourful and eye catching, frequently involving a series of shelves showing plants of different colours in layers ideal for carpet bedding. Colours were generally bright and vivid, ranging from pure white to deep crimson.

The provision of information in all formats played a crucial role in the commercialisation of gardening. Until the mid-eighteenth century, most gardening books had been primarily botanical in nature, such as John Evelyn's *Sylva, or A discourse of Forest-Trees and the Propagation of Timber* published in 1664, or Carl Linnaeus' *Systema Naturae* (1735).

John Abercrombie's *Every Man His Own Gardener* (1767) provided a different approach as it set out to be a work on practical gardening, although it did not initially refer to Abercrombie as the author – instead it carried the name of Thomas Mawe, gardener to the Duke of Leeds. This was possibly due to the fact that Mawe was more famous than Abercrombie and was given £20 for allowing his name to be associated with the work. The book provided detailed instructions on growing a variety of plants such as strawberries. It proved extremely popular and was frequently reprinted, with Abercrombie's name eventually being given as joint author in 1787. It was clear that there was a tremendous thirst for knowledge building up among the population.

Demand for books and magazines skyrocketed. Gardening was becoming a fashionable, popular leisure activity enjoyed by all sectors of the population, and as literacy levels rose, people wanted to read about the subject. Dedicated magazines began to appear. In 1787 the first issue of *The Botanical Magazine or Flower-Garden Displayed* (later renamed *Curtis's Botanical Magazine*) appeared. The first ever part work to be launched in Britain, it was the work of William Curtis, an apothecary and botanist who worked at Kew Gardens who sought to provide information on various ornamental and exotic plants, complete with detailed flower illustrations. Early issues saw massive demand, with over 3,000 copies being sold even though it cost 1 shilling per issue – an expensive publication for the period. In 1815, a competing magazine appeared: *The Botanical Register* by artist Sydenham Edwards, which also sought to focus on individual plants, while Loddiges, a prestigious London plant nursery, launched its own *Botanical Cabinet* two years later.

With the arrival of John Loudon in 1822, garden media publishing took a radical turn. By training a Scottish botanist and garden designer, Loudon recognised an opportunity for self-promotion as well as a potentially profitable opportunity. Entitled an *Encyclopaedia of Gardening*, his book provided details of garden history and all aspects of the theory and practice of horticulture, floriculture, arboriculture and landscape gardening. Loudon also highlighted what he called 'the latest improvements' in style and design, together with suggestions for future progress. It was instantly popular, with ultimately eleven editions being published during the nineteenth century.

Four years later, in 1826, he launched *The Gardener's Magazine*, the first ever magazine devoted solely to horticulture and garden design, costing 4 shillings per copy. It was a risky venture, as he was totally responsible all aspects of its publication. His initial aim was to help country gardeners achieve the same 'footing with those about the metropolis'. In his first issue Loudon stated: 'In an art so universally practised as gardening, and one daily undergoing so much improvement, a great many occurrences must take place worthy of being recorded, not only for the entertainment of gardening readers, but the for the instruction of practitioners in the art.' Within a short time, over 4,000 copies had been sold and Loudon had begun preparing his next issue. Initially he had planned to create a quarterly magazine, but given the demand and high level of sales, publication soon increased to bi-monthly, and then monthly at a cost of 1s 6d. Subsequent issues dealt with an ever wider range of topics of interest to gardeners, both professional and amateur, such as the need for self-education in techniques and knowledge, suggested improvements needed at Kensington Gardens, as well as highlighting management issues within the London Horticultural Society. He recommended the setting up of garden libraries, giving working gardeners especially in the big estates access to books like the *Hortus Britannicus* and the *Encyclopaedia of Plants*. *The Gardener's Magazine* was initially priced at 4 shillings a copy and according to Floud, this provided him with an annual income of around £500–£750. Within a few years, however, Loudon was forced to reduce prices substantially. By 1834, the price per copy had decreased to just 1s 2d, the main reason for this laying in the arrival of competing titles.

The success of *The Gardener's Magazine* had not gone unnoticed. Competitors quickly recognised an opportunity and had created alternative magazines. In 1831, Joseph Paxton and Joseph Harrison published the *Horticultural Register*, which was successfully published for five years. In 1832, George Glenny's *Horticultural Journal and Florists' Register* was launched in a bid to highlight the role of florists, stating in the first issue that:

> We shall go on our humble way till we can prove that florists' flowers belong to the highest instead of the lowest grade of floriculture, and that tailors, tinkers and weavers, who knew them and grew them a century ago, though not one in a hundred could read or write, were better judges than botanists of what constituted a good thing.

George Glenny founded a further magazine in 1837, the weekly *Gardener's Gazette*.

Despite such competition, Loudon become one of the most successful writers of the period with best-selling books such as *The Suburban Gardener and Villa Companion* (1838) and the *Suburban Horticulturist: or An Attempt to Teach the Science and Practice of the Management of the Kitchen, Fruit and Forcing Garden to Those Who Have No Previous Knowledge or Practice in the Department of Gardening* (1842). By 1838, he had achieved a fortune of over £15,000 from his work, but financial problems arose due to the sheer costs of producing his massive *Arboretum et Fruticetum Britannicum* that same year. When he died in 1843 the Loudon family were left in debt and *The Gardener's Magazine* died with him.

1841 saw the arrival of the biggest challenger to *The Gardener's Magazine* in the form of *The Gardeners' Chronicle*, published by Joseph Paxton and John Lindley. This became the most successful and longest lasting of the nineteenth-century magazines. A weekly magazine, each issue cost 6 pence and focused on horticultural subjects. The design was kept simple, with lots of text. Each issue contained sixteen pages of news, appearing on Saturdays and so timing its arrival with pay day and the following day of rest on Sundays, giving people time to read the magazine. Images were mostly provided by advertisers, which included seed companies like Suttons, as well as small nurseries, auctioneers, manufacturers of fashionable accessories, watering equipment, greenhouses – in fact, everything required to set up and maintain a garden. It became immensely influential, attracting garden designers, owners, professional gardeners and even an overseas readership. By 1851, its circulation had reached 6,500.

Nor was this a market which was confined to men. In 1846, Jane Loudon – who had not been involved in gardening until her marriage but soon became highly proficient – published *The Ladies' Companion to the Flower Garden* and sold over 20,000 copies. Initially printed as a monthly magazine, it was soon being sold as bound volumes for long-term reference. It proved a very successful project, staying in print for over thirty years.

In 1848, yet another magazine was launched, this time targeting low income, small gardeners. Costing just 3 pence per issue, it utilised a newspaper format. Published every Thursday, *The Cottage Gardener* was the brainchild of a barrister, George Johnson. Each issue focused on basic plants like cabbages, apples, mignonette, carrots and beans, rather than grand plants like pineapples and orchids. Advertising matched the readership, highlighting products like seeds, manure and garden netting. It was followed in 1850 by an even cheaper magazine, *The Gardener's Hive*, costing 2 pence. In 1857, George Johnson sought to target group sales by offering 'manuals for the many' at discount prices 'to clergymen and gentlemen who wished to distribute them to their parishioners.'

Over the next few years, *The Cottage Gardener* slowly widened its appeal and style, eventually becoming a 'gentleman's magazine' and in 1861 changed its name to the *Journal of Horticulture*. It was followed in 1865 by Shirley Hibberd's, *The Gardener's Magazine*, which became very popular.

Such a rise in magazines and newspaper-style publication devoted to gardening reflects the wider transformation that was taking place in society. The arrival of the railways made it much easier and cheaper to distribute publications nationwide, or to send them through the postal service. Circulations were high.

It was not just specialist magazines that took account of this burgeoning desire for information about gardening. In 1848, the *Edinburgh Weekly Journal* became the first general newspaper to include a regular gardening column. In 1852, the *Lloyds Weekly*, a London newspaper with a circulation of over 350,000, followed suit, appointing George Glenny to act as its gardening correspondent. Within a short time, *Lloyds Weekly* was also offering monthly garden guides for 1 penny, or a year's boxed version for 1s 6d. Alternatively, readers could buy short guides on specific flowers written by Glenny for 1 penny each.

The repeal of the tax on paper in 1861 had an immediate impact on the garden publishing industry. As a result of this decision, printing became much cheaper, leading to a rapid growth in the printing of all kinds of materials from catalogues to magazines. William Robinson was a trained gardener who decided to enter the publishing world. Having begun work as a garden boy in Ireland, he joined the Royal Botanic Garden at Kew and in 1869 spent £900 publishing a book entitled *The Parks, Promenades and Gardens of Paris*. Encouraged by its success, he went onto to launch *The Garden Magazine* in 1871. It took a very different approach to other magazines on the market, seeking instead to promote a garden style of the 'natural or English school free from rigid formalities, meretricious ornaments, gypsum, powdered bricks, cockle-shells, and bottle ends.' The magazine also adopted an innovative approach in its visual appeal, as for the first time, colour plates were included as well as several illustrations, and it possessed a decorative style, which was quickly adopted by competing publications.

In 1879, William Robinson launched another magazine, *Gardening Illustrated*, which cost just 1 penny per copy. In view of the number of gardening magazines on the market, Robinson included an editorial in the first issue asking, 'Why launch another garden magazine?' His answer was simple: there were 'fully a million persons deeply imbued with a love for gardening'. This was followed by *Cottage Gardening*, which he edited, and sold for a half penny – the cheapest magazine on the market. Publishing garden media made him very wealthy, and by 1885 he had purchased the estate of Gravetye Manor, East Grinstead.

Magazine and newspaper sales were undoubtedly helped by changing distribution patterns. With the fall in the cost of printing and the cost of paper, prices for publications had reduced dramatically, with many now available for as little as a penny. Instead of having to subscribe to a magazine, readers could now simply buy one whenever they chose. Spotting an opportunity, W.H. Smith had opened bookstalls on railway stations, enabling travellers to buy reading matter for the journey. It was also a quick, easy way for anyone to obtain a magazine and marked the arrival of a mass market readership.

Magazine numbers continued to increase, targeting different market sectors such as the 1901 title, *The Suburban Garden and What to Grow in It*. Soon every newspaper and magazine included regular columns written for gardeners. In 1919, *Ideal Home* noted that 'readers will find this journal of very decided assistance in not only the Ideal Home, but likewise the Ideal Garden with which the former would, of course, be incomplete.'

Along with this growth in magazines and newspapers, readers' demand for specialist books escalated. The rise of gardening publications encouraged book production, especially by magazine writers. Magazines frequently reviewed and recommended books. In 1834, *The Gardener's Magazine* recommended Charles Lawrence's *Practical Directions for the Cultivation of Cottage Gardens* alongside Loudon's own book, *Cottage Gardens*.

Evidence of the overall upswing in gardening books is reflected in the British Library catalogue. By law, the British Library must receive a copy of every book published within the country. During the 1820s, the catalogue listed 137 books containing the words 'garden' or 'gardening' in the title. Subsequent decades saw the number steadily growing until by 1909, there were 539 published, with some selling thousands of copies

Education was a key reason for the increase in gardening books. John Wright, chief instructor for the Kent and Surry County Councils, published *Garden Flowers and Plants, A Primer for Amateurs* (1895). His introduction included the words 'the importance of domestic gardening is now recognised by the Board of Education as a legitimate subject for teaching in elementary and continuation schools, and a great impetus will thus be given to the work in its various aspects, including floriculture.'

Companies like Suttons took advantage of this demand for information, providing a wide variety of materials, not always linked directly to gardening. In 1871, it published the first geological and railway map of England designed for agriculturalists. Over 16,000 copies had been sold by 1902. The company's 'My Garden Diary' offered monthly reminders of all the tasks that needed to be done in the garden, alongside details of the rising and setting of the sun and moon, plus miscellaneous facts such as historic events. Suttons Educational cabinets were highly popular. Made from polished oak, with glazed compartments and a sunblind, typical cases contained models of plant diseases, specimens of uneconomic grasses as well as cases of insects 'injurious and beneficial to farm and garden crops'. Its educational collection of twenty-four species of grasses suitable for permanent and temporary pastures contained not just examples, but also details of botanical names, soils, indications as to where they were most likely to be found, fresh and dry weights and seventy-five glazed tin boxes of grass and agricultural seeds. In 1910, the collection cost 40 shillings and such cases have become highly collectable. In recent years, a rare surviving example was brought on the *Antiques Road Show* TV programme and valued at £200.

Chapter 9

Plant Hunting and its Impact on Gardens

With attention increasingly focused on all aspects of a garden, people wanted to have plants they could show off to visitors. With plant hunters active around the world, demand for new, exotic plants and the creation of new varieties was intense. Fortunes could be made, but it was a risky business.

Considerable competition among nurserymen to be the first to introduce a desirable plant was the natural consequence of this movement, with some nurseries and horticultural associations sponsoring professional gardeners to take part in plant hunting expeditions. It was a potentially risky business, as the plant hunters faced the risk of robbery, theft and disease, not to mention problems caused by climate, storms, or travelling long distances in close-packed vessels. There could be hidden dangers, too. Plant hunter James Macrae had the task of collecting plants on route to Hawaii while travelling on board a ship carrying the bodies of King Kamehameha II and Queen Kamamalu, both of whom had died of measles. Numerous plant hunters died due to their work.

In her book *The Hidden Horticulturists: the Untold Story of the Men who Shaped Britain's Gardens* (2019), Fiona Davison highlights the extent to which people would go to obtain desirable plants. In 1828, John Lindley, assistant secretary at the Chiswick grounds, received a letter from a Hackney nurseryman called William Mackay, offering a selection of seeds at a cost of £12 (the equivalent of approximately six months' salary for an ordinary gardener). Lindley was instantly suspicious since Mackay's selection included rare seeds such as

Clarkia Pulchella, which had only just arrived at Chiswick having been sent by a plant collector active in America. Using the pseudonym Hortulaneus, Mackay wanted to meet Lindley in a Chiswick public house to arrange a deal. Instead, Lindley contacted William Ballard, a Bow Street Runner, who set a trap for Mackay by pretending to be the buyer and arranging to meet at the Flower Pot in Bishopsgate Street. Mackay did not turn up. Further investigations using *Chiswick's Handwriting Book* revealed that the handwritten script used in the letter was remarkably similar to that of gardener John Frederick Wood, who had lost his job at Chiswick due to 'improper conduct'. Ballard conducted a dawn raid on Wood's lodging and found a variety of seeds in a dish under his bed. Wood eventually admitted that he had purchased the seeds from a student labourer at Chiswick. Both Wood and the labourer were sent for trial at the Old Bailey, where they pleaded guilty and were sentenced to three months' imprisonment.

Sending seeds was one way in which exotic plants sourced overseas could be made available within a wider market. This did cause some problems, however, since germination rates could be low. Sending living specimens was an ideal option, but trying to ensure their survival during long ocean voyages amid varying climatic conditions and uncertain care was not easy. Often, the cases of specimens were placed in the hands of the crew rather than being accompanied by the plant hunter. Even if the plant hunter was present, plant care could be difficult due to changing levels of light and darkness, temperature variations and even simply the issue of watering if supplies of water ran low on a long voyage that might be lengthened due to storms or lack of wind.

A chance discovery in 1829 by Nathaniel Bagshaw Ward revolutionised plant hunting. Fascinated by botany, Dr Ward had been attempting to raise a hawk moth within a sealed glass bottle. Having placed damp leaf mould at the bottom of the bottle before sealing it, he discovered seed from ferns and grasses had germinated in the moist environment. His attention was caught by this discovery and he subsequently worked to develop it with the aid of the prestigious nurserymen, Loddiges of Hoxton. His innovative Wardian cases created a sealed environment that allowed plants to survive despite any seasonal changes around them. The decision was made to send two Wardian cases packed with plants on a long sea voyage to Sydney in 1833. All the plants survived. In Sydney, the cases were replanted with a variety of Australian plants and arrived in London the following year in 'the most healthy and vigorous condition'. Throughout the long voyages, the Wardian cases had not been opened and the plants had not been watered. They had also withstood deck temperatures ranging from -7-49°C (20-120°F).

The invention of Wardian cases proved an instant success, with demand rocketing from plant hunters everywhere. It facilitated the creation of an international plant trade, with plant hunters able to send new species safely around the world and new plant introductions from nurseries to be distributed worldwide. In 1842, the *Quarterly Review* noted:

> There are few ships that now arrive from the East Indies without carrying on deck several cases of this description, belonging to one or other of our chief nurserymen, filled with orchideous plants and other new and tender varieties from the East, which formerly baffled the utmost care to land them here in a healthy state. These cases, frequently furnished by the extreme liberality of Dr Wallich the enterprising and scientific director of the Hon. Company's gardens in the neighbourhood of Calcutta, form on shipboard a source of great interest to the passengers of a four-month's voyage, and after having deposited their precious contents on the shores, return again by the same ships filled with the common flowers of England… This interchange of sweets was a few years ago almost unattainable, the sea-air and

spray, as is well known, being most injurious to every kind of plant; but their evil effects are now completely avoided by these air-tight cases, which admit no exterior influence but the light.

The scale of successful new introductions following the invention of the Wardian case skyrocketed. It enabled a new industry cultivating tea plants to be established in India and Sri Lanka after tea seeds and plants were successfully transported from China using the same method. Plant hunter Robert Fortune, for example, travelled to China in 1842 and was subsequently responsible for discovering countless new introductions such as the Kerria Japonica, Dicentra, Weigela Rosea, Jasminum nudiflorum, Daphne Fortunei, Berberis Fortunei, Gardenia Fortuniana, Viburnum, Spirea, Azaleas, the Chusan daisy-style chrysanthemum and many varieties of prunus.

Expeditions might be financed privately or as part of a government activity. Joseph Dalton Hooker was a naval surgeon with a deep interest in botany. His father, Sir William Jackson Hooker, was director of Kew Gardens. In 1849-50, he was placed on half pay as a naval surgeon and given £400 by the Treasury to embark on two years of plant hunting in the Himalayas, accompanied by a retinue of fifty-five servants, porters, an escort of Nepalese sepoys, an interpreter and a personal servant. Despite obstacles placed in his way by the local Rajah, Joseph Hooker continued to collect seeds accompanied by Dr Archibald Campbell. Eventually, the two men were imprisoned, beaten and tortured until being later rescued by the British authorities. Despite their ordeal, they managed to collect ripe rhododendron seeds of which forty-three were new species.

Plant hunting could be a dangerous business. The majority of plant hunters were exploring uncharted terrain and rarely knew in advance what type of conditions or circumstances they might face. Sudden torrential storms could turn rivers into raging torrents, or they might encounter wild animals as they traversed thick forests, while climbing mountains in search of rare, unknown rock plants could lead to falls. There was also the ever-present risk of piracy, robbery, theft, inadequate food and disease during months of arduous travel, while ships returning plants home could be lost at sea. Plant hunters exploring the River Orinoco in South America in search of rare orchids encountered major problems with dysentery, and their stock was stolen by rivals. At least two plant hunters are known to have died: William Arnold drowned in the Orinoco, while Gustavo Wallis died from malaria and yellow fever. In 1901, a plant hunting expedition searching for orchids within the jungles of the Philippines resulted in five people never being seen again. Another was eaten by a tiger and yet another burnt to death. Among the many reports sent back were comments like that of Joseph Hooker, writing to his father William from Darjeeling in 1849, recalling an expedition to acquire rhododendron seeds:

> I staid [*sic*] at 13,000ft very much on purpose to collect there seeds of the Rhododendrons and with cold fingers it is not very easy... Botanizing, during March is difficult. Sometimes the jungle is so dense that you have enough to do to keep hat and spectacles in company, or it is precipitous... Certainly one often progresses spread-eagle fashion against the cliff, for some distance, & crosses narrow planks over profound Abysses, with no hand-hold whatever.

Meanwhile, Robert Lyall noted that in Mauritius, he was 'made a prisoner, for being a Sorcerer, exiled, and finally banished'.

Heading off to America, Victorian plant hunter David Douglas wrote that:

> An intermittent fever dreadfully fatal broke out...not a soul remains!! The houses empty and the flocks of famished dogs howling and dead bodies in every direction... I am one of the

few among the persons of the [Hudson Bay] Company who have stood it... The ship which sailed with us was totally wrecked on entering the River but I am glad to say no lives were lost. To this ship I was at first appointed and...I should have lost my all.

Later on, Douglas travelled down the Fraser River in British Columbia and recorded: 'At the "Stony Islands" of Fraser's River...my canoo [*sic*] was dashed to pieces when I lost every article I then possessed...the collection of plants was about 400 species, of which 250 were mosses – a few of them were new. I cannot tell you how much this has worn me down.'

The vast quantities of plants collected could pose problems when it came to arranging their propagation and care. The United States Department of Agriculture (USDA) set up a plant collecting project during the 1890s, placing David Fairchild as head of the section. The first official collector was Professor Niels Ebbesen Hansen, who headed off to Russia. David Fairchild recalled 'almost the moment I was settled in our first location, tons of seeds and plants began to pour in upon me from Russia. Hansen felt that he had been sent out to collect, and he collected everything and collected it in quantity. It was all most embarrassing, as no provision whatever had been made to take care of his shipments.' The resultant plants included apples, alfalfa, pears, crab apples and proved extremely useful, meeting the requirements of the USDA for produce that was cold hardy and drought tolerant. Another plant hunter working with the USDA was Mark Carleton, who discovered a type of durum wheat in Russia that was extremely productive in dry conditions. Within five years, farmers were growing over 20 million bushels of this new durum wheat.

By the late nineteenth century, plant hunters were actively seeking to fulfil orders from all types of buyers. Royal Botanic Gardens, Kew has a letter in its archives that was sent to the assistant director, Sir William Thiselton-Dyer from George King, who was based at the

Government Chinchona Plantation near Darjeeling, India. Apart from thanking Sir William for three Wardian cases and a box of plants that included various Malayan specimens, he wrote that he had struck cuttings of Aesculus *punduana* and promised he would try to get seeds of Rhododendron *griffithii*, as well as Bassia *butyacea*, but wanted to know if more tubers of Amorphophallus *campanulatus* were required.

Nurserymen often financed expeditions for plants. Seeing a specimen of the rare Hankerchief tree at Kew in 1899, nurseryman Henry Veitch commissioned a young botanist from Kew, Ernest Wilson, to travel to China and bring back seeds. Wilson's experience reflects the difficulties that plant hunters faced. Although the tree had been identified in a remote area of the Yuan province, Wilson only had a hand-drawn map plus a few instructions to guide him. His letters recall the problems he faced which included encountering bandits, almost drowning when his boat overturned in a rocky river, surviving a deadly fever and being imprisoned as a suspected spy. To make matters worse, when he found the reported location of the tree it had been cut down and used to build a house. Fortunately, another specimen was encountered while searching for other plants, but he had to wait weeks for the seeds to develop. Despite these experiences, Wilson retained his enthusiasm and undertook other successful plant hunting expeditions, resulting in the introduction of over 1,000 species of plants and thus creating a vast new market among gardeners keen to incorporate the latest exotic plants into their gardens. Discovering a really desirable plant could prove very profitable.

It was not just men seeking out new, rare plants. Women also made their mark on the sector. Travelling with her husband on postings in North America and India during the 1820s and 1830s, self-taught botanist Lady Dalhousie created extensive dried flower collections of rare native plants, some of which are now in the herbarium at the Royal Botanic Garden, Edinburgh. Others such as Ellen Willmott financed plant hunting expeditions by Ernest 'Chinese' Wilson to China. Mary Anne Robb, meanwhile, the granddaughter of industrialist Matthew Boulton, enjoyed travelling and seeking out unusual plants. It is said that when she visited Turkey in the early 1890s, she spotted a desirable euphorbia growing by the roadside. Lacking a Wardian case or similar container, she simply took one of her hat boxes, removed the hat and replaced it with the plant to keep it safe. The euphorbia survived and later became known as Mrs Robb's Bonnet.

Returning visitors from overseas, especially visitors to places like China, Africa, Australasia and India, would retell stories of the plants they had seen, arousing considerable interest among their families back home in Britain. In 1812, the travel writer Maria Graham provided detailed plant descriptions in her *Journal of a Residence in India*: 'The Saguerus Rumphii, a kind of palm, from which an excellent kind of sago is made. It is also valuable on account of the black fibres surrounding the trunk at the insertion of the leaves, which afford a cordage for ships, said to be stronger and more durable than that made from any other vegetable substance.'

While visiting the Calcutta Botanic Gardens, Graham noted that a 31-year-old banyan tree had a 'monstrous warty trunk, of soft useless wood. Crowned with a few ragged branches and palmated leaves,' and that 'carefully preserved there is a cajeput, from the leaves of one species of which (*Melelucca cajeputi*) the famous cajeput oil is extracted, which is used by the inhabitants of Malacca and the eastern isles, of which the tree is a native, as a sovereign remedy for rheumatisms, swellings and bruises.'

There was a flourishing market in botanical illustrations for both decorative and educational purposes. Women played a major role in providing these paintings. Ellen Hutchins (1785-1815) has been described as the first female botanist in Ireland, creating drawings of non-flowering plants such as seaweeds and lichens. Lady Charlotte Wheeler-Cuffe accompanied her husband on a posting to Burma, where she spent years painting and analysing plants, including a white flowered rhododendron discovered at Nat Ma Taung, which was subsequently named Rhododendron *cuffeanum*.

During the latter part of the nineteenth century, Marianne North travelled on her own between 1871 to 1885 to fifteen different countries, including India, painting the flowers she saw there. What made her paintings unique was the fact that she used oil paints and painted plants within their environment rather than as individuals against a white background. This made the paintings extremely valuable botanical records. She returned to Britain with 240 oil paintings, which she subsequently gave to Kew Gardens, along with an offer to build a gallery to house them. While the gallery was being constructed, Marianne decided to travel around Australia, Tasmania and New Zealand creating more illustrations. Yet more paintings were created on other journeys to Canada, the USA, Jamaica and Brazil, where she explored the Amazon rainforests. By 1882, over 800 botanical paintings and drawings created during her travels were hung in the gallery and attracted considerable attention from visitors.

Not surprisingly, exotic plants were highly prized and sought after, often becoming status symbols within Victorian society. People would try to outdo each other in terms of the number and rarity of the plants held in their glasshouses and gardens. It could be highly profitable for nurserymen and growers who managed to successfully propagate and bring to market such rare plants.

Frederick Sander was one such person. Known as the 'Orchid King', he became the official royal orchid grower to Queen Victoria. Sander owned a large orchid farm based at St Albans, which had over sixty greenhouses devoted to growing and propagating orchids. He also employed twenty-three orchid hunters working in a variety of locations worldwide, bringing back vast quantities for the European market. Sander is said to have claimed that he imported over a million orchids from just one species from New Guinea.

The problem was that these bulbs were extremely delicate, and all too frequently less than 1 per cent of bulbs sent back by plant hunters actually survived. Archives at Kew Gardens reveal the dangers experienced by his plant hunters. Correspondence between Sander and orchid hunter Wilhelm Micholitz highlighted Micholitz's fear of the natives since they practised ritual sacrifice. When his ship caught fire and destroyed a cargo of orchids, Sander simply ordered Micholitz to 'Return, recollect'. Allowed an armed guard, Micholtiz successfully found more orchids, although these were apparently growing on human remains.

Plant hunting often had unforeseen circumstances. It was not unknown for plant hunters of choice plants such as orchids to strip an area so as to prevent any of their competitors obtaining the desired plants. Having introduced malaria to South America and finding that indigenous people treated fevers with bark from the cinchona tree, the discovery of a process to extract quinine from the bark in 1820 led to its use in tackling malaria worldwide, especially in Africa and Asia. The high levels of demand led to attempts to obtain cinchona seeds and plants, but unfortunately, the newly independent republics of Peru, Ecuador, Colombia and Bolivia had imposed strict export restrictions in order to safeguard their own profits. Plant hunters from European countries like Britain, the Netherlands and France took part in illegal expeditions to try to obtain seeds and plants. It was only when plant hunter Charles Ledger, with the aid of a young Inca man, managed to find ideal plants which were smuggled out and eventually sold to the Dutch, that the successful cultivation and improvement in the species in the East Indies became possible. These plants eventually formed the basis for the world's quinine supply. Unfortunately, the young Inca man, Manuel Incra Mamani, had a less happy ending. Regarded as a traitor by local people, during a later seed collecting expedition in 1871 he was arrested and severely beaten, resulting ultimately in his death.

There were also occasions when plant hunters worked with the British authorities to create new industries derived from plants. Plant hunter Robert Fortune smuggled camellia sinensis seedlings using Wardian cases from China to create a tea trade in Assam, Ceylon and India. He had already made detailed notes from a previous visit to China exploring their cultivation and harvesting techniques. On another occasion, plant hunters worked with the British India Office to unofficially obtain seeds that would provide access to rubber supplies. Henry Wickham, a British citizen living in the Amazon, collected 70,000 seeds of the Brazilian rubber tree Hevea *brasiliensis*. He then shipped them out secretly using a fast steamer and delivered them to Kew Gardens. Within four days, the seeds had been germinated and resulted in 1,900 viable plants. In August 1876, these young plants were packed in Wardian cases, sent to Ceylon and Singapore and ultimately formed the nucleus of massive rubber plantations in South East Asia.

Although the nineteenth century has become known as the major period of plant exploration and discovery, such activity did not cease with the dawn of the twentieth century. George Forrest made his first plant hunting expedition to China in 1904, and narrowly escaped death from Tibetan monks rebelling against Chinese missionaries. His escape was dramatic, involving tumbling down a 60-metre slope through dense jungle, hiding under rocks, climbing up 900 metres of rock and jungle, wading through waist-deep water and having poisoned arrows shot through his hat. He eventually reached a safe village, barefoot and almost starving, having lost all his specimens. Subsequent expeditions were more successful and he ultimately collected over 31,000 specimens and discovered more than 1,200 new plant species, including fifty varieties of primula, camellias and large magnolia trees.

Correspondence at Kew records the activities of botanist William Robert Price and plant collector Henry John Elwes in Formosa (now Taiwan) during 1912. After four months exploring the forests, Elwes left for Japan but Price stayed on to collect plants for Kew. He wrote to Kew's director, Sir David Prain, saying, 'I go off to the east coast, where savages, malaria and plague are rampant! So I am in for a fine time.' During his visit, he collected 1,133 plant specimens including seeds of Taiwania and the orchid *pleione*. He was definitely impressed by what he saw as he wrote to Prain, saying, 'The mountains too fascinate, & the more one travels in them, the more one wishes to penetrate, the more one penetrates the more hopeless it seems of ever seeing more than a few isolated glimpses of them.'

From the 1920s onwards, Isobel Wylie Hutchison was involved in plant hunting within the Arctic region, especially Iceland, Greenland, Alaska and the Aleutian Islands. She collected seed and live specimens as well as taking countless photographs of hundreds of arctic species of alpine plants, which were then sent to the Royal Botanic Gardens in Kew and Edinburgh.

In 1925, Lieutenant Colonel Edward Bolitho inherited a house and garden at Trengwainton in Cornwall. Having travelled extensively during his career, he wanted to transform the garden and sponsored a plant hunting expedition to Assam and the Mishmi Hills of Burma. This resulted in the discovery of many rare species unknown in Britain, and the sending of numerous seeds and plants for propagation at Trengwainton, such as the Rhododendron *macabeanum*.

Plant hunting continued to be a dangerous activity. At one point in the 1930s, Francis Kingdon-Ward combined his plant hunting with spying for the British India Office. This led him to being arrested by Tibetans for entering an area without permission. Apart from this, he survived numerous accidents while exploring Tibet, Northwestern China and Northeastern India. Writing to his sister, he commented 'If I survive another month without going dotty or white-haired it will be a miracle; if my firm gets any seeds at all this year it will be another.' During his career as a plant hunter he was impaled on a bamboo spike, fell off a cliff (only to be saved by falling on a tree growing out of the cliff), lost in the jungle without food and forced to survive by sucking nectar from flowers, had his tent crushed by a tree during a storm and was close to the epicentre of a massive earthquake in August 1950 during an expedition to Assam.

Chapter 10

Technological Innovation

The Industrial Revolution in the eighteenth century saw massive changes taking place in the production of metal, fabrics and agriculture, as well as the introduction of canals and steam power. These were changes that ultimately helped to transform gardening on both a domestic and commercial scale, resulting in the creation of new products and materials, and even labour-saving devices like the lawnmower.

It was a period when almost everything relating to the garden underwent some kind of transformation. Basic cultivation tools like spades and forks were made lighter with the advent of steel, including the introduction of smaller sizes for use by ladies and children. Experiments were even made on a domestic level to try to find ways of improving basic cultivation. Tucked away among the exhibits at the Gressenhall Farm and Workhouse Museum in Norfolk are handmade double-bladed shears, a pitchfork turned into a fork with the aid of a horizontal metal bar and a sharp prong in the centre, plus a handmade cultivator involving a hand fork connected by wooden struts to a wheel. The introduction of flexible hosepipes in 1845 made the task of watering much easier and efficient, as they were much easier to use than traditional bulky, leather or tarred canvas hoses measuring 3 or 4 inches in diameter.

Great swathes of green lawns have always played a role in garden design among the great houses and estates. The work of designers such as Capability Brown stressed the need for openness and natural landscapes. Keeping grass at a manageable level meant using grazing animals like cows and deer, while areas closer to the house were painstakingly hand mowed using scythes. For smaller houses, especially for the working people, lawns were an undreamt-of luxury.

The year 1830 marked the beginning of a dramatic transformation. Over in Stroud, Gloucestershire, a textile mill worker called Edward Budding had created a machine designed to trim the fuzzy surface (known as a nap) off the surface of cloth used to make Guardsmen's uniforms. Recognising an opportunity, he went into a partnership with John Ferrabee, a local engineer, to create an innovative machine that could cut grass much faster and shorter than men using scythes. Budding placed rotating cutting blades into a wheeled frame pulled by horses, allowing it to cut the grass as it was pulled along. His initial plans met with considerable scepticism, as the British Lawnmower Museum points out: 'At the time, people thought he was a lunatic and a madman to invent such a contraption, so he had to test the machine at night so no one could see him.'

The resultant patent referred to 'a new combination and application of machinery for the purpose of cropping or shearing the vegetable surface of lawns, grass-plats and pleasure grounds.' These early machines were made of cast iron, with cutting blades placed in front of a large rear roller. It was quite expensive for the period, costing 10 guineas to buy, and needed two men and a horse to operate. Despite this, sales were good. Early customers included Regent's Park Zoological Gardens and various Oxford University colleges. Rather than focus on manufacturing machines themselves, Budding and Ferrabee opted to allow other companies to build them under license. This enabled the market for lawnmowers to expand quickly. Ransomes of Ipswich was among those early pioneers of the lawnmower industry, acquiring a licence from Budding and Ferrabee in 1832. A major producer of 'self-sharpening' ploughshares and other agricultural machinery, Ransomes was ideally placed to exploit this new market sector, becoming a key lawnmower producer.

Lawns became an integral part of all kinds and sizes of gardens. The presence of flat green spaces helped transform the way people looked at their gardens, making them a place of relaxation, leisure and social activities. Garden games appeared such as lawn tennis and croquet, which became an essential part of social lives, especially for women.

When Budding's patent lapsed in the 1850s, soon numerous other companies began experimenting with new designs. In Leeds, Thomas Green and Son created a lighter, quicker and quieter machine known as the Silens Messor (silent cutter), which used chains to transmit power from the rear roller to the cutter. Ransomes launched a gear-driven Automaton, possessing an optional grass collection box. Further developments followed and in 1885, Ransomes' latest Automaton won silver medals the Inventions Exhibition, as well as the Liverpool Exhibition the following year. Prices ranged from £2 5s to £10 10s depending on the size of blades, which themselves ranged from 8 to 24 inches. Other variations included steam-driven machines and extremely popular side-wheel versions without a rear roller, which sold worldwide, especially in North America.

By 1870, *The Gardeners' Chronicle* magazine indicated that lawnmowers were now almost universally used. Petrol versions appeared early in the twentieth century and by 1921, the first lightweight Atco mower costing just £75 was introduced. It was selling in the tens of thousands by the mid-1920s, with an even cheaper £15 Qualcast motor mower being launched a few years later.

Throughout the latter part of the nineteenth century, patents were issued for all manner of gardening products. This was a period of innovation, of exploring technology and how things worked. People were constantly looking for new ways to solve problems and were incredibly inventive. A spade with a small arch in the middle of the blade was seen as a way of quickly removing caterpillars from cabbages and cauliflower. The arch fitted around the stem of the vegetable, enabling the gardener to shake it and the caterpillars would fall off onto the spade for disposal. Glass tubes were placed over each cucumber plant to encourage them to grow long and straight. A desire to extend the storage time of grapes led to the invention of a patented bottle. Usually square in the centre, it could be laid in rows on a shelf. A hole in the centre allowed it to be filled and refilled as needed. In the autumn, gardeners would collect bunches of grapes with their adjoin stems, which would then be placed into the neck of the bottle so that they rested in the water, and the grapes would be left to hang down from the mouth of the bottle.

In 1843, the Utility Designs Act made it cheaper to apply for short-term copyright protection lasting just three years. This provision only cost £10, compared to the more conventional £400 for fourteen years' protection. As a result, levels of experimentation were high and often ingenious – not all were successful. Among the gadgets put forward for this short-term protection were instruments for picking up fruit, a gadget to protect peaches, and a racket with its own in-built device for collecting balls. Joseph Paxton devised a structure resembling a crinoline skirt that could be used when cultivating strawberries. The idea was to enable the shoots and fruit to be kept clean and dry by being lifted off the soil. An added advantage was said to be that it would also help protect the fruit from slugs. In 1851, umbrella manufacturers William and John Sangster patented a system for destroying insects on trees. Their idea involved using an umbrella-style cover to be hung like a veil over a tree and wrapped around the trunk to enclose the branches. The nozzle of a fumigator was inserted into a hole enabling the user to pump in pesticides in the form of tobacco fumes.

Technological innovations also contributed to the growth in popularity of landscape garden styles such as rockeries and garden ornaments.

Gentlemen heading off on a Grand Tour of Europe frequently brought back large quantities of classical statues to install in their gardens. Much admired, demand often outstripped supply, especially when war with France broke out, thus making it much harder to travel overseas. Eleanor Coade found the perfect answer to the problem. An entrepreneur, she developed a partnership with Londoner Daniel Pincot making artificial stone. It was a short-lived partnership, however, and by 1771 she had replaced Pincot with sculptor John Bacon. The resultant business of Coade Artificial Stone Company was a resounding success, with Eleanor Coade controlling the company until her death in 1821. She devised a hard-wearing, realistic sculptural ceramic material containing a mix of clay, terracotta, silicates and glass which was fired for four days in very hot kilns. It was also extremely versatile, enabling it to be used for monuments, cast-stone sculptures, garden furniture and even ornamentation for buildings. The Cobham Monument at the Stowe Landscape Gardens, Buckinghamshire is a typical example of the use of Coade artificial stone.

Visits to mountainous regions of Europe as well as the activities of plant hunters worldwide resulted in much greater appreciation of plants suited to rocky locations. Gardeners increasingly sought to include these plants within their own gardens, but it quickly became clear that creating mounds of broken stone, bricks and other rubble did not create suitable growing conditions. Bringing in large pieces of natural rock was expensive. Recognising this, attempts were increasingly made to create artificial rocks and sculptural materials that could cater for this demand.

Pulhamite was a patented rock material devised by James Pulham of Pulham and Sons, Broxbourne in Hertfordshire. Made from a secret formula of sand, Portland cement, and clinker, it was sculpted over a core of rubble and crushed bricks to create very realistic-looking rocks. Once complete, it looked like a pinkish, gritty, extremely hard-wearing sandstone. Extremely versatile, garden designers quickly recognised its potential, utilising it for an array of garden features such as rockeries, caves, grottos, water features and even underground tunnels. Among the many sites known to incorporate Pulhamite features are Waddesdon Manor, Buckinghamshire; Heythrop Park Oxfordshire; Felixstowe Spa and Winter Gardens, Suffolk; the rockery at Burslem Park and Rock Cliff, Bawdsey Manor, Suffolk; as well as the islands on the lake in St James' Park, Westminster. One of the most spectacular examples of Pulhamite was created for Henry Oakley at Dewstow Gardens, Caerwent. A recluse, Oakley commissioned a large rock garden complete with a labyrinth of underground tunnels, caves, grottos and ferneries. After his death, the rock garden fell into disuse and was eventually buried in topsoil from the creation of the M4. A chance sighting of buried rock pieces led to its rediscovery and reopening to the public in 2000. Very little maintenance had to be undertaken on the Pulhamite rock constructions, bearing witness to its strength and longevity.

Another key garden feature that achieved widespread use was the development of greenhouses, or glasshouses as they were often known. These were widely used in the gardens of great estates like Chatsworth. The possession of a greenhouse represented wealth and status. At Chatsworth, Joseph Paxton undertook numerous experiments with glasshouse construction. He introduced the concept of a sloping roof, containing ridges that allowed rainwater to be directed into tanks below. It was a design that also allowed the heat of the sun to permeate into the glasshouse during the early and latter part of the day, while reducing the risk of over-heating during the midday hours. In 1836, Paxton began the construction of the Great Conservatory, or Great Stove, at Chatsworth, incorporating this ridged roof system. Designed by Paxton and architect Decimus Burton, it was the largest glasshouse in the country when completed in 1841 at a cost of £33,099. The Great Stove immediately attracted massive attention due to its sheer size – 277 feet long, 123 feet wide and 61 feet high. Queen Victoria came to see it and was able to drive through it in her carriage. Filled with all kinds of plants, visitors were amazed, describing the interior as being like 'a fairyland'.

Until 1845, glass had been an expensive commodity costing around 2 shillings per square foot. The repeal of the glass tax made an instant difference, leading to a drop in the price to just 2 pence per square foot. This was followed by the repeal of the window tax in 1851. Until then, homeowners had been taxed on the number of windows in their properties, including windows in conservatories. Although the window tax was replaced by a new house tax, the overall taxation payments were lower. The effect of these two changes, combined with the effect of industrialisation allowing the cheap manufacture of identical parts like bolts and struts, and the creation of new techniques to manufacture large sheets of flat plate glass, made glasshouses much more affordable since costs had been reduced by around 90 percent.

The attention of the world was drawn to the potential now being offered through the use of glass and glasshouses when another massive innovative glasshouse designed by Joseph Paxton was used to house the Great Exhibition of 1851. Located in Hyde Park between May to October of that year, it was the first ever international exhibition of its kind and was visited by over 6 million people. Nicknamed the 'Crystal Palace' by *Punch* magazine, the glasshouse comprised a gigantic pre-fabricated building of metal and glass capable of accommodating a vast array of objects from steam locomotives to the Koh-i-Noor diamond. The barrel-vaulted roof was designed to accommodate three elm trees that were already growing on the site, as well as a 27-feet-high pink glass fountain weighing 4 tonnes. In total, over 293,000 panes of glass were produced, creating a glazed surface of 900,000 square feet supported by 3,300 iron columns, 2,224 girders and 205 miles of sash bar. Constructed in a modular fashion, it could be dismantled just as quickly as it was installed. It even included a newly invented form of guttering created by Paxton, together with an ingenious machine enabling eighty men to install 8,000 panes of glass each week during the construction period.

Greenhouses became a very desirable element within gardens of all sizes. On larger estates, it was not unknown for considerable attention to be paid to the aesthetic quality of a building. At Kew, the magnificent Palm House hid facilities required for heating and dealing with the resultant smoke. Instead of adding chimneys to the Palm House, underground tunnels took the smoke away, allowing it eventually to disperse into air from a smokestack disguised as an Italian-style bell tower.

Manufacturers quickly responded, aiming to create durable structures that would provide access to maximum sunlight along with good ventilation and minimal maintenance. Frames tended to be a combination of wood and metal. Initial designs focused mainly on lean-to versions, which could take advantage of existing brick walls, although standalone structures soon became common, as did conservatories forming an integral part of a house. Writing in *The Daisy Chain*, C.M. Yonge noted in 1856 that the conservatory had become 'a real bower for a maiden of romance with its rich green fragrance. In the midst of winter…a picture in a dream…a fairyland, where no care or grief or weariness would come.' A little over ten years later, in 1868, George Whyte-Melville wrote a novel called *The White Rose* in which the heroine's visit to a conservatory involves 'quaintly-twisted pillars, the inlaid pavement, the glittering fountain, and the painted lanterns hanging amongst broad-leafed tropical plants and gorgeous flowers.'

Garden designers like Paxton worked with manufacturers to take advantage of the potential market. Paxton linked up with Samuel Hereman to produce and sell Paxton's designs for a 'portable hothouse…of unparalleled cheapness,' marketing it under the name 'Hothouses for the Millions'. Typical advertisements read:

> These buildings are of unparalleled cheapness, and being composed of simple parts can be enlarged, removed, or adapted to any Horticultural purpose by ordinary labourers. They are calculated for gardens of the highest order, or gentlemen's

gardens generally, for market gardens where they may be used to cover any extent and surface, and also for suburban villa and cottage gardens.

Paxton's idea was based on a folding hut frame he had previously devised for use during the Crimean War. All the buyer had to provide was basic masonry – everything else was provided in the kit such as supporting walls, pillars, sash bars and glass.

Horticultural engineers W.G. Smith & Co., of Bury St Edmunds, were the sole manufacturers of Beard's patent metallic 'All Steel' non-conducting glasshouses and hot water apparatus. These patent glass-walled buildings comprised thick sheets of rough plate glass mounted on iron frames, which could be driven into the ground for short periods or mounted on permanent foundations. Such an invention appealed both to gardeners seeking a long-term building, and people such as market gardeners or allotment holders needing buildings that could be moved whenever necessary. In 1860, J. Lewis Horticultural Works was advertising greenhouses measuring 30x16 feet for just £30, or 60x24 feet for £90.

Demand grew inexorably with new styles, designs and concepts expanding faster than ever before, as can be seen in advertising literature produced by Norwich manufacturer Boulton & Paul Ltd. Potential buyers could choose from a vast array of garden houses, decorative footbridges, portable bungalows, aviaries, pheasantries, greenhouses, vineries, peacheries, conservatories, marquees and palm courts. By the end of the nineteenth century, almost every middle-class house had its own conservatory.

Greenhouses became an essential element in gardens, large and small. By the 1920s, the Straw family living in the small town of Worksop, Nottinghamshire and possessing their own grocery store could afford a standard greenhouse complete with a 7s 6d book by

A.J. MacSelf entitled *The Amateur's Greenhouse,* providing all the advice they needed to operate it.

Garden innovation spread to other items and techniques, marking a change in practice that affected not just gardeners, but the wider horticultural/agricultural sectors as well. Until the mid-nineteenth century, organic manures were the main form of fertiliser applied to the land to maintain fertility. In 1847, the English firm of Antony Gibbs gained a monopoly to export guano – centuries of seabird droppings – from Peru to Europe and North America, where it could be used as fertiliser. Mining the guano was undertaken in atrocious working conditions by Chinese labourers and it quickly became very profitable. In the 1850s, Gibbs was reporting annual profits of between £50 to £65 million. William Gibbs, one of the firm's owners, was described as being the richest non-noble in England and he used his wealth to buy the Tyntesfield estate in Somerset. By 1863, over 435,000 tonnes of guano were being mined each year, and demand soon outstripped supply resulting in the provision of adulterated goods.

The opportunities presented by the creation of artificial compounds and chemical products were attracting the attention of other companies. German scientist Justus Freiherr von Liebig, professor of chemistry at the University of Giessen, has been described as the 'father of the fertiliser industry' due to his research into plant nutrients, particularly nitrogen and trace minerals. Further experimentation by John Bennet Lawes and Joseph Henry Gilbert discovered that calcium phosphate could be treated with sulphuric acid to make an artificial fertiliser known as super phosphate. It was an invention that made both men extremely rich. Soon, people were buying nitrate of soda, nitrate of potash, sulphate of ammonia and various potash manures to dig into the soil. By the 1860s Lawes was reporting an annual income of around £50,000 (approximately £31 million today). It enabled him to establish the Rothamstead

Experimental Station, Hertfordshire, which is believed to be the oldest agricultural research centre in the world.

The first insecticides designed to deal with common garden pests were advertised in *The Gardeners' Chronicle* in 1860. Typical examples included Tobacco Paper for use in fumigating and killing all insects, except red spider mite; Keatings' Persian Insect destroying powder; Gilshurst Compound for dealing with red spider mite; and Bordeaux Mixture (copper fungicide) for use against the dreaded potato blight. Strychnine, mercury and arsenic were regularly used to deal with cockroaches, ants, mice and rats. Gardeners were also recommended that if paraffin emulsion failed to work in dealing with unwanted insects and weeds, they could try using arsenate of lead, cyanide of potassium and Paris Green (a toxic combination of copper acetate and arsenic trioxide), hellebore powder, and quicklime. With such poisonous products readily available in the garden shed, it is no surprise to find that whenever police investigated murders potentially involving poison, the garden shed was the first place they searched!

The arrival of electricity led to yet more experimentation and innovation. There were suggestions that electricity might be used to change the climate. Loudon reported that a Mr J. Williams had suggested it would be a good idea to 'erect large electrical machines, to be driven by wind, over the general face of the country, for the purpose of improving the climate', since this would prevent too much evaporation, and thus improve growing conditions.

Using electricity to extend the growing season or to adjust to requirements was a more practical option, which became the subject of considerable experimentation. Research by botanist Hervé Mangon in 1861 revealed that plants produced chlorophyll when exposed to electric light, and that plants leaned towards a light source. It was a finding that caught the attention of other botanists and growers, as well as the leading industrialist Sir William Siemens, whose background was in the development of electric lighting. At his home at Sherwood Park, Tunbridge Wells, Siemens had built a steam engine which produced enough electricity to provide lighting for the house and garden, in addition to pumping water around the estate and saw wood. Waste steam was used for heating.

Siemens' company provided lighting for the 1879 RHS Summer Show and he was approached by *The Gardeners' Chronicle* to 'contrive a few simple experiments on the action of the light on plants…to see whether tulips or dandelions, once closed would re-open by exposure to the electric light? Whether their period of expansion could be lengthened?' Siemens' attention was caught, and he subsequently spent the next three years carrying out experiments within his own garden with the aid of his head gardener, David Buchanan. Among the experiments undertaken were attempts to grow quick-growing vegetables such as mustard, carrots, beans, cucumbers and melons in varying levels of light, from total darkness to normal light and electric light. Siemens came to the conclusion that electric light could have a similar effect to that of sunlight and reported that a banana palm exposed to electric light at night during its early growth and then later when fruit was maturing, produced fruit weighing 75 lbs, 'unsurpassed in flavour'.

Throughout the Victorian era, there was increasing concern about product quality and safety. Scientist Friedrich Accum caught public attention in 1820 when he published *A Treatise on the Adulterations of Food and Culinary Poisons*. Upon reading the treatise, a *Literary Gazette* reviewer wrote:

> It is so horribly pleasant to reflect how we are in this way beswindled, be-trayed, be-drugged and be-devilled that we are almost angry with Mr Accum for the great service he has done the community by opening our eyes, at the risk of shutting our mouths for ever…our pickles are made green by copper, our vinegar rendered sharp by sulphuric acid; our cream

composed of rice powder or arrow root in bad milk, our comfits mixed with sugar, starch and clay and formed of the dregs of distilled walnuts with a decoction of the outer green husk of the walnuts, and seasoned with all-spice, cayenne, pimento and common salt – or if founded on mushrooms, done with those in a putrefactive state remaining unsold at market; our mustard is composed of mustard, wheaten flour, cayenne, bay salt, radish seed, turmeric and pease flour, and our citric acid, our lemonade and our punch to refresh or exhilarate, usually cheap tartareous acid modified for the occasion.

Opting to buy fresh vegetables and fruit instead did not avoid the problems – shop keepers were known to wash strawberries in spit and make vegetables seem greener by cooking them in brass. Alternatively, produce like plums or cherries might be sold in containers with faulty bottoms, ensuring that customers received less than they should have done.

House owners who could grow their own produce avoided some of these issues. Head gardeners on the big estates owned by the aristocracy and gentry were accustomed to filling locked boxes with fresh produce from kitchen gardens for use by the estate owners when they were in London or elsewhere. Numerous gardening treatises contained detailed recommendations on how to pack and present produce. Vegetables had to be trimmed neatly in order to maximise space and reduce weight. Melons, cabbages and cauliflower were placed at the bottom of the box, with softer fruit and vegetables placed in separate boxes on top. Flowers, too, could be sent around the country the same way.

Risks still remained for both the seed company and the end user. As previously discussed, selling seeds through catalogues or sending large quantities to shops for weighing out and selling as required could result in unscrupulous merchants taking advantage of customers by adulterating the contents. Fraud was common. Dead mustard seed were frequently mixed with more expensive cauliflower or cabbage seed. Loose seed could be sold in short quantities due to faulty scales, or scales altered to make them heavier on one side than the other. Seed killing machines were available allowing unscrupulous merchants to kill off cheap seed, thus preventing germination before mixing it with more expensive seeds. The price differential could be huge, such as broccoli (10s per pound) and old rape seed (3d per pound).

Suttons Seeds led the way in trying to reduce these problems. In 1839, Suttons began working with Essex seed growers to supply crop exclusively. The company set up its first laboratory designed to test all its seeds for quality in 1840, and a decade later, it began selling seeds in sealed, named and labelled packets specific to Suttons. The presence of such clear branding enabled Suttons to stress the reliability and quality of its produce, and to promote its business using aggressive advertising designed to make the Suttons name pre-eminent among seed companies. Other seed companies quickly followed in their wake.

Unfortunately, it was difficult to erase the potential opportunities for adulteration or corruption completely. An anonymous English critic wrote in 1855 that 'there is not a country in the world where commercial roguery is so generally and successfully practiced as in Great Britain.'

The following year, *The Gardeners' Chronicle* noted indignantly that 'it is notorious that some seeds are indistinguishable by the eye, although they can produce totally different plants. No one for instance can tell the varieties of Carrot, Beet, Turnip, Cabbage, Radish & Co from each other by their seeds.' The magazine also reported a letter sent by a wholesale supplier to seedsmen, saying, 'I have sold this day some Indian Rape seed for mixing with Turnip seed… If you want some seeds for mixing, I shall be happy to serve you.'

Suttons campaigned vigorously about the problems of adulteration, holding meetings and discussions. In 1868, the Royal Horticultural Society studied Martin Hope's collection of killed seed, and evidence of the various threats made against him. Committee members anonymously purchased packets of seed from eighteen seed companies in London. This included one packet from each dealer of the five commonest vegetables: cauliflower, broccoli, carrots, white and yellow turnips. Each packet held 100 seeds. All the packets were planted, variety by variety, and recorded by dealer as to how many seeds germinated. The results were shocking. Looking at the cauliflower seeds, the highest germination rate was just eighty-six in one packet, compared to twenty-four for the lowest germination rate. For broccoli, the highest was eighty-six, the lowest at thirty-five. Germination of yellow turnips dropped rapidly by packet from ninety-five to twenty-eight. Carrots were a little more successful, with one packet producing ninety-eight plants and the lowest fifty-seven, while white turnip germination rates were generally regarded as 'reasonable'.

The resultant report indicated that the majority of seeds sold to the public were of poor quality. Dealers often kept seed too long, selling it even when it had lost all its vitality. Seed was doctored to look good by dyeing, sulphur-smoking or oil dressing it. The report called for government action to protect 'the very large numbers of ignorant and uneducated people who have to purchase seeds'. Their findings forced the government to act. In 1869 the Adulteration Act made it illegal for anyone to sell adulterated goods, but it would take a long time for the issue to become an unusual occurrence rather than the norm. The food crisis following the end of the First World War finally persuaded the government to enforce penalties for infringing the 1869 Seed Adulteration Act. A new Seeds Act laid down minimum germination standards, forcing all seed companies to invest in seed testing equipment and use qualified people to undertake the tests.

The search for technological innovation continued unabated throughout the sector. In 1915, Suttons carried out a series of experiments into fertilisers using radium ore. It was concluded that radium ore benefited rape, clover, lettuce and radish but had no effect on peas, tomatoes, nasturtiums or other flowers. Users were recommended to use it at a rate of one pound per square foot. Despite these findings, radium ore was never eventually used as a commercial fertiliser for any crop.

Chapter 11

Workhouse Gardening

The workhouse was the place of last resort for anyone in distress. It was a place where people who had no income of any kind, the poorest of the poor, could seek refuge. During the nineteenth century it became a place to be feared and dreaded; a view that remained until the final workhouses were eventually closed in the twentieth century.

Operated by a parish or group of parishes, a workhouse would provide a basic level of food and accommodation in return for some form of work. People could be admitted to a workhouse and stay briefly, even overnight, or become long term inmates. It might be individuals, children or whole families; many were infirm or sick. All the costs were borne by the parish, particularly the more well-off members such as the gentry and aristocracy, in the form of poor relief.

Operating workhouses was expensive and frequently incurred considerable reluctance from landowners who were being asked for yet more money to fund the facilities. As a result, there was a move towards being as self-financing as possible, with inmates being required to undertake work such as laundry, construction, rope picking or agriculture. Gardening became one of the ways in which costs could be reduced, as Peter Collinge points out in his study on workhouse gardens and gardening, published in the *Journal for Eighteenth Century Studies*: 'Workhouse gardening was not simply about food, costs and pauper employment but also about managing the expectations and resentments of ratepayers, vestries, theorists and politicians.'

Some workhouses did succeed in reducing costs through the use of productive gardens. In Keswick, a workhouse garden was 'cultivated by the poor, who in return are supplied with vegetables from it…a large quantity of vegetables are every year sold out of [it], and the money applied towards the maintenance of the house.' It is known that some workhouses added decorative plants for use as screening the workhouse from the houses of wealthy merchants. For example, in 1793 the Liverpool workhouse arranged for a nurseryman to supply and plant 645 trees and 150 shrubs, including lime, beech, willow, sugar maple, black Italian poplar, horse chestnut and dwarf apple trees.

Information relating to Poor Law provision on a parish basis submitted to parliament in 1804 revealed that there was a total of 15,000 parishes across England and Wales. There were 3,765 workhouses, but only fifteen referred to the presence of gardens or farms on site.

In the early nineteenth century, landscape designer Humphry Repton was asked for ideas on workhouse design. His son, Reverend Edward Repton, had been considering how to improve conditions for parishioners living in his local workhouse. The building had been constructed on waterlogged land and so he was considering that it ought to be moved to a drier location.

Repton's design was published in his book *Fragments on the Theory and Practice of Landscape Gardening* in 1816. It shows a thoughtful design, in which considerable attention is placed on the role of a garden within workhouse life, as well as acting as an incentive to good behaviour. His sketched-out design placed the workhouse building in the centre, with wings on either side providing accommodation for the governor and matron, respectively. A south-facing terrace provided seating for the 'aged and infirm' as well as an outdoor classroom for the children. Grape vines were to be grown on trellises along the side of the building.

Descending from the terrace was a vegetable garden divided by a wide path and a pond providing a water source for the workhouse and grounds. Children are shown at work in the garden hoeing vegetables while other children are being trained as potential soldiers. The children would be able to see the benefits of their work and feel part of the wider community. A simple fence divided the front of the garden from the outside world, and villagers could buy food and flowers from tables at the gate.

Repton commented: 'This might be considered as the reward of good conduct: the Children, supplied with spades and hoes, and tools, proportioned to their strength, should be taught and exercised in the cultivation of the Garden, and perhaps drilled to become the future defenders of their Country.'

The back of the workhouse offered a different atmosphere, emphasising the use of courtyards. Repton wrote: 'Let the back-yard be considered as a sort of punishment for misbehaviour and refractory conduct, where, shut up between four buildings, nothing can be seen to enliven the prospect.'

Although Repton's design was initially welcomed, cost issues led to its rejection. Complaints relating to the cost of providing poor relief were all too common, accompanied by suggestions that inmates lived in idleness. John Loudon wrote in 1829 recommending, 'Let a source of agreeable and productive labour, such as large gardens, be found for the inmates of our workhouses, and let efficient gardeners be set over them, and we have no doubt that the poor in many parishes would nearly, or wholly support themselves.'

Loudon added that the produce 'would, in great part, be consumed by the poor themselves, and the remainder might be sold', recommending that there ought to be at least 1 acre cultivated for every four people in a workhouse. Loudon also believed that involvement in a garden would be good even for infirm inmates, suggesting that 'if, instead of being placed upon benches, with nothing to gaze at but a brick wall, these persons were led into a garden, where they could see numbers of their fellow inmates at work, breathe the fresh air, see and smell the flowers, and hear the birds…their miserable lot would have some little alleviation.'

Detailed information on resources and inmates was very much hit and miss. Complex variations existed in terms of financial control, external scrutiny, employment, diet and living conditions within workhouses. By the time the Royal Commission into the Poor Laws was set up in 1832, only 1,200 rural parishes and 380 urban parishes had provided recent information to parliament, with 109 parishes indicating that their workhouses possessed access to some form of land, of which 105 had gardens.

Even the eventual report issued by the commissioners in 1834 contained inaccuracies. Cumberland, for example, only lists workhouses in Keswick and Penrith as possessing land, but Brampton, Dalston and Wigton workhouses were also active in cultivating land. Staffordshire was not mentioned in the report, but as Peter Collinge indicates in his study, 'at least seven out of the thirteen workhouses in the county possessed gardens: Darlaston, Gnosall, Haughton, St Mary's Lichfield, Tettenhall, Uttoxeter, Wednesbury.'

Given the size of the various counties listed in the report, it does raise questions over numbers. For example, Yorkshire had twenty workhouses with adjacent land, while others like Warwickshire, Westmoreland, Dorset and Essex only had one such workhouse with land. Some also had farmland, potato fields and pasture.

As Peter Collinge points out:

The size of gardens and cultivated land per workhouse did not reflect the size or number of inmates. Much depended on the attitudes of local workhouse governors and land availability eg Gedling Nottinghamshire possessed a one and a half acre garden and 53 inmates; while Bedford had 104 inmates and was supplied by 22 acres including pastures. Great Ouseburn, Yorkshire possessed a garden of three quarters of an acre which was said to be 'kept in very good order by the paupers'.

Some workhouse gardens were undoubtedly successful. At Uttoxeter, produce sales between 1826-27 provided an income of £4 1s 3d, while in 1831, it amounted to £11 10s 9d. In October 1831, Basford raised £22 3s 9d from produce sales. However, Basford did enjoy two major advantages: the governor was a market gardener by trade, and the workhouse inmates were able to cultivate 24 acres of land. They also had a ready market in the nearby town of Nottingham.

A major problem with the report's findings was the fact that it did not take into account the number and type of inmates, or the additional costs such as buying seeds and tools. The number of able-bodied inmates often varied according to season or need. Meanwhile, many of the long-term inmates were infirm and unable to undertake garden tasks. At Penrith, for example, out of sixty-two inmates only one was physically able to work in the garden, while gardening was not regarded as a suitable task for women. Lack of knowledge was also an issue. At St Mary's in Reading, 'a piece of ground was taken for a garden to supply the poorhouse, but was given up the wages paid for the work done making it too expensive. This arises from the master of the poorhouse not being able to give that vigilant attention such an undertaking requires, his other avocations taking him away.' Over in the Isle of Wight, the workhouse had 667 inmates in 1832 requiring that 'such men, resident in the house as can work are employed in the garden', but that 'at present there are scarcely any men of this description'.

The Poor Law Act of 1834 introduced major changes into the way in which workhouses operated. It centralised the workhouse system with the aim of reducing costs and discouraging laziness, but in doing so created bleak workhouses that became infamous for forced labour and starvation rations, resulting in the vivid portrayal of living conditions given in Charles Dickens' novel, *Oliver Twist* (1838). Families were separated, with men, women and children living in separate areas and little social contact allowed between them. At Gressenhall workhouse in Norfolk, for example, high walls separated the bleak exercise yards between the men and women's sections.

Until this point, the design of workhouses had varied from place to place but generally came to comprise of a large, somewhat forbidding, building containing basic accommodation, plus facilities for overseers such as matrons and the workhouse beadle, who was responsible for its day-to-day operation.

Given the high standing in which Humphry Repton's name was held, it is not hard to imagine that his design ultimately had some bearing on workhouses built following the passing of the Poor Law Amendment Act of 1834. These workhouses were utilitarian in design, but many did incorporate gardens and growing areas. At Abingdon, the new workhouse included 10 acres of land at the rear of the building that was to be used for housing twelve pigs and growing a range of vegetables, particularly swedes, mangelwurzels, parsnips, carrots, potatoes, peas and barley.

All inmates were expected to work while at the workhouse. Vagrants and others admitted overnight had to undertake work before they were allowed to leave the premises. Able-bodied men and older boys were generally put to work in gardens and farms if available or might be set to work on tasks like picking oakum (teasing out fibres from old hemp ropes to be combined with tar for use in sealing liners of wooden ships), chopping wood, breaking stones for sale to road makers, or grinding corn using heavy millstones. Women were generally required to undertake domestic duties such as cleaning, cooking and laundry work.

In 1849, Abingdon's workhouse master, Richard Ellis, reported their experiences of cultivation to the Poor Law Commissioners investigating the 'profitable employment of paupers on workhouse land', indicating how they had made it a profitable enterprise. He stated:

> You understood me rightly that the produce of the ten acres of land adjacent to the Abingdon workhouse had enabled me, besides supplying vegetables for the use of the inmates, to credit the guardians with £100.
>
> The potato crop, although a failure in most places, has not been so to any great extent here. The soil being of a light description, and the system of planting in the autumn having been followed...the preservation of this valuable crop. The quality of the potatoes was such that they were eagerly sought after and realised an average price of 11s 3d per sack.
>
> By keeping, upon average, twelve large pigs, which we purchase in a very poor condition...We can use all our spare offal from the garden, and this description of pigs will eat it... We obtain a large quantity of manure from them, and, with a small purchase of stable dung, are enabled to manure the ground sufficiently. The liquid obtained from the washhouses, privies &c, is all conveyed into close cesspools in the garden, from which it is pumped and conveyed between the rows of the crops, particularly mangelwurzel, by which means this plant attains a weight of from 20 to 25lbs each and sells at 20s per ton. In winter, the liquid manure is pumped up and distributed over such parts of the count as are dug in, and the ground is trenched and prepared for spring crops... The seeds we grow ourselves, so that no extra charge is made upon that account in this return.
>
> In employing paupers in the garden, or on out-door work, one thing must be particularly attended to, that is, the character of

the persons so employed. Unless upon particular occasions, I do not employ young able-bodied men, or even married men with families, if I can learn that they became inmates by their own misconduct. I make it a matter of favour to employ them there, and for those who do not work well while there, some sort of employment within the house is found. The old men and boys occasionally work in the garden, which makes them cheerful and keeps them in good health. The ground is worked by the spade and a light harrow, which is drawn by the boys. You will perceive by the return herewith sent, that the common charges are credited with £52 for vegetables consumed by the officers and paupers, which number, including children, on average about 200 weekly.

Where gardens and cultivated areas were available, it is interesting to see the range of produce that was grown and the clear links within the local economy that were established. The operation of Southwell workhouse in Nottinghamshire is a good example of this. From the beginning, gardening was seen an integral part of the daily life of the workhouse. Formed in 1824 by a group of forty-nine parishes, its charter stated that 'land fit for gardens, orchards and the keeping of a cow or cows shall be purchased in the parish of Upton'. The first inmates entered the workhouse in December 1824, and records indicate that spades and shovels for garden cultivation were immediately purchased. By the end of February 1825, seeds were being ordered from John Sandaver, a local seedsman trading in Southwell. He supplied a variety of seeds including leeks, peas, beans, parsley, potatoes, onions, carrots, turnips, radishes and lettuce. In May of that year, a further order for pea and bean seeds was made.

Southwell's use of local seedsmen was normal practice. Seeds, young plants and associated items were generally supplied by local businesses. R&A Taylor of King's Lynn supplied vegetable seeds to its local workhouse. George Foster, John Gee, William Rogers, John Smith and Robert Brassington supplied seeds to the Uttoxeter workhouse – all were local seedsmen. The workhouse received supplies of a very varied range of vegetables including celery, savoy cabbages, radishes, lettuces, Windsor beans, turnips, peas, Prussian and marrowfat peas, onions, leeks, cauliflowers, broccoli, swede and spinach. Over at Lichfield St Mary's, the workhouse ordered mustard, cress, radish, onion, lettuce, cabbage, Savoy cabbage, cauliflower, celery, turnip, carrots, Prussian peas and imperial peas, plus Cockney potatoes. Some more enlightened workhouses even took account of recent developments. Lichfield workhouse, for example, deliberately purchased Altrincham carrot seed because it had been tested in the Horticultural Society's garden and proved to be a good variety.

The emphasis was always on practical, seasonal vegetables as opposed to exotic or luxury items grown in kitchen gardens elsewhere, although exceptions could be made for produce destined for those responsible for overseeing the workhouse. Records at Southwell indicate that in 1825, twelve standard plum trees, fifty gooseberry bushes, thirty current bushes and an unspecified number of raspberry plants were acquired. It is believed that this was mainly for the use of the workhouse master and his direct household.

Attention was also paid to maintenance and cultivation methods. Tools and garden items were kept in a dedicated building at Southwell. At Uttoxeter workhouse, accounts refer to the purchase quantities of Archangel or Bass mats (similar to modern horticultural fleece), while Southwell account books indicate payments to local labourers for repairing ladders, wheelbarrows and a watering pan. Archaeological excavations at Southwell have revealed that burnt charcoal was being added to the soil as fertiliser for growing turnips and carrots, while elsewhere pig manure, ash from the fire and night soil from the privies were utilised.

Expectations that inmates should contribute to the running of the workhouse via their work clearly continued over succeeding decades. Records at Southwell indicate that in May 1851, it was ordered that boys should no longer be put to work in the garden alongside old men, while vagrants were routinely put to work in the gardens. At a meeting of the house committee in December 1910, a letter was read out from Mr A.J. Metcalfe, clerk to the justices. It referred to the case of a vagrant being brought before the justices on a charge of absconding. The letter rebuked the workhouse as the magistrates felt that given the 'state of the man's boots, the task set him, viz, digging in the garden, was most unreasonable, and expressing the hope that the Master might be instructed to exercise more discretion in his selection of tasks for casuals.'

By the 1930s, Southwell records indicate that there was a shortage of inmates capable of cultivating the garden, while the former exercise yard for elderly and infirm inhabitants was now a garden for the workhouse master.

The initial utilitarian nature of workhouses remained a dominant feature throughout their existence. Although both Repton and Loudon had suggested that some measure of decorative planting ought to be considered as a health benefit, particularly for the infirm, this was rare. In 1895, representatives of the *British Medical Journal* visited a range of workhouses throughout Britain and discovered that the growing of flowers was an exception rather than the rule. Among the few examples they found were: Truro, where men's airing courts included grass and flowers; a north Dublin workhouse, where the master had created a garden with benches, flowers, trees and shrubs for elderly residents; while in a south Dublin workhouse, elderly women lived in huts surrounding three sides of a garden possessing grass, flowers and seats. Most workhouses were far less attractive in appearance. At Hatfield, the *British Medical Journal* representatives reported:

> The airing courts are dreary prison-like yards, asphalted, the garden with its wealth of flowers, being behind the house out of sight. We are at a loss for the reason why the sick poor are so carefully excluded from the use of the gardens; it would surely relieve the monotony of their lives to be allowed to walk among the flower beds.

As the years progressed, many workhouses did become more friendly and domestic in style, with outdoor areas incorporating glasshouses, cold-frames and flowers. At the Gressenhall workhouse, elderly married residents were allowed to live together in small houses with adjacent gardens rather than being separated into male and female wards. Changing attitudes meant that alternative options were being provided for those in need, such as the arrival of pensions for elderly people in 1909. In 1929, new legislation enabled local authorities to transform workhouses into hospitals, and inmates were steadily found alternative accommodation.

Chapter 12

The Allotment Movement

Throughout the nineteenth century there was increasing recognition of the need to encourage the agricultural workers, villagers and the industrial working classes to grow their own produce to help feed their families. Changes in agricultural practices such as the introduction of threshing machines, along with poor harvests and the enclosure of land resulted in less demand for labour. Food became more expensive, especially after the imposition of the controversial Corn Laws in 1815, which prevented the import of cheap wheat and other grains from overseas. This ensured a steady market for wheat produced on British estates, thus protecting the income of the landowners. Many agricultural workers were forced to enter workhouses as they could not feed their families, which in turn resulted in increased demands for money to pay for the operation of workhouses. Consequently, riots and general discontent were common, particularly since they had no other form of improving their situation. Demand for political reform increased, especially regarding universal male suffrage, which would allow ordinary men to be able to vote for their MPs.

Landowners and philanthropists sought ways to deal with these issues, and encouraging gardening was increasingly seen as an answer since it would be a way of enabling labourers to grow their own food. Gardening itself was seen as typifying Victorian virtues such as hard work, self-help and discipline. As Jenny Uglow points out in her *Little History of British Gardening* (2004), there was an increasing social belief emerging that gardening was a cure all. 'It brought one closer to God – who, after all, created Eden. It was cure for depression, political agitation, drunkenness and ambition, keeping men off the streets and out of the pubs. All in all, gardening was a healthy, hard-working, wholesome democratic art.'

In order to achieve such results, houses needed outdoor space and encouragement to plant without fearing eviction and loss of their hard-earned produce. In Loudon's *Manual of Cottage Gardening, Husbandry and Architecture* (1830), he recommended that in terms of space, one eighth of an acre was ideal, indicating that it could be easily divided to provide enough space to grow leeks, onions, carrots, parsnips, beans, cabbages, and potatoes. Soft fruit could be placed against the house and the hedges thickened with fruit trees.

Not all houses designed for the working class were built with access to outdoor garden space, however, and so increasing stress was placed on the need for small allotments. Some areas already had a tradition of setting space aside for use as allotments, also known as 'garden ground'. The Earl of Dorchester had introduced the idea of renting a quarter of an acre of waste ground to poor people who needed to feed their families, enabling them to cultivate potatoes. In 1826, William Cobbett noted in his *Rural Rides* that while riding from Devizes to Highworth, 'I saw great numbers of labourers either digging potatoes for their Sunday dinner, or coming home with them, or going out to dig them. The landowners or occupiers let small pieces of land to the labourers and these they then cultivated with the spade for their own use.'

Organisations emerged advocating the creation of allotments. Typical of these movements was the Labourer's Friend Society, which set out to help improve the living conditions of the poorest in society. Benjamin Wills, a London surgeon who was also a member of the gentry, played a prominent part in the society. Although he supported enclosure, he believed that surplus land should be rented for small farms or allotments, which would encourage self-respect and independence among labourers. The Young England movement took a slightly different view, regarding allotments as a revival of old customs.

Throughout the nineteenth century, the number of allotments grew steadily, especially after periods of dissent or disruption such as the Captain Swing riots in 1830, when hayricks and farm buildings were burned following the introduction of threshing machines impacting on the number of labourers required on farms. The lack of work left people hungry and for many, the ability to grow produce on allotments and in back gardens proved to be lifesaving. The range of produce grown on these allotments was extensive, with the most popular items being wheat, potatoes, peas, beans and cabbage. A small number even grew lettuce, leeks, artichokes and mangelwurzel (a type of beet). Yields could be high, often higher than on the farms where many of the allotment holders worked. In 1832, an assistant poor law commissioner named Mr D.C. Moylan noted that 'the amount of produce from these small allotments, particularly in the neighbourhood of towns where manure may be had cheap, is quite astonishing – I understand not less than ten or twelve sacks (thirty or thirty-six bushels) of potatoes to the eighth of an acre.' A few years later, land agent Robert Hughes told the House of Lords Select Committee on agriculture that labourers were growing twenty sacks of potatoes on a quarter of an acre of land.

Observers commented on the way allotments could improve behaviour. Speaking to the 1834 Select Committee on the Labouring Poor, James Brooks stated:

> An individual that I know myself, the first time that I spoke to him was when he was in a state of intoxication, and that man has become a sober man from his allotment. His wife, before I came up, thanked me very much. She was so glad because her husband had become acquainted with me; she said he had left off drinking and abusing her and her children, she said that if he only kept sober, they should do tolerably well.

Small organisations were established across the country to develop allotments in various localities. Typical of these was the Nottingham Independent Garden Society, set up by James Orange in 1842. It aimed to provide 400 allotments that could be rented for just £1 per annum and proved extremely successful, ultimately providing over 5,000 plots being let mainly to hosiery workers.

By the time the House of Commons was exploring the issue of allotments in 1843, there was a focus on the way in which working on allotments reduced rural crime. During a discussion in parliament on enclosures, Mr Cowper, the MP for Hertford, commented that allotments:

> Would prevent the labourer from having recourse to the ordinary excitements of dissipation, and that a change of character must be effected by teaching him to rely on his own exertions for the improvement of his condition. In West Kent, 3,000 allotments had been made, and in 1841 and 1842 none of those holding them committed offences against the laws, though many of them previously lived by poaching, and in other disreputable ways. The eagerness with which the labouring people caught at a favourite day-dream of the Chartists, that every man should have a bit of land of his own, showed how great a desire existed to become proprietors of land.

Labourers became more possessive of their property and less inclined to support people who misbehaved, as James Brooks indicated:

> The greater part of the people had sympathy with an individual who broke the laws; they felt sorry for him and felt as if he were wronged; but now the case of those individuals is very different, if anything happens to their crops, or an individual robs them, they feel that there is some injury done to them, and

that if it were not for the laws, the property they have laboured hard for would not be secure.

As a result, theft from gardens and orchards declined. The report by the West Kent Labourer's Friend Society noted in 1844 that crime in the area had decreased significantly and that since gaining allotments, tenants who had previously appeared before magistrates were no longer doing so.

Allotment holders were proud of their work and the amount of produce they could raise, often being heard to speak of 'my potatoes' and 'my beans'. It became a matter of pride to grow the best possible produce. Often other family members such as children provided help. In *Lark Rise to Candleford* (1945), Flora Thompson recalled:

> Allotment plots were divided into two, and one half planted with potatoes and one half with wheat or barley. The garden was reserved for green vegetables, currant and gooseberry bushes, and a few old-fashioned flowers. Proud as they were of their celery, peas and beans, cauliflowers and marrows, and fine were the specimens they could show of these, their potatoes were their special care, for they had to grow enough of these to last the year round. They grew all the old-fashioned varieties – Ashleaf kidney, Early Rose, American Rose, Magnum Bonum and the huge misshaped White Elephant. Everybody knew the Elephant was an unsatisfactory potato, that it was awkward to handle when paring and that it boiled down to a white pulp in cooking, but it produced tubers of such astonishing size that none of the men could resist the temptation to plant it. Every year specimens were taken to the inn to be weighed on the only pair of scales in the hamlet, then handed round for guesses to be made of the weight. As the men said, when a patch of Elephants was dug up and spread out, 'You'd got summat to put in your eye and look at'.

Obtaining land for allotments was not easy, and did encounter considerable opposition. It was not unknown for local farmers and landowners to express the belief that if labourers had access to their own growing space, they would work so hard on it that they would be unable to do a day's work for the farmer the next day. William Davis, member of the Bath Society for the Investigation and Relief of Occasional Distress, Encouragement of Industry and Suppression of Vagrants, commented that space should be 'large enough to produce plenty of roots for the cottager's family, but not so extensive as to tempt him to withdraw his attention from daily labour for his master, nor to make his produce much of an article for sale.' As a consequence of these fears, many allotments were only let on the basis that tenants would not let maintenance of their garden space interfere with their employment at any point.

Allotment provision was also attacked on the basis that it encouraged criminality. Farmers and landowners suggested that the reason many allotment holders were experiencing such huge crops was because they were stealing produce from farms rather than growing it themselves.

The *Northampton Herald* reported landowner Sir Henry Dryden as saying that 'the allotment system tended to make labourers a set of thieves...produce did not come off poor lots – it came off the farmer.' Meanwhile, at the Brockley Petty Sessions in Northamptonshire 'a woman was convicted of robbing her neighbour of sprouts'. Over at Stradbroke, a Mr Gessin reported in the Suffolk Report on the Employment of Women and Children in Agriculture that the allotments 'are all planted with fruit trees, which is a great objection, it makes boys trespass after the fruit, and injure the corn to get at it, they secrete themselves in it.'

Countering such arguments, Lord Carnarvon noted that it should not be forgotten 'how much more labour a man can perform who is well fed and clothed, and possessed of comfort and competence.' Many examples of the beneficial nature of allotment provision were provided to the 1843 committee. John Brooks informed the committee that in Hinckley, 'one of the lecturers of the Chartists, from Leicester, came there a week or two ago, and made a great noise, but none of the allotment tenants visited him, instead of going to the meeting, they went with their spades on their shoulders to their gardens.' As Jeremy Burchardt concludes in his book *The Allotment Movement in England 1793-1873* (2002), 'taken together, the evidence that allotments decreased rural crime is much more extensive and on the whole persuasive than the evidence that they increased crime.'

In 1845, the Inclosure Act included provision for the landless poor to have access to 'field gardens' occupying no more than a quarter of an acre, identifying that space proved harder to achieve, especially where landowners were unsympathetic to the concept.

The clergy ultimately played a key role in allotment provision. Churches frequently had land that could be utilised for this purpose. Churchgoers would be more likely to be granted such allotments, thus encouraging people to go to church regularly. The Nottinghamshire village of Lambley experienced a transformation in attitudes after the local rector set aside land for use as allotments. Parishioners stopped talking about politics, Chartism and parliamentary reform in favour of discussing their allotments and growing food for their families. Church attendance also increased. In 1847, the Reverend Philip Gordon of Norfolk wrote that 'I am not aware of a single instance of dishonesty…having occurred, that can be considered as arising out of the allotment system.' Using allotment provision to decrease dissent was a common feature in many areas, a fact recognised by the Chartists, who argued that allotments were just 'a sticking plaster' and could not deal with the underlying problems in society.

Many local clergy were keen practical gardeners themselves and were keen to promote its values. In *Pride and Prejudice*, Mr Collins spends much of his time at work in his garden. Following the arrival of Elizabeth Bennet, Sir William Lucas and Maria Lucas:

> Mr Collins invited them to take a stroll in the garden, which was large and well laid out, and to the cultivation of which he attended himself. To work in this garden was one of his most respectable pleasures; and Elizabeth admired the command of countenance with which Charlotte talked of the healthfulness of the exercise, and owned she encouraged it as much as possible. Here, leading the way through every walk and cross walk, and scarcely allowing them an interval to utter the praises he asked for, every view was pointed out with a minuteness which left beauty entirely behind. He could number the fields in every direction, and could tell how many trees there were in the most distant clump.

In Hitcham, the arrival of Reverend Henslow as rector marked a transformation in the fortunes of the village. Henslow was a professor of botany at Cambridge and an active proponent of gardening as an activity. Aiming to reduce unemployment and criminality among his parishioners, he encouraged the development of self-help clubs, the provision of allotments and the teaching of botany in the village school. His friend John Lindley provided quantities of guano for use on the plots, and Henslow acquired seeds from a contact in Ipswich, although local farmers initially accused the allotment holders of stealing seeds.

Men such as Reverend William Wilks, who was actively involved in the Royal Horticultural Society and introduced the Shirley Poppy, a variant of the field poppy common in arable fields, took an active role in promoting gardening among their congregations. Not surprisingly, such clergy encouraged the development of garden schemes, giving cuttings and distributing seeds to get people started.

The number of allotments grew steadily during the nineteenth century. A new form of allotment provision appeared following the growth of railway companies, mining companies and the various utilities such as water and gas, which acquired land for their business use. When construction was complete, leftover surplus land was kept on the basis that it may be needed at some point in the future and in the meantime, was rented out as allotments for their employees. These employees tended to spend time on their allotments before and after work, allowing them to provide food for their families if working hours were cut back at any point.

Allotment holders tended to take advantage of any opportunities that arose. In York, for example, the railway passed by the entrance to the allotments in Bootham Stray. It became an accepted practice for the allotment holders to replenish their stock of coke for heating boilers used in their greenhouses from the railway bunker beside the crossing keeper's cabin. Ingenuity also played a part in keeping costs to a minimum. In 1939, a collier described his allotment in *Practical Gardening & Food Production in Pictures*: 'I purchased some old window frames from a dismantled colliery, a few bags of cement, some sand and glass and with an old bedframe and wire netting, I built a small glasshouse in which I grow grapes (forty bunches this year), tomatoes (with a surplus which I sell to the neighbours) and plants for planting out in spring.' He also grew large quantities of blackcurrants, loganberries, gooseberries, rhubarb and apples.

Many landowners kept a paternal eye over the horticultural activities of their tenants. At Holkham, the Earl of Leicester ordered the creation of seventy-three allotments close to the village sited at the bottom of his drive. Regular competitions were held for the allotment holders, as well as gardens attached to the cottages with titles like the 'most productive', 'best garden', 'nicest garden', 'most attractive garden' etc. The earl undertook all the judging himself.

Working on the allotments increasingly became a social activity, replacing beer houses as a place to meet friends. According to Jeremy Burchardt, allotments played a significant role in the transformation of the countryside and lifestyles of the allotment holders. He states that allotments provided labourers with land which had:

> The effect of enhancing their self-respect... There is also evidence of the symbiosis between allotment and the development of horticultural shows, fostering individual competitiveness... Mutuality was an important feature of allotment sites, which by their form and from the exigencies of their cultivation promoted the exchange of seed, crops and on occasion labour... Allotments reduced criminality and, at least in the view of the most contemporary authorities, encouraged industrious habits.

He also states that the combined effort of these changes was to make villages less 'rough' and more 'respectable' and that they controlled and channelled social conflict into more regularised, peaceable and legal channels. According to Burchardt, the total number of allotments doubled between 1845 and 1873, although exact numbers are difficult to ascertain since there are no specific numbers available on a national basis. Looking just at one area, the East Midlands, it is known that it had had almost 35,000 plots available. Burchardt indicates that by 1873, there appears to have been over 242,542 plots in existence nationwide, covering a total acreage of 58,966.

The passing of the Third Reform Act in 1884 enabled working-class men to have the vote for the first time. Politicians began to pay more attention to the interests of these new voters, and consequently to the issues of land reform giving ordinary people more access to the land supply.

In 1908, the Smallholdings and Allotment Act became law, requiring councils to provide growing areas for the 'labouring population'. Within four years, contemporary estimates were indicating that 81 percent of households had access to allotments and by 1914, there were said to be between 450,000 to 600,000 allotments nationwide.

Chapter 13

Garden Tourism

Visitors have long enjoyed exploring gardens within Britain, especially in search of picturesque landscapes and unusual plants. During the late eighteenth and early nineteenth centuries, garden visiting was very much a pastime enjoyed by the upper class. Walking or driving through parkland and gardens formed an important way for aristocrats to spend their leisure time when staying in the countryside. 'Polite visiting' focused on architecture and scenic vistas, resulting in landowners focusing on creating suitable landscapes within their grounds. Many country houses attracted tourists travelling on circuits of the country, or on short visits from towns.

Daniel Defoe's classic 1742 tour included accounts of numerous gardens that he had visited along the way. In July 1748, Jemima Yorke, 2nd Marchioness Grey wrote an account of her visit to the Stowe Landscape gardens in Buckinghamshire, saying, 'There is scarcely anything concealed in it, or Object you come upon without having seen it a Mile off and in fifty different Views in your journey of Five Miles around the Enclosure.' She continued, 'That side of the Garden first Finished is so Crowded with Buildings that as you see them at a distance seem almost on Top of One Another that each loses its Effect.' Visiting grand landscaped parks such as Stowe and Stourhead became de rigueur among ladies and gentlemen of fashion – and those who aspired to it.

Landowners regarded their gardens as being highly important and wanted to make them better known. This was the era of landscape gardening, with gardens blending into their setting. Circuit walks were created so that people would encounter all the desired elements and miss none. These walks were usually gravelled paths that led round the garden, through all picturesque areas utilising curving paths that approached focal points obliquely. It usually included a mixture of shrubberies, statues, buildings, a pool or lake, woods and fields. Such walks might last several miles or were so short they could be completed in less than half an hour. Typical examples included Kedleston, Derbyshire where the main walk from the house led along a winding path, passing through areas darkened by thick planting of trees and shrubs before suddenly widening out to provide open viewpoints across the park and into the hills beyond. At Netheravon, Wiltshire, Thomas Wright designed a circuit walk for the Duchess of Beaufort, maximising the potential offered by just a small area of 140x140 feet. It included an array of features including a central lawn, alcove seat, pool, and a resting places with views around a circular path edged on either side by the lawn and woods.

Writing in *Observations on Modern Gardening* in 1770, Thomas Whately relates his travels around England and all he has learned about gardening. He states: 'Gardening, in the perfection to which it has lately brought in England, is entitled to a place of considerable rank among the liberal arts.' He added that 'Many gardens are nothing more than such a walk around a field; that field is often raised to the character of a lawn; and sometimes the enclosure is, in fact a paddock; whatever it be, the walk is certainly a garden.' He encourages readers to visit places like Stowe, Hagley and Painshill, where according to him:

> The disposition of the gardens affords frequent opportunities of seeing the different parts, the one from the other, across the park in a variety of advantageous situations... In the midst of a thicket...is a parterre, and an orangery, where the exotic plants are, during the summer, intermixed with common shrubs, and

a constant succession of flowers. The space before the house is full of ornament, the ground is prettily varied.

By comparison, Hagley is 'surrounded by a lawn, of fine uneven ground, and diversified with large clumps, little groups and single trees.' Whately notes that there are numerous vistas to be explored linking the grounds with the countryside around, as well as exploring garden buildings such as a rotunda and a Doric portico called 'Pope's Building, with part of the lawn before it, the scene is very simple, the principle features are great, they prevail over all the rest, and are intimately connected with each other.' A wilderness attracts his attention, with its 'large airy forest glade, thinly skirted with wood, caress of drifts and much overgrown with fern.' Stowe, on the other hand, offers a circuit of up to 4 miles along 'a very broad gravel walk, planted with rows of trees', offering access to Doric pavilions and Corinthian arches.

The very first public guidebook to a large garden was published in 1774, when Benton Seeley, a Buckinghamshire printer, created a guide to the Stowe gardens. Garden visiting was clearly becoming popular, as Mrs Jael Pye indicated in 1775 that garden visiting in England had become the female equivalent of the Grand Tour of Europe enjoyed by young men. She created a short guidebook that year entitled *A Sort Account of the Principal Seats and Gardens in and about Twickenham*, specifically targeting young women. She was concerned that many young ladies visited such gardens 'without answering any other end than barely saying they have been there, but neither receiving any instruction from it themselves, nor rendering their conversation more amusing.'

Another guidebook, this time for the highly unusual gardens at Hawkstone in Shropshire, was published in 1784. Compiled by Mr T. Rodenhurst, it was entitled *A Description of Hawkstone, the*

Seat of Sir Richard Hill, Bart, Shrewsbury. It quickly aroused interest, resulting in sufficient sales to warrant several editions being published. The gardens had been created by Sir Richard as both a sublime garden possessing a religious message as well as being a circuit garden with a long path leading around the various vantage points. A typical section highlights the walk through to the St Francis Cave: 'After having groped around for some yards in total darkness, you are suddenly transported into the cheerful light of day, and whichever way you turn yourself, the most enchanting prospect, intermixed with woods, hills, lawn and water are enlivened with the busy scenes of Agriculture, meets your view.'

Steamboat trips were organised down the River Thames to Gravesend in 1816 to take visitors to Cobham Park. Horsedrawn wagons provided access between Gravesend and the estate, enabling visitors to explore the house and garden with ease.

By the time Jane Austen wrote *Pride and Prejudice*, garden visiting had become an organised part of travels by the gentry and other wealthy people. They would frequently visit stately homes and apply to the housekeeper for a tour of the house, later followed by a tour of the gardens led by the gardener. During a tour to Derbyshire, Elizabeth Bennet and the Gardiners visit Chatsworth as well as Pemberley. When suggesting the visit to the latter, Mrs Gardiner points out that the 'grounds are delightful'. After the housekeeper had given them a tour of the interior of the house, Elizabeth and the Gardiners 'were consigned over to the gardener, who met them at the hall door' ready to take them round the grounds showing them all the important pints via a circuit walk: 'They had now entered a beautiful walk by the side of the water, and every step was bringing forward a nobler fall of ground, or a finer reach of the woods to which they were approaching... They pursued the accustomed circuit which brought them back again...to a descent among the hanging woods, to the edge of the water.'

During the Victorian period, country house visiting became ever more popular, partly as a result of better transport facilities, increased mobility, and curiosity about life on the country estates, as well as the general benevolence of the landed gentry. Although landowners regarded opening their properties to the general public as being a financial and logistical burden, it was felt that they had a social obligation to encourage people to develop worthwhile, improving interests.

The arrival of glasshouses proved to be a fashionable novelty attracting considerable interest both in terms of the construction and the exotic species grown within them. In London, the arrival of a Grand Palm House complete with steam heating and sprinkler system to keep plants moist at the Loddiges Nursery attracted large numbers of people. Visitors arrived just to see the Palm House and the plants within it since it offered something new in relation to gardening. By 1826, the Palm House contained 120 species of palm from over thirty countries. Other nurseries around the country steadily followed suit, opening up grounds to visitors of all kinds.

Joseph Paxton's massive Great Stove at Chatsworth was a major lure for visitors, especially after Queen Victoria drove through it in her carriage during a visit in 1843. A couple of years later, Loddiges added yet another hothouse to its London nursery site, together with two camellia houses containing a total of 1,900 species and eighty varieties of ferns. Outside the hot houses, visitors could follow a carefully laid out spiral path leading through an arboretum comprising of 3,075 trees and shrubs before reaching a display of 1,000 rose varieties. Visitors thronged the site keen to see all these plants, leading *The Gardener's Magazine* to comment 'There is no garden scene about London so interesting.' In 1849, Thomas Cook arranged the first organised trip by road to Chatsworth, subsequently arranging similar excursions to other historic houses.

That same year, the *Penny* magazine published by the Society for Diffusion of Useful Knowledge reported:

> With Oxford holiday-seekers of all classes, Nuneham Courtney is one of the favourite resorts. It lies at an easy distance from the city, being about five miles by road, and not more than seven by the river, and as the row to it is one of the pleasantest on the Thames, few make an aquatic excursion from Oxford without Nuneham serving as the goal: and it deserves the favour in which it is held. Few parts of the river are pleasanter, and fewer of the parks along its banks are so beautiful in themselves, or afford so rich a variety of views.

Further evidence of the interest in plants and gardens as a tourist attraction can be seen from the creation of botanic gardens in major towns and cities around the country, including West Park in Wolverhampton and Sefton Park in Liverpool. Sheffield Botanical Garden was among the first to be opened to the public, albeit only for four days a year. The remaining days were reserved for shareholders and annual subscribers who paid 10s 6d per year for the privilege of visiting whenever they wished.

In Cambridge, the newly appointed Professor of Botany John Henslow insisted that the existing botanic garden within the centre of the city was too small, especially if experimental botany was to become a key part of natural science studies within the university. As a result, a 16-hectare site was acquired 1 mile south of the city centre, enabling the curator, Andrew Murray, to design a circuit garden. This involved the creation of a winding path following the circumference of the garden, bisected by a main walk comprising a variety of stately conifers. A u-shaped lake was placed just beyond the main walk, and to the south a variety of herbaceous beds.

In Birmingham, the Botanical and Horticultural Society established a large garden occupying 18 acres, initially providing access solely to members. The creation of glasshouses was a cause of dispute since the garden designer, John Loudon, wanted a large circular house. Members felt this was too expensive and commissioned a smaller building from a local firm, eventually adding extra houses for tropical and subtropical plants. When the general public was admitted, it quickly became a popular venue with Sunday concerts in the bandstand, flower shows and even political meetings.

In 1840, Kew Gardens opened to the general public for the first time, enabling visitors to explore the gardens every weekday afternoon. Queen Victoria was not happy with this decision by the director William Hooker, saying that it was the only place she could exercise. Her views were overruled, however, and Kew became a very popular destination. By 1841, 9,000 people had visited the glasshouses, and by the end of the nineteenth century it had attracted over 1 million people. Buildings like the Palm House, Herbarium and Temperate House provided continued interest, as did the vast array of flower beds and walks. Visitors did have to comply with certain conditions to be allowed entry: no food, no smoking, no refreshments, no playing, no prams and everyone had to wear 'decent attire'. It was not until 1888 that a Tea Pavilion was opened within the gardens.

Individual plants could cause a sensation. The Titan Arum (Corpse Flower) rarely flowers in the wild or in cultivation, and its first flowering at the Royal Botanic Gardens, Kew in 1889 was so memorable that Kew's assistant director remarked on it in a letter to plant hunter George King in India. It achieved a similar effect when it bloomed in 1926. So many visitors wanted to see it that the police had to be called to deal with the crowds. Reasons why people were so keen to see this plant were not hard to find: apart from the rarity of its blooms, when they do appear the blooms form the world's largest flowers at over

3 metres tall. A Titan Arum blooms for just a couple of days, emitting a characteristic foul rotting odour for a single one evening.

The development of the railways providing quick, reliable transport throughout the country resulted in increasing numbers of people seeking to travel as a leisure activity. The Railway Act of 1844 established a principle of a penny for every mile travelled. Special excursion trains were often laid on for groups. Such excursions might be held at weekends, especially if they were targeting the working population, or during the week for more specialist groups such as artisans and small business owners. In June 1849, a train excursion group arrived at Chatsworth House and Robert Aughtie, the under gardener there, recorded their visit in his diary: 'A large company of Derby folks came today by a special train to see Chatsworth – they were taken round in parties of from twenty to thirty. The Duke seemed much pleased with them, walking about and among them.'

A wider group arrived one Whit Monday to participate in a general open day. *The Gardener's Magazine* included a description of their visit:

> Here were pale-faced men and women from the cotton factories of Manchester, dark denizens of the Staffordshire Potteries and the sharp, active looking mechanics of Leeds, Bradford and Halifax all brought hither on special trains and, in the full heyday of an English holiday, rushing through the gorgeously fitted up rooms of the ducal mansion – admiring the conservatories, rockeries and fountains.

Increasing numbers of workers now expected to have leisure time available each week, and most took Saturday afternoons and Sundays off. The 1871 Bank Holiday Act established the concept of public holidays when everyone had the right to a day off. Annual excursions were arranged by employers, especially in the mill towns of northern England, such as the Wakes Weeks, and provided additional opportunities for trips.

Opening gardens to visitors on Sundays did provoke some opposition as it was felt that it would take people away from religious worship and create a 'continental view of the Sabbath'. Such opposition was in vain, as people increasingly sought to determine how they used their free time. Even *The Times* newspaper added its support saying that it was wrong to expect a 'working Londoner to spend his Sunday in his own dark and dismal hole, breathing the reeking atmosphere of close courts and yards.' Sundays became a popular day for leisure activities, ranging from visits to gardens to trips to the seaside by train.

A new style of garden tourism emerged in the latter part of the nineteenth century with the advent of seaside towns providing a popular mass market holiday and days out. Going to the seaside was extremely popular with ordinary folk and industrial workers. An important part of the experience was to stroll down the promenades and admire the vast flower beds filled with carpet bedding and decorative flower designs. Equally important was the concept of visiting an indoor winter palace; a massive glasshouse on the promenade containing exotic plants and water features. A typical example still exists at Great Yarmouth and is the last surviving winter garden of its type. Initially built between 1878 and 1881 by Torquay architects John Watson and William Harvey, at a cost of £12,783, it was used as a pleasure palace within the town. In 1903, J.W. Cockrill acquired the gardens on behalf of Great Yarmouth Town Council for £1,300. The building was taken apart and transported by barge, where it was reconstructed on the promenade.

Further impetus encouraging people to visit gardens resulted from the foundation of the National Trust in 1895 with the aim 'to set aside the best and most beautiful parts of Britain for the public and posterity, and to provide sitting rooms for the poor in the countryside'.

The following year, it acquired Alfriston Clergy House in East Sussex for £10. Octavia Hill, founder of the National Trust, described it as 'tiny but beautiful, with orchard and a sweep of lowland river behind it' while the restored Arts and Crafts style gardens now form a series of 'garden rooms', each surrounded by hedges and trellis.

The popularity of country house and garden visiting led to consideration of ways to control numbers. Some began charging a small entry fee or placing a strict entry limit on the number of tickets available daily, while others adopted timed ticket entry. The scale of the problem can be seen from correspondence between Thomas Speed, head gardener at Chatsworth in 1883, and various colleagues in other gardens around the country. Speed was seeking information about arrangements being made to manage visitor numbers, and the costs they were incurring. Responses included charging a nominal fee of 1 shilling for each visitor to Blenheim and Eaton, and those who were not currently charging but were considering doing so. George Glass, head gardener at Enville Hall, commented that the garden attracted large crowds resulting in a decision to:

> Place a man at the entrance and he admits all who come. We do not allow any bottles or baskets to be taken into the grounds. They can be left at the gate. All parties are requested not to walk on the grass. I have a few men about the grounds just to see that parties are behaving themselves... We do not allow any picnics or games to be carried on inside the grounds, only to walk quietly around.

Belvoir had a different response. It charged just 2 pence for entry and stated 'the increased facilities offered by Railways bring a great invasion of visitors and I am sorry to say that no regulations exist to meet such circumstances... Should the Duke take up his residence at the Castle in the summertime, he would find it annoying to have people all over the place.'

All the respondents shared concern about charging visitors because no one wanted to prevent respectable working-class people from visiting, preferring a more informal system with no entry charge. Instead, the visitors could give tips to gardeners and servants. Despite this, by 1900 it had become normal practice to introduce an entry charge since this was the only way they could regulate visitor numbers and subsidise the costs involved with opening to the public. The Marquess of Winchester set out to attract visitors to Eaton Hall by setting up specific opening times, and proceeds from entry fees were used to pay four men to take visitors round the house and garden. Any surplus was given to charities. At Warwick Castle, guides were employed to take visitors around the castle and grounds in return for an increased entry fee. This resulted in making the enterprise profitable, as well as greater visitor numbers: 20,000 in 1886 compared to 40,000 in 1905, when five guides were employed.

Travel books and guides frequently referred to gardens as a key attraction within an area. Editorials ranged from detailed descriptions of specific gardens to general descriptions designed to inspire and encourage visitors. Writing in the 1909 edition of *The English Rivera, The Queen Newspaper Book of Travel: A Guide to Home and Foreign Resorts*, S.L. Bastin stressed the pleasure provided by the luxurious gardens and general vegetation, commenting 'Geraniums clamber up to the first-floor windows of the amazing villas in Penzance, bearing literally hundreds of bunches of blooms. Groves of palms and tree ferns are delightful features of many gardens, whilst there are many places where the banana tree attains to fine proportions.'

Garden tourism reached new heights in the aftermath of the First World War and the subsequent economic problems. Paid holidays became widespread during the 1920s and 1930s, creating more time for people to visit gardens and other locations. In 1927, members of a fundraising committee were discussing potential initiatives at the Institute for Nurses, which provided endowments for district nurses. One member, Elsie Wrag, suggested creating a National Garden Week and persuaded several members of the committee, together with their friends, to open their gardens to the general public for a specific period. A total of 609 gardens were involved. The committee persuaded train companies and charabanc companies to provide transport, and garden writer Marion Cran mentioned the event in her radio programme. It turned out to be an incredible success. At one house, Ham House in Surrey, 100 visitors had been anticipated, but 900 turned up, each paying a shilling to enter. The scheme raised £8,000 and it became an annual event, involving ever increasing numbers of gardens nationwide. Within four years there were 1,000 gardens taking part. It was the forerunner of the National Gardens Scheme and its *Little Yellow Book*, which has continued to raise money for charity by opening private gardens.

The number of gardens being opened to the public on a regular basis increased steadily. In 1938, Vita Sackville-West opened her garden at Sissinghurst in Kent, with visitors paying a shilling to enter. It was so popular that it raised £25 on the first day, resulting in Sackville-West describing these new visitors as 'the shillingses'.

Access to gardens linked to major estates became increasingly possible and formed a popular destination for charabanc companies. These companies were developing a market providing excursions for town dwellers wanting to visit places of interest. Faced with financial problems following the death of so many family members during the First World War, many landowners were struggling to survive and sought solutions to their problems. *Country Life* magazine drew up a list of properties that must be saved for the nation. In 1931, the National Trust for Places of Historic Interest or Natural Beauty took on specific responsibility for the garden as well as the house at

Montecute in Somerset. The success of their projects resulted in the 1937 National Trust Act, which allowed the National Trust to acquire and hold land or investments, acting as endowments for country houses. This meant that the original owners were no longer liable for tax but could stay in parts of the property. In 1940, the National Trust acquired Blickling Hall and Wightwick Manor, both with substantial gardens. Later acquisitions included other properties with important gardens such as Cotehele, Hardwick Hall, Ickworth House, Penryhn Castle and Sissinghurst Castle Garden. It was a move which acted as a catalyst for future action that would take post-war garden tourism to new heights.

Chapter 14

The First World War and Its Impact

The twentieth century was marked by two world wars involving the total mobilisation of entire nations. This had an immediate effect on all aspects of gardening, not just the people involved in day-to-day tasks but also the style, practice and commercialisation. Cultivation for food became essential and the role of women in the garden changed dramatically.

The outbreak of war in 1914 marked the beginning of a major transformation in the way politicians and individuals regarded gardening and horticulture.

Initially, there was a general feeling that this was a war that would not last long. Most people believed that it would all be over by Christmas. There had been no major continental war involving Britain for nearly a hundred years, resulting in an attitude of complacency. Young men rushed to serve in the armed forces, believing that if they did not take the opportunity now it would be over before they had a chance of experiencing warfare and travelling outside their home areas. Thousands of young men left their jobs, including those working in estate kitchen gardens, allotments, market gardens and farms, having been promised that their jobs would be waiting for them on their return. Whole groups of workers signed up, forming platoons of friends. As 1915 dawned, realisation had begun to emerge that this would be a war that would be much more drawn out than anticipated.

With the death rate mounting, volunteer enlistment numbers were no longer enough and compulsory military service was introduced. The government paid little attention to the needs of the agricultural and horticultural sectors, regarding all available men as being ideal for serving in the forces. As a result, market gardens, farms and horticultural companies faced problems as there were now fewer men available to cultivate the crops needed to feed the armed forces, as well as the civilian population. Demand was outstripping supply. Food shortages began to occur. Women and children spent hours standing in long queues outside shops for what food was available.

At the end of 1916, the Cultivation of Land Orders was issued under the Defence of the Realm Act (DORA). Everyone was encouraged to grow food, with the Board of Agriculture issuing informative pamphlets and leaflets. Even tennis courts and golf courses were transformed into growing areas. Flower beds outside Buckingham Palace were replaced with potatoes, while glasshouses in city parks grew tomatoes for sale to the public. It was reported that King George V, a keen gardener, when holding a lunch party expected participants to undertake some work afterwards. Half the guests would go to work on an allotment with the king, while the other half would assist Queen Mary to serve meals to workers.

Land was acquired nationwide for use as allotments and market gardens. Women undertook much of the labour, with married women encouraged to take on allotments. *The Gardeners' Chronicle* was soon listing requests for female gardeners to take up employment opportunities. Trained female gardeners took up employment at Kew, replacing the male gardeners who had joined the services. All these female gardeners had been trained at Swanley and soon became involved in most areas of the botanical gardens, with the exception of the Palm House. They were even invited to join Kew's Mutual Improvement Society and attend its talks.

In 1917, the Women's Land Army was formed, recruiting girls aged 20 years and over who could provide paperwork proving they were educated and literate and had suitable references. They worked on a six-month or one-year contract and were paid between 20 and

25 shillings a week. Each girl had to pay 17 shillings each week for room and board. According to the *Women's Land Army Handbook*, they also had to agree to 'behave quietly', 'avoid entering the bar of a public house', 'not smoke in public' and 'never wear the uniform after work without her overall, nor walk about with her hands in her breeches pockets.'

Within a year, over 23,000 Land Girls were active on farms, market gardens and kitchen gardens undertaking all the tasks normally done by men. The arrival of Land Girls cultivating crops was met with some opposition, with some believing that they were just using it as way to catch a husband and that their real place was in the home. Writing in *Women on the Land* (1990), Carol Twinch noted that the government used posters feminizing the new roles in a bid to change engrained attitudes, quoting the surprise encountered by a Land Girls parade in Birmingham. It was reported that 'the procession attracted much attention, and to many of the watchers, it was a novelty to see the girls in their working clothes, and to realize that the girls of England are really working on the land, and not merely playing about in print frocks in the haymaking time.'

A small number of women gardeners also took on roles within the armed forces. In 1917, twenty women belonging to the Women's Army Auxiliary Corps (WAAC) and Queen Mary's Army Auxiliary Corps (QMAAC) were sent to France to work as gardeners in the numerous military cemeteries located throughout the Western Front.

The impact of the First World War was slow to hit seed companies. Men working in the seed growing industry were placed on the list of reserved occupations, thus reducing the number of employees conscripted into the forces. Order levels were high. At Suttons, staff were processing around 400 to 500 orders daily but were receiving around 600 to 700 in high season. As a result, there were times when the management sought volunteers to work through the night to relieve the pressure of orders. There was still considerable variety of seeds available. In 1916, R&A Taylor in King's Lynn issued twenty-two-page catalogues containing a vast array of seeds and other merchandise. This included fifty-one varieties of peas, eight varieties of carrots, as well as seeds like artichokes, asparagus, savoy cabbage, capsicum, chilli and chervil, plus lawn grass and seed potatoes. In addition, there were two pages full of sweet pea varieties, numerous florist flowers, collections of choice flower seeds, bulbs and roots, plus horticultural sundries. The cover was brightly coloured and there were lots of black and white illustrations inside the catalogue.

As the war continued, the government appealed to private gardeners to provide seeds for allotment holders, and to give up space in their gardens for growing food. The number of allotment holders increased rapidly, with even the city parks starting to grow tomatoes in their greenhouses and selling these to the public. By 1917, gardeners everywhere in the country were steadily growing more and more food. Demand for traditional medicinal plants such as marigolds, foxgloves and dandelions increased.

By June 1918, seed companies were facing a very different type of problem in the form of paper shortages. This led Suttons to issue a statement to its staff on 6 June stating:

> New postal rates and paper restrictions order. Need for increased economy. Postcards should be used whenever possible for brief correspondence. Stamped reply envelopes should not be enclosed, except when necessary, and postcards should generally be used for this purpose. The paper shortage is so acute that paper and envelopes must be used sparingly. Small envelopes and memorandum pages are provided, which can be obtained from the stationery room, and these should be made the best use of.

With the signing of the Armistice in November 1918, men began returning home from the war. Thousands more were being released from hospitals into civilian life, frequently disabled or suffering from the effects of their wartime experiences. They anticipated they would immediately return to their old lives and jobs. In reality, it was not quite as easy as anticipated. For some men, life changing injuries incurred during their military service meant that their original occupations were no longer possible. Many employers, meanwhile, discovered there were financial implications. Suttons stated, 'In re-absorbing our men, they should be taken back with the old wage, plus necessary War Bonus. Every care should be taken to keep departmental expenses within existing bounds. The case of boys who are now men needs special treatment.'

It also meant changes for the thousands of women who had adopted new roles during wartime and now found that their jobs had been taken away. In the gardening sector, the number of women being employed, whether in nurseries, gardens or with producers such as seed companies, declined rapidly as men took their places. For younger women this posed new problems. Many were reluctant to give up the independence they had achieved, especially given that marriage might not be an option due to the vast number of deaths that had occurred in wartime, meaning there were now numerous 'surplus women' at all levels of society.

The pressures of war had changed society forever, and it raised major issues that would have a long-term impact, including within the garden sector.

Chapter 15

Between the Wars

The end of the First World War saw millions of soldiers returning to civilian life. The Land Army ceased, and women were expected to resume their traditional roles with the home, especially if they were married. Although many people expected that the pre-war social status quo would return, this did not happen. Too much had changed. Women had shown that they could take on a much wider role than before, and their demand for the vote and a say in politics was eventually granted in the Representation of the People Act 1928.

One of the biggest promises was also the hardest to deliver. Prime Minister David Lloyd George had declared that returning soldiers would have 'homes fit for heroes'. Such houses were to include gardens, since this would encourage family life and reduce the need for men to spend time in pubs. Having gardens would also enable housewives to keep an eye on children playing outside while undertaking tasks around the house. As a result, the Housing Act of 1919 set out to provide a better standard of living for ordinary people, most of whom had previously been living in slums and tenements within towns and cities. Under the terms of the Housing Act, councils were given money to build 'council houses'. These were built on large estates, usually with three bedrooms, a bathroom, indoor toilet, living room and kitchen. Hot and cold running water and electricity were also provided. Some had an extra downstairs room on the basis that such rooms could double up as a bedroom for injured soldiers who could not easily get upstairs. Gardens were provided at the front and back of the house, and council officials were required to ensure that tenants kept gardens in good condition. The intention was to build half a million homes within three years. In reality, however, only around 200,000 'homes for heroes' were ever built, due mainly to the worsening economic situation. Another major round of council house building was launched during the 1930s following an Act of Parliament requiring local authorities to clear all remaining slum housing.

For many occupants of these new estates, the transition could be hard. It often involved moving from the centre of a town or city to the suburbs. At Burnage, Manchester a recent Heritage Lottery funded project 'Burnage: A place called Home' highlighted the sheer scale of change the new tenants experienced, with tenants surprised by the sheer amount of green around them: 'Our old house, it was a very poor house, it was a slum really. My father called it "The Hovel". The grate fell off the wall and nearly killed my brother. When we got the Corporation house in Ferndale Gardens, off Kingsway, we thought it was heaven on earth.'

Writing in *The Gardens of the British Working Class*, Margaret Willes points out that the council authorities could be very strict in their requirements. Advice might be available from an experienced gardener employed by the council, but standards had to be kept.

> These standards would seem amazingly demanding today. For example, Mr Pennington in 1932 was asked to remove a trellis he had erected next to his path to grow his sweet peas. When he ignored the directive, the council sent two men to pull it down. Charlie Hammond was likewise reprimanded for building a trellis to keep his son off his flowerpots. Those who retained what were described as slum habits would face eviction, though the threat would seem to have been sufficient, for only six notices to quit for 'non-cultivation of a garden' were served in the whole of the Manchester district between 1921 and 1933.

In Bristol, the new developments were described as garden suburbs, following the ideas of Ebenezer Howard. Following a survey on housing needs conducted in 1931, it was reported that development of Seahill and other locations in Bristol had proved successful:

> Considering the conditions under which they had lived, with insufficient accommodation and lack of proper facilities for cooking, washing, drying and other domestic duties, without gardens to afford relaxation or to stimulate interest in pursuits other than ordinary daily toil, it is generally regarded as highly satisfactory that the response of tenants to improved conditions has been so marked. They take a real pride in their new homes and gardens are well cultivated.

London County Council was responsible for the creation of the largest of all these council house projects. Known as Becontree, it took fifteen years to complete and covered vast areas around Ilford, Dagenham and Barking. The inhabitants of these new council houses were people who had lived within the tenements of inner London. Reports from the time indicate that many tenants were surprised to see grass in their new gardens. Garden clubs were set up on these new estates to enable people to learn how to garden, exchange or sell plants and provide help when necessary. Such clubs would buy seeds and other garden necessities in bulk, thus cutting the cost of gardening. Most of the new tenants became very keen gardeners, proud of what they could achieve. Resultant garden designs varied from lawns, circular flower beds and a few vegetables surrounded by a privet hedge grown from cuttings to ornate designs complete with paths made from crazy paving, rose covered arches, productive vegetable patches, flower beds and trees. Among the most popular plants to be seen on these estates were traditional cottage garden varieties such as violas, mignonettes, roses, hollyhocks and daisies. Garden gnomes also began to make an appearance.

So popular had gardening become nationwide that there were even cigarette card series focusing on garden designs. Help and advice was widely available from many sources. At the Daily Mail Ideal Home Show, held at Olympia in 1920, Suttons created vegetable gardens to accompany various cottages on show. Later in the 1920s, several unnamed crowned heads of Europe were said to have designed gardens accompanying the full size 'Tudorbethan' houses on display. These gardens were lit by special gas lamps which mimicked daylight enabling visitors to see the real colours of the flowers. Over at the Chelsea Flower Show, there was a model garden designed as a suburban plot. In 1922, the *Reading Mercury* recorded that the Suttons Seed Garden at Chelsea was:

> One of the most attractive exhibits of the whole show, and one which many visitors considered alone worth the gate money. This remarkable plant breeding garden, which extends to no less than half an acre, must be the most comprehensive example of its kind that has ever been staged at any show in the world. One portion is devoted to experiments showing how the improvements are affected in plants both for agricultural purposes and the vegetable garden. Another section shows the work carried out for improvement of grasses and clovers... the formation of sporting turf from seed is depicted by a miniature tennis court, bowling green, croquet lawn and putting green... Botanists will be delighted with the 'grass garden' and horticulturalists in the methods shown for the production of vegetables and flowers for the show bench; all this embellished by beautiful beds of annuals and others which Suttons are justly famed for in all parts of the country. At the end of the garden they have created a pavilion furnished as a botanical museum.

Garden magazines were widely read, and part works offered an easy way for working class gardeners to build up a reference library. Typical titles included Associated Press's *Popular Encyclopaedia of Gardening* in fifty-two weekly parts each costing 6d. In 1928, a new weekly magazine was launched entitled *Home Gardening* with the strapline 'the gardening paper for the millions'. Costing 2d, it included a section designed to encourage children to take up gardening by following the activities of Peter, Pam and Pat, a free advice service and the first issue even included a free 'monster packet of flower seeds'.

Garden publications provided lots of inspiration in terms of colour combinations for experimental gardeners. In 1937, *Oldham's Illustrated Gardening Encyclopaedia* suggested gardeners could try

> A blue, mauve and white border with occasional groups of shell pink. Start with pinks, whites and red, increase to blues, yellow and orange and back to pinks and reds for grouping. Try Salvia Virgata Nemerosa (purple) with Helenium July Sun (orange) Lavender with Nepeta Mussini, deep blue delphiniums with white Madonna Lilies, Cheiranthus (deep orange) with Viola Cornuta or Royal Blue Forget-me-Nots.

The advent of the wireless and radio services offered new ways to talk to gardeners, and gardening talks were one of the first programmes provided by the BBC after its launch in 1922. For several years, these talks were given by a variety of gardeners ranging from Vita Sackville-West to Marion Cran, but it was in 1931 when the most popular voice of gardening emerged: C.H. Middleton. Employed as a garden instructor for Surrey County Council, after his first broadcast in 1931 he was giving weekly talks by 1934 with the title 'In the Garden', which eventually attracted mass audiences of up to 3.5 million. Such was his popularity that he was recruited in 1937 to make the first television programme in a specially created garden at Alexandra Palace, as well as making a number of school radio broadcasts.

Considerable emphasis was placed on the use of competitions to encourage new gardeners in their efforts. London County Council held regular competitions offering certificates, medals and small amounts of money for first prize winners on their various housing estates. In the 1930s the launch of the London Gardens Society led to the creation of competitions open to anyone living within the city. Participation was high: in 1938, their best kept garden competition attracted 65,000 participants, which were steadily whittled down to a short list of 1,611 gardens for the final judging.

Attention was also focused on the need to improve the general environment for people living within cities. Local authorities began to plant trees and flowers, improving public parks and the general municipal environment. In Bermondsey, the council undertook a major campaign aiming to plant all waste ground, whether public or private, with trees and shrubs. Plans to provide tubs, window boxes, rockeries and fountains if requested by residents fell by the wayside due to the cost, but the council did provide householders with free plants and compost. Over 9,000 trees were planted, and 9 acres of formerly waste ground were turned into public gardens and children's playgrounds. In the Wilson Grove area, the council created a garden suburb complete with cottage-style housing, silver birches and climbing roses. By the end of 1923, the council's superintendent of gardens, Mr Johns, was responsible for fifty flower beds, 168 window boxes and over 150,000 square feet of flower borders. His aim was to provide as much colour as possible all year round, which resulted in mass plantings of pansies, bulbs and polyanthus for winter and spring. The summer saw displays of plants like foxgloves, lupins, irises, snapdragons, columbines, geums and Sweet William while in the autumn attention switched to dahlias, chrysanthemums and Michaelmas daisies.

With the increasing fear of bolshevism in the wake of the Russian Revolution, many politicians began to consider ways to decrease discontent at home. Just as in the Victorian period, when dissent was high, gardening was seen as a potential answer to social problems. In 1920, Neville Chamberlain noted that 'every spadeful of manure dug in, every fruit tree planted' helped to convert possible revolutionaries into happy citizens.

The 1920s had been a boom period, but this came to an abrupt end in October 1929 when the Wall Street Crash led to stock markets losing over half of their value. This situation soon began to impact all aspects of life, with businesses closing as they no longer had the money to keep going. Unemployment rates rose as most countries plunged into what became known as the Great Depression. By the end of 1930, unemployment had doubled to 20 percent, public spending was severely reduced, and taxes increased leading ultimately to yet more job losses. Poverty and unemployment became a major issue throughout much of the 1930s, especially in northern England. Recovery within London and southern England came quicker than elsewhere, fuelled partly by a building boom. Demand for gardeners remained steady, with around 300,000 people being employed in the sector by 1931.

Access to allotments became crucial for many working-class families. It was a way of providing much needed food as well as a social activity. Demand for allotments was extremely high, but available land outstripped supply. Much of the requisitioned land taken for allotments in 1917 onwards had been returned to the original owners. This meant that many of the wartime allotment holders – especially women – no longer had access to growing space. Likewise, the countless returning soldiers traumatised by the experience of the First World War needed not just a facility to provide food for themselves and their families, but a space for peace and quiet. Gardening became their lifeline.

Overall, demand for gardens throughout these two decades was extremely high. According to research undertaken by Mass

Observation in the 1930s, up to 94 percent of people living in towns wanted a garden. Contemporary literature often included scenes in gardens portraying them as pleasant places to relax, or as places of adventure. Examples of this include the *Just William* books by Richmal Crompton, first published in 1922, where every garden possesses key features like a tennis court, vegetable patch, roses, lawns and flower beds. Gardening became a favourite weekend pastime, celebrated during the summer months at flower shows with added family interest such as craft stalls, races for children and prizes for jams, cakes, pot plants and cacti. Gardens were being created everywhere. A feature on London gardens published in the *Picture Post* in June 1939 contained the words 'Every Londoner longs for a garden. Few can afford a big one. But thousands grow glorious flowers in backyards, and window boxes, even on rooftops.'

One of the more innovative gardening projects undertaken during the inter-war period was the creation of a rooftop garden at Derry & Toms, a department store on Kensington High Street, London. Having been taken over some years earlier by Barker & Co., a new building had been constructed on the site. Trevor Bowen, the chairman of Barkers, decided to offer customers something slightly different in terms of facilities. Both Selfridges and Barkers had pioneered the idea of small roof gardens complete with tearooms during the Edwardian period, but the new Derry & Toms garden was designed to be totally innovative. Ralph Hancock, a Welsh landscape architect, was commissioned to design and build the new facility. Rather than putting on the final floor as had been originally intended, he suggested it should be placed on the roof itself. By laying concrete, screed, asphalt, bricks, and clinker breeze concrete, followed by turf and up to 36 inches of topsoil, it became possible to design a garden without affecting the load-bearing capacity of the floors underneath. It took two years to design, construct and plant with over 500 species of plants and shrubs. Water was pumped up from Derry & Toms' own artesian wells underneath the building.

The garden contained three themed areas:

- A Spanish garden based on the Moorish gardens found in the Alhambra, in southern Spain, with palm trees, a courtyard complete with fountains, colonnades and vine covered walkways.
- An English woodland garden filled with over 100 trees, a flowing stream complete with fish, ducks and resident flamingos.
- A formal Tudor style garden with herringbone brickwork paths, Tudor inspired arches, a wrought iron pump, flower and herb beds.

On completion in 1938, the garden had cost Barkers £25,000. It was deemed money well spent attracting large numbers of people keen to explore the garden and visit the tearoom. Opened in 1938 by the Earl of Athol, the new 1.5-acre garden formed an oasis of greenery 100 feet above the road below, making it the largest intensive green roof in Europe. Among the early visitors were Queen Mary and other members of the Royal Family.

Outside the cities and towns, the big estates continued to operate their gardens much as they had done before the war, although usually with fewer staff. In many cases the pre-war gardeners had not returned. At Heligan, in Cornwall, the gardening staff had all signed up together and formed one platoon – all died in battle. Some gardens fell into neglect due to financing and staffing problems, but many others maintained much of their pre-war gardening activities. At Windsor, King George V automatically expected a daily fresh gardenia on the breakfast table ready for him to insert into his buttonhole. Over at Easton Park, the gardener was expected to have all the flowers done inside the house before breakfast.

Quite often, staffing in the big estates mainly comprised the head gardener, a foreman and some trainees. At Penrhyn Castle, trainee Norman Thomas earned 22 shillings a week and gave 12 shillings to the foreman to pay for his food and lodging. Just like gardeners in Victorian times, Thomas was expected to pack and send fruit and vegetables to Lord Penrhyn wherever he was staying in the country. He wrote that 'all fruit was placed in special paper with wool and wood wool surrounding them. They were then placed in special boxes… packing took place three times a week. On Sunday this operation would take five hours to complete.' Once packed, the boxes would be transported by rail to Lord Penrhyn.

Another gardener, Harry Dodgson, recalled the process of sending produce from Chilton Gardens to Belgrave Square, London. Jennifer Davies recorded his memories in *The Victorian Kitchen Garden*:

> There were long hampers for flowers and separate square hampers for fruit and vegetables. The only fruit that was put into the vegetable hamper was cooking apples or pears. The kitchen garden foreman picked the outside produce and packed the vegetables but the fruit boxes and hampers were always packed by the inside foreman supervised by the head gardener. Root vegetables were washed and put into the bottom of the hamper. On top of these went the more solid vegetables such as heads of cabbage and cauliflowers. Next came peas and beans and, on top, tender salading such as lettuce and tomatoes. Before the hamper was strapped down, the contents were topped with a covering of spinach. This was the vegetable least able to withstand any crushing and putting it on top also provided a cushion for the other vegetables packed in beneath.

Equal care was given to the fruit hamper. Fruit would be packed into smaller boxes before being placed into the main hamper, for example a felt-lined box held twelve peaches and a cushion of bleached wadding was placed on top of the fruit. Dessert plums and gages formed a layer in another box, with each fruit being separately wrapped in a leaf or piece of tissue paper. There were even 10-inch boxes for individual strawberries or figs. According to Harry Dodgson 'the skills required to pack a hamper properly was a closely guarded and handed down secret,' learned from watching a head gardener in action.

Arthur Hooper was a newcomer to the world of estate gardens, starting as a garden boy in 1922. By 1926, he was responsible for seven glasshouses at Fonthill House, Wiltshire, the home of Hugh Morrison MP. He recalled that the door handles in the hothouses had to be kept totally clean 'as Mr Morrison's family or their guests would be most annoyed if they soiled their hands or gloves when walking through the greenhouses'. Hooper subsequently worked at Gatton Park, Surrey, an estate owned by Sir Jeremiah Colman, where he oversaw seventeen glasshouses and twelve orchid houses, as well as supplying and arranging flowers and pot plants for the house. Later, at Highbury Hall, he was in charge of thirty-seven gardeners plus another seven who worked in the kitchen garden.

The inter-war years were a time of opportunity for companies involved in the garden sector. Not only was there a massive demand for seeds and garden products, new ways of communicating with potential customers now existed. Suttons Seeds were quick to take advantage of this. Cinema advertising was considered, and ideas developed, but transport systems provided the greatest opportunities. In 1920 the number of rail journeys reached over 2 million, while the buses and charabancs become increasingly comfortable forms of transport for work, excursions or holidays. Consequently, Suttons devoted considerable resources to maximising its involvement. Coloured advertisements were introduced into first-class carriages on the London & South Eastern Railway during the 1920s, and in the 1930s it expanded its activities to the London & North Eastern Railway, with advertising presented 'as a card divided into three sections; on the left there was a coloured picture of flowers, on the right a coloured picture of vegetables and in the centre Suttons Seeds of Reading.'

Earley Local History group have noted that 'This advertising was further extended to Southern Railway through Kent and the great central suburban district, to signs on bridges and on main roads with a reflector pointing to Reading, "The Home of Suttons Seeds".'

Sales were high, especially of garden sundries. Although manufactured by various suppliers, they were branded with the Suttons name. The range was extensive and included a Suttons' garden syringe, a Suttons' thermometer boxwood scale, Suttons' artificial manures and even a Suttons' lawnmower. The company even created its own garden construction company, announcing the new venture in 1922:

> For the enduring success of a garden, good planning inspired by imagination and directed by experience is the only sure foundation. In order that we may meet all the requirements of our customers in this respect we have arranged for the professional co-operation of Messrs Millner Son & White, the well-known firm of garden architects, who have been responsible for the arrangement of so many of the more famous public, private parks and gardens in this country and on the continent.

Over the next few years, the new venture installed hard landscaping and created rockeries, pools, flower beds, lawns, water gardens and lily ponds.

Demand for flowers was not limited to houses, estates and public parks. The increasing numbers of cars and other vehicles led to the creation of more, and better, roads. The Council of the Roads Beautifying Association, possessing a membership that included botanists and horticulturalists, set out to ensure that the roads were aesthetically pleasing by improving the surrounding planting areas. Roger Notcutt, of Suffolk Notcutts Nurseries, was one of the people involved in this project. The company was ideally placed since most of its business was involved in supplying country houses with the large quantities of flowers and vegetables needed to fill their gardens.

The art of flower arranging gained new impetus between the wars due to the activities of Constance Spry. Having divorced her abusive husband, she set out to create a career involving flowers. In 1928, she opened a flower shop trading as 'Flower Decoration' and adopted a revolutionary approach to floristry, which became socially dominant. As Catherine Horwood points out, the title 'Flower Decoration' was 'part of the snobbish vocabulary of the time – floristry was something done for money, flower arranging by suburban women, flower decoration by upper middle-class women with country homes'. In due course, Spry became the expert on flower décor. Instead of elaborate vases, she recommended using soup tureens, bowls from old dinner services or unusual containers, crumpling up wire to hold flower stems allowing flowers to tumble over the edges.

> Rather than focusing on expensive, select flowers, she [Spry] was inspired by styles from Dutch Old Masters such as the work of Rachel Ruysch to combine traditional flowers with unusual ones like kale and pussy willow. She summed up her approach with the words 'Do whatever you please. Follow your own star: be original if you want to be and don't if you don't want to be. Just be natural and gay and light-hearted and pretty and simple and overflowing and general and baroque and bare and austere and stylized and wild and daring and conservative. And learn and learn and learn. Open your mind to every form of beauty.'

Equally influential within the gardening sector at this time was Margery Fish, who developed an informal, cottage garden style at her home at East Lambrook Manor. It was a style far removed from the more conventional formal, structured lawns and flower beds that dominated the period. Elsewhere Vita Sackville-West had created an outstanding garden at Sissinghurst, likewise Heather Murat at Kiftsgate and Sybil Burnett at Crathes Castle.

Chapter 16

The Second World War and a Different Approach

As the 1930s drew to a close, awareness of another imminent war resulted in a very different approach by the government, businesses and ordinary people. Preparations were made well in advance of the official announcement of war to maximise and safeguard food production via the Food (Defence Plans) Department. The government was quick to take action to control the entire food production system, and the Land Army was re-introduced.

A major publicity campaign stressing the need to 'Grow More Food' was instantly launched but was soon replaced by the more memorable, catchy title, 'Dig for Victory'. The focus was on economy, essential crops and avoiding practices seen as extravagant, such as forcing early vegetables or growing exotic fruits. Practicality and volume were the order of the day. Dig for Victory exhibitions and talks were held all over the country, with horticultural specialists, nurserymen and growers giving lectures. Popular radio gardener Cecil Middleton's programmes became a major source of information and essential listening for countless home gardeners following the decision of the BBC to commission a weekly series, 'Your Garden in War-Time'. The first programme under this banner took place on 4 September 1939, just one day after war had been declared. There was even a light-hearted play broadcast called 'Digging for Victory', designed to encourage amateur gardeners. In the play, the hero starts as a total beginner, knowing absolutely nothing about gardening but eventually becomes so knowledgeable that he gives talks to the local horticultural society. The play ends with the words:

'There's an obvious moral in Christopher Grigg
If he can grow turnips, we also can dig
So back to the land – and if you are able
Contribute a sprout to the national table.'

In 1941, a midday gardening programme targeting women was launched, involving two women discussing garden problems and how to cook the produce they grew. R&A Taylor included a suggested outline plan for a 300-yard allotment in its wartime seed catalogues. Far less serious but extremely popular since it provided some levity from the general tension was Peter Ender's *Up the Garden Path*, which set out to entertain by providing spoof advice. Dedicated to the government's Dig-for-Dear-Life-Campaign, it included numerous cartoons and suggestions, such as 'Devote a space in your garden to horseradish which, folded in half, makes an excellent stopper to gin bottles!'

The Ministry of Agriculture soon called for yet more space to be given to food production, announcing that 'half a million more allotments will feed another million adults and one and a half million children for eight months of the year, so let's get going and let "Dig for Victory" be the motto for everyone with a garden or allotment and every man and woman capable of digging an allotment in their spare time.' Lord Woolton, Minister of Food, declared 'every extra row of vegetables in allotments saves shipping.'

Gardens around the country were transformed, including big estates which frequently dug up large sections of lawns or landscape areas. At Ickworth House in Suffolk, much of the surrounding grassland was dug up for cultivation, while at Kew Gardens, considerable space was devoted to growing vegetables and medicinal plants. The Royal Parks in London were turned into allotments and air shelters and in 1941, Miss Tarver from Kew Gardens was appointed to organise the Ministry of Agriculture model allotments in Hyde Park. Businesses and commercial organisations joined in the allotment frenzy. BBC outside broadcast staff took on a 90x30-feet allotment in a London's West End Square and quickly turned their project into a Radio Allotment. At St Helens, Lancashire Pilkington Glass created greenhouses within their factory, as well as fourteen allotments on their playing fields. LMS Railway created 22,000 allotments on their land, resulting in an estimate that if placed end to end, they would stretch from London to Dumfries. Wolseley Motors created marrow and cucumber frames from the windscreens of old cars. Any space that could be transformed was used, including bomb sites. Schoolchildren worked on allotments located on playing fields, while ARP wardens, police and fire officers cultivated spots near to their premises.

Problems did arise, however. Many sites proved to be unsuitable due to soil infertility thanks to previous industrial use resulting in massive amounts of copper, nickel, zinc and lead being present in the soil. Allotment holders often experienced difficulties trying to find enough time to work on the allotment, as well as undertake wartime duties in the Home Guard or fire watching, not to mention doing their normal jobs and having a family life. Problems of theft also occurred. At Ipswich magistrates court a man was sent to prison for a month having stolen vegetables worth 1s 6d from an allotment, while in Oldbury, some Home Guard members were charged with stealing three pods of peas and three carrots. The case was dismissed, but they had to pay 4s each to the allotment holder.

Professional gardeners, horticultural staff and fruit growers aged 25 or over were generally exempt from call up due to their food growing skills and were classed as reserved. It was felt that they could be better employed growing the produce needed to keep people alive. By 1940, the reserved age category had been reduced to 21, but certain jobs such as general gardener and bulb grower found their reserved status withdrawn. Younger gardeners possessed less knowledge and so were regarded as being best employed within the armed forces. Retired gardeners were often called back into the workforce. An unexpected aspect of this situation meant that under gardeners found their wages being increased, earning almost as much as a head gardener. In 1939, under gardeners earned £1 14s per week, but by September 1945 their weekly wage had risen to £3 10s. Head gardeners, on the other hand, received no such increase and were simply told by their employers that they could retain any profits made on the sale of garden produce.

Girls were encouraged to consider careers in gardening as part of their wartime service. In 1940, the Women's Garden Association introduced free training for any woman aged 18 or over working as apprentices under head gardeners. It attracted a lot of attention, both from potential trainees and from the media keen to take photos of these new gardeners. Their arrival was equally surprising in many communities, as a Mass Observation interview with Judith Hill, a newly trained gardener indicates. She reported that she was a 'great sensation in the village' since they had not previously known any female gardeners and was regarded as an expert despite having only six weeks' training. Not all head gardeners were happy with the situation. An unhappy head gardener wrote to *The Gardeners' Chronicle* complaining:

> Many gardeners with life experience have now to train young lady gardeners sent out from horticultural schools, women's farm and garden associations, etc, to fill up the places of men called up. Some of these girls are very good, but others have had little or no training. A gardener is expected to give practical experience acquired by him during twenty or thirty years to these girls. The gardener is expected to do all this for the ordinary gardener's small wage! Yet men who train girls at the

machine or bench are paid an instructor's wage of £7 or £8 per week. Is this fair?

Demand for female gardeners grew quickly and in 1941, the Women's Farm and Garden Association reported that demand was outstripping supply for trained women gardeners. At Kew there were just twenty-seven women gardeners when war commenced and numbers rose quickly, with employees including girls from Australia, Canada and Denmark. The Kew Guild noted that:

> Women gardeners have come to Kew once more... The fashion in clogs remains the same...they are employed in the Propagating Pits, Decorative Department, and Flower and Rock Gardens and in certain sections of the Tropical Department... And by endeavouring to set up a high standard of work, disprove the saying for all time that Nepeta Mussinii is the only plant a woman can't kill! In fact, Kew women gardeners are now part of the Kew landscape.

Working hours were long and arduous. Most started work at 6.30am and continued late in the evening. Vegetables were cultivated in some of the famous beds and hothouses at Kew, as well as herbs and drugs. Bananas, too, were cultivated in the hot houses and the fruit sent to hospitals.

For many plant breeders, nurseries and market gardens, wartime requirements meant that cherished plants had to be uprooted, and many had to sell or destroy long-established breeding lines of roses and other plants in order to convert land to crop growing. They were only allowed to keep a small proportion of their available land and glasshouse space for the purpose of growing such plants so that they would be able to rebuild their businesses after the war. Rare collections could be kept, although growers of orchids, lilies and pot plants had to remove them from commercial glasshouses. If they did not, then they could be prosecuted and ordered to remove the offending plants. By the end of 1944, it was estimated that hardy nursery stock had been reduced by half compared to pre-war figures, and outdoor bulbs and flowers by three quarters. In order to comply with the government requirements, many nurserymen became very creative in their growing. Jennifer Davies in *The Wartime Kitchen and Garden* relates the story of a ministry inspector working in the Evesham area:

> Ron Sidwell remembered that during the war years flower growing was profitable and nurserymen could be wily…he used to encounter a glorious mixture of cabbage plants and asters along greenhouse benches, so much so that it was difficult to assess whether the amount of flowers complied with the restriction on their number or not! It was uneconomic in terms of officials' time to calculate the relative quantities of the two categories of plants, and game set and match to the grower. He also remembered a grower who was building up his stocks of gladioli for the cut-flower trade. In order to keep within the restricted acreage, the grower put corms closer and closer together. When eventually the restrictions were lifted, his acreage jumped fourfold.

Everyone was encouraged to be creative with space and not miss any potential opportunities. In due course, even bomb sites were turned into growing areas. Any vacant space near ARP or fire stations was quickly transformed. Climbing nasturtiums were grown over air raid shelters, as were strawberries and marrows. *The London Evening News* ran a series of columns suggesting how vegetables could be grown in very small areas such as 'window box salads. Beans on your Bedroom Sill. Tomatoes in Tubs'.

During one of his weekly radio programmes, Cecil Middleton commented that he believed much more could be done if areas worked together. He declared that 'In the urban and industrial areas, the allotment movement has grown to such an extent that in some places, the difficulty now is to find land to satisfy the demand, and some enthusiastic gardeners I know of have to travel long distances after the day's work to get to their allotment.' He argued that there was scope to identify derelict gardens and similar locations with odd plots of land 'which nationwide could amount to thousands of fertile areas.' It seems the authorities were not enforcing such use, even though they had the power to do so. He pointed out that the National Vegetable Marketing Company, operating under the aegis of the Ministry of Food, could buy onions and carrots from allotments and growers working on less than an acre of land if the combined produce weighed a tonne or more.

Detailed plans were widely distributed showing how to maximise production in gardens and allotments. The government frequently issued information leaflets containing such plans. People were encouraged to grow crops with names like potato Home Guard, Onward and Advance Guard Peas. As an extra incentive, numerous competitions were held offering certificates of merit to suitable entrants. Out of 10,000 potential competitors, just 4,000 met the required standard making it a cherished statement of quality. Anyone could buy a Digging for Victory badge, costing just 3d.

Vast quantities of literature were produced to provide ideas and information on every possible topic from beekeeping to chicken keeping. There was a booklet on the use of cloches with the title *Cloches v Hitler*. The National Federation of Women's Institutes published a *Gardener's Guide* targeting WI vegetable producers to grow more produce. National and regional newspapers included columns of gardening advice such as the *News Chronicle Vegetable Gardening* by Albert Gurie (costing just 7 pence). Magazines like *Amateur Gardening* published paperbacks such as *The War Time Greenhouse*. Oldham Press with its *How to Grow and Produce Your own Food* was just one of many publishers creating books to meet demand. Baker Nurseries of Wolverhampton issued *The Vegetable Growers Handbook*, which quickly proved to be a best seller, while the 1941 RHS manual *The Vegetable Garden Displayed* costing just 1 shilling sold over half a million copies and negotiations were soon underway to obtain more paper for reprints.

The government had established strict control over all aspects of production, including the provision of paper and printing and this impacted on the way in which the seed companies operated. Looking at the seed catalogues issued by R&A Taylor, the impact on its business is clearly seen. In 1940, it produced a consumer catalogue incorporating a glossy colour picture on the cover as well as black and white photographs inside. Anyone wanting to include some decorative colour and fragrance in the garden could do so with ease as the catalogue included a vast array of sweet peas, bulbs, lilies, ranunculus and ornamental grasses.

The following year, 1941, R&A Taylor's spring catalogue also incorporated a coloured image on the cover highlighting a range of vegetables on display as if in a horticultural show. Large quantities of flower seeds, annuals and pot herbs could be purchased alongside extensive vegetable ranges like thirty-two varieties of peas, eight tomato varieties and vegetable marrows.

By 1942 the situation was clearly getting harder. R&A Taylor had shrunk its catalogue to just sixteen pages. Although there was still a colour image on the front showing vegetable produce on display, there were gaps allowing the shelves behind to be seen. Consumers still had a good choice of seeds, with thirty-two types of peas, seven types of carrot, and eight varieties of tomatoes among the vegetable offer, as well as a couple of hundred varieties of flower seeds including ten types of wallflower and eight types of stocks.

Taylor's 1943 spring booklet had reduced still further in size to just eight pages, no illustrations, and only a little colour on the cover. Most of the focus was now on providing a wide range of vegetables such as thirty-two types of peas, fourteen types of broccoli, and twenty-five varieties of potato. The following year, all colour had been dropped in favour of a simple black and white cover and no illustrations inside. The range of seeds was from the previous year, laid out in neat lists. Very few garden sundries were available. Gardeners were definitely under pressure to produce as many vegetables as possible – a factor which impacted on seed demand since seed producers struggled to obtain sufficient seed to match order levels. Seed donations from overseas including America, Canada, Australia and New Zealand helped plug the gaps, with 90 tonnes of donated American seeds distributed among members of the National Allotment Society in 1943.

Costs could be minimised by joining forces with other gardeners, especially in horticultural societies. Cecil Middleton pointed out that a small horticultural society in the Midlands 'brought over £35 worth of small seeds wholesale, nearly seven tons of Scotch seed potatoes, and two or three tons of lime and other things.' He calculated that on these items alone 'members not only got their shilling subscription back, but were on average, two or three shillings in pocket on the deal.'

The government constantly called for householders to stop growing flowers or at least to substantially reduce the amount of space allotted to them. A typical call to action was that of Mr Hudson, Minister of Agriculture in 1940, who indicated that every household should turn a large section of their flower beds to vegetable growing. Despite this, people were still keen to grow flowers. Annual seed catalogues always included a selection of flower seeds ready for purchasing, even though quantities were lower. There were reports of air raid shelters being given a decorative, colourful touch with honeysuckle, ivy and periwinkle growing over them. Many suggestions were put forward to reconcile the demand for food production with the pleasures of flowers. Excavated flower bulbs were dropped into trenches, attractive herbs could be grown, and it was pointed out that some vegetables could be attractive in their own right, such as the purple leaves of beetroot, or the flowers of runner beans, while carrots had feathery foliage. In 1940, Steven Cheveley wrote in *A Garden Goes to War*:

> Our general plan will be to discard a large number of perennials and have fewer annuals. This will free the front half of each border for vegetables. The remaining perennials will be transferred to the back of the borders, so that one can imagine, next summer, dwarf vegetable crops against a background of flowering plants.

Writer E. Graham noted in 1940 that while 'green leafy vegetables, green salads, carrots, peas and potatoes – all are particularly important', it was essential to remember that the cheerfulness and colour provided by flowers helped boost morale. Visiting gardens like Kew were also popular as the 'ceaseless streams and large queues' indicated that people wanted calm and peace, and to enjoy the beauty of flowers providing an escape, albeit for a short time, from the pressures of wartime life.

Cecil Middleton pointed out in his radio programme in 1941 that people were still asking him for advice on growing rambler roses, dahlias, fuchsias, geraniums, hydrangeas and many other flowers. 'Why not a nice show of spring flowers? They can cheer us up wonderfully after a long dark winter.' He spoke frequently about the need to encourage flower growing because it was good for morale, and that even in wartime the pleasure of sowing even just a packet of hardy annuals and seeing them grow and bloom brought some joy into dark days.

For the same reason he defended the need to hold garden shows, although he recognised that it was not easy holding a garden show in wartime. There were many difficulties to overcome such as petrol restrictions and problems trying to arrange refreshments, acknowledging that 'many people maintain that a show is a waste of time, and that the men would be better employed in their gardens and allotments, that the expense is unjustified and that to introduce the holiday atmosphere is quite wrong and unpatriotic.'

But there were advantages and good reasons for holding a show. He noted that a horticultural show 'brings a bit of light and pleasure to what otherwise is a rather drab routine. We all know, the enormous value, the refreshing influence of ENSA concerts to the troops and the lunch-hour entertainments in the munitions factories, the local flower and vegetable show brings the same happy influence to the diggers for victory.'

Such shows were highly popular and a good way of generating funds for charities like the Red Cross. Recalling one show that he had been involved in organising, Middleton pointed out that:

> The Women's Institute members were overwhelmed by the hungry and thirsty and soon sold out what they had regarded as vast and impossible quantities…we sent £120 to the Red Cross Agricultural Fund and a lorry load of vegetables to the local Army unit, and fired all the gardening fraternity with so much enthusiasm that they are still talking about it and making plans for next year.

Any problems with regulations could be easily overcome, with Middleton advising people to 'invite the village policeman in and give him a pint of beer and all will be well.'

Chapter 17

Post-War Gardening and the Arrival of Garden Centres

The end of the Second World War resulted in yet more change taking place within UK gardens. Recruitment of women to work at Kew and other big gardens quickly ceased. Their numbers declined as men returned to civilian employment. Married women too tended to leave their employment – they were not expected to work outside the home.

The extensive bombing and resultant damage that occurred during the war resulted in another major housing programme. With millions of people rendered homeless, it was important to create homes as quickly as possible. Pre-fabricated standalone houses proved to be the perfect answer. These were single-storey buildings divided into rooms including bathrooms and kitchens complete with indoor toilets and facilities like hot running water. Constructed offsite, the buildings were brought on lorries to a newly cleared site, placed on pre-laid foundations and bolted together. All that remained was for the final interior work to be completed, which usually took just a few hours. Each pre-fab had its own small garden surrounding it, which was quickly filled with vegetables and fruit. Sheds were provided, although these were sometimes just Anderson shelters with bricked-up rear walls and a door at the front. New householders unfamiliar with gardening could seek help from the Women's Voluntary Service Garden Gift Scheme. Apart from providing advice, they also distributed donations of seeds, flowers, vegetable seedlings, shrubs, trees and hedging. The

Women's Voluntary Service also ran annual competitions offering a silver trophy presented by Queen Mary to the best prefab garden, while in 1947 Princess Elizabeth visited the prize-winning garden of Mr W.C. Bodger, a railway foreman.

Rationing and shortages combined to ensure that people continued to be encouraged to grow as much food as possible within their gardens. A government survey in 1948 estimated that 72 percent of households in England, Scotland and Wales now had their own garden or allotment, and many also had window boxes and lots of indoor plants. Homes became the centre of leisure activity especially among the working-class population, resulting in a focus on gardens as a space for leisure and the need to create an attractive environment. Visiting gardens was a way of collecting ideas. Between 1947 and 1955, the Chelsea Flower Show featured a Women's Voluntary Service replica pre-fab house designed to show visitors how to maximise produce from their pre-fab gardens. The displays were extremely popular, attracting considerable attention, and on one occasion, in 1949, the Queen Mother sheltered in the prefab during a rainstorm.

During lectures to Women's Institutes, Julia Clements used to tell her listeners: 'We can't get new curtains, we can't paint our house, we've got nothing…except flowers.' Flower arranging became a popular activity, with competitions being held in towns and villages nationwide. Special flower arranging societies emerged, leading ultimately to the creation of the National Association of Flower Arranging Societies, which had more members than the RHS. Garden open days held by flower arrangers like Sheila Macqueen were so popular that roads were jammed with cars.

As austerity slowly eased at the beginning of the 1950s, so gardens began to experience changes. While vegetable areas were still popular, gardeners were paying more attention to decorative planting, introducing brightly coloured flower borders surrounding neat lawns. As time went on, greenhouses, summer houses, pools and fountains appeared alongside children's swings and see-saws. The Festival of Britain in 1951 aimed to raise spirits and provide a cultural uplift, despite the austerity that was still prevalent. Gardens were much in evidence with special pleasure gardens set up along the South Bank, which included a wine garden surrounded by miniature pavilions and foaming fountains, while at Battersea Park, additional facilities included the creation of extensive flower gardens complete with a Grand Vista and Fountain Lake. Two years later, the sense of exuberance was reinforced by preparations for the coronation of Queen Elizabeth II. Many gardeners celebrated throughout the year with lots of red, white and blue plant combinations.

Gardening was no longer seen as primarily a male activity, either: women were now equally as keen and demand for information widened away from traditional subject matters like growing vegetables, and cultivation techniques to seek ideas on decorative planting. Specialist gardeners were asked all kinds of questions on the new *Gardener's Question Time* radio programme, while talks on subjects like plant collecting, botany and landscape design were much in demand.

Demand for televisions grew rapidly following the decision to televise the coronation. As more and more people experienced television programmes, and prices dropped, the number of households with televisions grew rapidly. Gardeners were among the first to benefit from the range of visual programmes being transmitted. In 1951, Percy Thrower made his first televisions appearance, and five years later, he became the host for the long-running BBC *Gardening Club*, although it did not originally involve a specific garden – the first programmes were actually filmed in a Birmingham-based former wrestling arena. Percy Thrower would talk about gardening, demonstrate techniques and planting styles within a pretty garden space, which was then totally dismantled at the end of the programme. This involved removing all the soil, all the plants, greenhouse and potting shed each time!

The use of artificial fertilisers and chemicals dominated garden practice, just as they had during the Second World War. It was seen as a way of ensuring high-volume cropping and abundant planting, but there were also signs of alternative attitudes taking root. Margery Fish, a key contributor to magazines like *Amateur Gardening* and *Popular Gardening*, was steadily encouraging her readers to pay attention to composting, and pointing out that by using compost there was no need to add lime each year.

Garden tourism and preservation of historic gardens grew equally quickly. People wanted to visit gardens and seek out ideas. Coach and train trips were popular, and car ownership was increasing. In 1947, Hidcote Manor became the first property taken on by the National Trust specifically for its garden, and was quickly followed by other locations like Nymans, Bodnant and Mount Stewart. In 1949, the Marquess of Bath decided to open Longleat House and grounds, recognising the sheer popularity of nearby sites like the show caves at Cheddar Gorge in attracting paying visitors. During its first year of being open to the public, it attracted 134,000 visitors. He was not alone identifying the potential profits that could be made. Owners of landed estates and historic houses newly returned to private ownership following requisition during the war saw visitor interest as a way of raising funds and helping keep their properties within their families. Around a million people visited stately homes and gardens around the country in 1951. Blenheim Palace was one of those locations that opened buildings and grounds to paying visitors, attracting 126,000 people, while 90,000 explored Longleat. Chatsworth, meanwhile, attracted 205,000 visitors in 1954. By 1956, approximately 250 historic estates were open to the public on a regular basis.

Many botanic gardens throughout the country began introducing new concepts and new garden styles in a bid to extend their activities and attract more visitors. At Cambridge Botanic Gardens, a large winter garden was created, along with a limestone rock garden. *Sport and Country Magazine* noted in 1957 that 'the garden is not only a teaching centre, an amenity for casual visitors and a living catalogue of plants for amateur gardeners and plant-lovers, but it also plays a part in the practical distribution of plant species.'

Watching and listening to garden programmes, reading magazines and visiting gardens meant that more and more people wanted to recreate styles, ideas and planting concepts in their own gardens. People were becoming more optimistic, seeking new ways of making their lives more exciting. There was much more consumer confidence resulting from increased employment opportunities, along with the end of rationing and desirable products appearing in shops. In 1957, Prime Minister Harold Macmillan told voters that 'we have never had it so good'. With incomes rising, people could afford to improve and wanted to do so quickly. These were gardeners who wanted plants to create rapid transformations rather than having to wait. The problem was that almost all plants had to be grown from seed or were supplied bare rooted and ordered months in advance.

A visit to the USA in search of ideas by Dorset-based nurseryman Edward Stewart provided the solution. His family had been operating a nursery in Dorset for many years but had been badly affected by the aftermath of the Second World War. The former RAF wartime pilot was offered an opportunity in 1955 to return a plane to Miami. Stewart had many contacts in America and exported plants across the Atlantic. As a result of those contacts, he had an inkling that something was happening regarding the way plants were being sold there. Being offered the opportunity to fly a plane over to the USA provided the ideal opportunity to discover more. Having delivered the plane, Stewart travelled by air to Atlanta, and eventually made his way by train up the west coast to Toronto, Canada, visiting various businesses along the way. This led him to discover the concept of garden centres; one stop shops that incorporated a large, undercover sales area selling all kinds of sundries, gifts, equipment and plants, as well as refreshments. He also discovered that plants were being grown and sold in containers, thus ensuring they were available all year round for people to take home and install instantly into their gardens.

Writing from his hotel in Toronto, Stewart told his family:

> I have a belief that it is time to separate the general propagation and growing side of the average British nursery from the sales side. A 'Centre' can be set up in a comparatively small area (an acre or two) and display prepared shrubs, trees, prepared pre-packed roses for customers to take away. Combined with sundries and as wide an interest as possible, a certain amount of self-service could be planned but here one must go with care (we are in England). Salesmen would concentrate on selling and foremen would stick at their proper jobs somewhere in the background. Here in Toronto a large nursery actually maintains a most successful sales depot in Montreal (350 miles away). A small depot placed some where there are new housing estates is the ideal, even if not for permanence or even the development of the area at Ferndown.

On returning to Britain, Stewart began to transform the family business by cutting into some of the propagation sheds and adjacent buildings to create an instant selling area. Thus, the first garden centre in Britain was formed. It proved very popular, and so Stewart set out to create the first, purpose-built garden centre nearby in Christchurch. An artist's concept drawing of both sites revealed the transformation being introduced and how it reflected the style of trading common in North America. The central covered retail area was surrounded by parking at the front, and lines of plant displays on the remaining three sides. The whole area was surrounded by a landscaped garden area, which visitors could explore and gain inspiration for their own gardens.

Admitting to a degree of nervousness, Edward Stewart started trading from the new premises in 1961, inviting Percy Thrower to undertake the opening ceremony. The results exceeded expectations as Edward's son, Martin, indicates:

> It was packed. Six thousand people clogged the roads as people came to see it and use it. They couldn't get enough of it. It was a bit higgledy piggledy inside, but on sale were a wide range of items like sundries, seeds, equipment, gifts and container-based plants that they could take away immediately. It also had the first ever coffee shop in a garden centre. There were nurserymen from all over the UK coming to see it. Harry Wheatcroft sent his two sons, both nurserymen to see it.

Quite apart from the retail concept, Stewarts had shown the way forward for the industry was through provision of plants in containers that people could instantly take home. Finding suitable containers had been a problem, with the company recycling used 'catering cans' from schools and hospitals. Edward Stewart's innovations had created a mass market for retailing and provision of plants and garden products and in doing so, saved their family business as well as countless others.

Even before that first purpose-built garden centre had opened, other nurseries had begun to utilise some of the ideas Stewarts were introducing. Nurserymen and retailers became frequent visitors to the Stewarts initial retail site. In Suffolk, Notcutts decided to relocate their Woodbridge town centre store to its nursery site, half a mile away. Opening in 1958, the new premises offered car parking available on site. It soon became popular with both local people and customers keen to travel further in order to spend an afternoon browsing the extensive range of plants that could be purchased immediately for use in the garden. The arrival of plastic plant pots made this even easier as they were less likely to be damaged when moving plants from one place to another.

The age of self-service retail and instant gardening gratification had begun.

Conclusion

As the 1950s drew to a close, many people were experiencing greater prosperity with increased wages, new work opportunities and lifestyle changes. Almost everyone was able to afford a car, and gardeners were able to spend more money and look more widely for plants and sundries. This was the dawn of a consumerist society, in which people wanted everything new. As the years progressed, this trend became even more apparent with traditional urban townscapes being ripped up and replaced with Brutalist concrete shopping centres and tower blocks. There was no sudden leap from thrift to prosperity, but rather an evolving situation. A post-industrial society emerged, with the loss of heavy industry devastating former industrial, mining and steel communities, while providing prosperity elsewhere. The financial crash of the late eighties caused problems, as did subsequent economic difficulties in subsequent decades.

Gardening was not exempt from these changes. The growth of consumerism brought with it demand for instant gratification: instant gardening that could be created quickly without waiting for plants to grow and develop. Cheap, inexpensive products were in demand and were replaced quickly as fashions changed. Plastic, which was cheap and lightweight, dominated this new consumerist style of gardening, while easily replaced bags of peat-based compost were purchased from garden centres rather than creating compost heaps at home. At the same time, mass produced chemicals were used to combat every plant problem from fungicides to insect killers.

The arrival of DIY superstore chains in the 1980s offered a new style of retailing for garden products. Instead of heading for the high street, car-owning customers would head to retail parks on the outskirts of urban areas, where everything from plants to conservatories, paint to plumbing could be purchased and taken home instantly. Many observers believed it would mark the end of independent high street retailers and garden centres. In reality, the impact of DIY superstores was far less than anticipated, as many independent stores and garden centres focused more on service, knowledge and high quality products. DIY stores only ever provided a limited range of plants, especially annuals, which could be sold at low prices. Gardeners seeking a wide range of plants, or specialist advice, continued to head for the plant nurseries and garden centres.

Garden makeover programmes such as *Ground Force* and *Garden Rescue* became popular, transforming outdoor spaces into stunning gardens within a short time. Instant gardens were very much in demand. Despite these changes in practice and retailing over the past decades, there has always a hardcore number of gardeners using their gardens and allotments to produce fruit and vegetables as well as flowers. Television programmes like *Gardeners' World* were popular with the public eagerly following the activities of gardeners like Percy Thrower, Peter Seabrook and Geoff Hamilton. Gardening magazines such as *BBC Gardeners' World*, *Garden News*, and *Kitchen Garden* remain widely popular. One popular title, *Amateur Gardening*, set up in 1884, has achieved the distinction of being the world's oldest continually published gardening magazine. It nearly closed in 2023 but was then taken over by Kelsey Media.

Garden tourism has flourished with ever increasing numbers of visitors flocking to historic and display gardens, as well as shows such as the RHS Chelsea Flower Show, the RHS Flower Show Tatton Court and the Hampton Court Flower Show. Almost 100 years since the launch of the National Garden Scheme, millions of pounds have been raised for charity by people opening up their private gardens to visitors.

Women have also steadily taken an ever-increasing share of the landscaping sector. In 1977, Beth Chatto won the first of ten consecutive Gold Medals at the RHS Chelsea Flower Show. Her book, *The Dry Garden*, published in 1978, became a best seller, highlighting the need to match plants to the appropriate soil and landscape, resulting in the creation of naturalistic planting and wildlife friendly gardens.

By far the biggest impact on modern UK gardening has been environmental issues, resulting in many aspects of gardening turning full circle, bringing about a revival of practices focusing on sustainability, while maintaining its role in food production, leisure and relaxation.

The campaign against peat extraction was one of the earliest impacts to be experienced in gardens. Between 1950 and 1990, thousands of acres of natural peat bogs in the UK had been destroyed forever by commercial extraction. In 1990 a campaign began to stop peat use, highlighting the fact that peat is a finite resource – once removed from its original site it cannot be replaced. Harvesting peat damages the environment, especially since it helps deal with water retention and acts as a carbon sink. It is a campaign that has proved successful. It took time, but by 2024 peat-based composts have been almost completely replaced by environmentally friendly non-peat alternatives. Today, even shows such as the RHS Chelsea Flower Show insist that designers use non-peat compost. Meanwhile, home composting has regained supremacy it once had.

Just like gardeners in the past, repair, recycling and reusing has now become the norm for gardeners today. More and more people are exploring ways of reusing items within gardens rather than simply throwing them away. At the RHS Flower Show Tatton Court, landscape designer Sophie Godber created an innovative sustainable display garden using a variety of recycled materials, including bicycle chains that had been turned into supports for climbing plants, while corrugated sheeting from a skip had been transformed into a tin wall.

The RHS is actively encouraging gardeners to adopt planet friendly gardening practices, highlighting the way in which every gardener can contribute towards capturing CO_2 emissions, reverse habitat destruction, encourage plant diversity, as well as protecting wildlife and pollinating insects. This approach was clearly evident in the 'Tomies Cuisine the Nobonsai' balcony display garden at the RHS Chelsea Flower Show in 2024, which highlighted water efficiency and permaculture, with lush planting allowing all creatures including fungi and micro-organisms to grow together.

Gardening is now much less influenced by fashion and major television shows. Although there has been a return to traditional chemical-free and plastic-free gardening, it is not a simple throwback to years gone by. Green roofs are becoming commonplace on top of garages, sheds and outdoor buildings. The advent of cheap solar lighting and outdoor cooking has meant that the garden is increasingly seen as an extra living room, particularly for small houses and flats. Garden furniture, especially vintage styles, has become a massive market. Changes in energy provision and global trade mean that the cost of food is increasing, resulting in gardeners focusing more on growing food such as salads and small crops that can be grown in containers within the smallest area. Sadly, climate change is already affecting gardens due to the longer periods of dryness, and more violent storms, floods and high winds. For twenty-first-century gardeners it is a time of challenge and transformation, just like gardeners of the nineteenth and twentieth centuries.

Resources

The Hidden Horticulturalists: the Untold Story of the Men who Shaped Britain's Gardens, Fiona Davison (Atlantic Books, 2019)
A Little History of British Gardening, Jenny Uglow (Chatto & Windus, 2004)
The History of Norfolk and Norwich Horticultural Society 1829-1929, compiled by Arthur W. Preston and John E.T. Pollard (1929)
The Model Village, Alexander Harvey (Batsford, 1906)
Digging for Victory: Wartime Gardening with Mr Middleton, C.H. Middleton (Aurum Press, 2008)
'The Allotment Movement in England 1793-1873', Jeremy Burchardt, *Studies in History Past & Present* (Boydella & Brewer Ltd., 2002)
From Plot to Pauper's Plate, John Devlin and Philip Jones Southwell (Workhouse 2006 (adapted 2011))
'"He shall have care of the garden, it's cultivation and produce": Workhouse Gardens and Gardening 1780-1835', Peter Collinge, *Journal for Eighteenth Century Studies* (Volume 44, March 2021)
An Economic History of the Garden, Roderick Floud (Allen Lane, 2019)
A History of Kitchen Gardening, Susan Campbell (Unicorn Publishing Group, 2015)
Swindled: From Poison Sweets to Counterfeit Coffee – The Dark History of the Food Cheats, Bee Wilson (John Murray, 2008)
The Electric Melon: Experiment in Electro-horticulture at Sherwood Park Tunbridge Wells, Kate Minnis (Kent Garden History, 2015)
The Gardens of the British Working Class, Margaret Willes (Yale University Press, 2015)
Suttons Seeds: A History 1806-2006, Earley Local History Group (2006)
Gardening Women: Their Stories from 1600 to the Present, Catherine Horwood (Virago Press, 2020)

Women on the Land: Their Story During Two World Wars, Carol Twinch (Lutterworth Press, 2021)
Life in the Gardeners' Bothy, Arthur Hooper (Malthouse Press, 2000)
The Head Gardener: Heroes of Horticulture, Toby Musgrave (Arum Press, 2007)
The Victorian Kitchen Garden, Jennifer Davies (BBC Books, 1987)
The Victorian Flower Garden, Jennifer Davies (BBC Books, 1991)
The Wartime Kitchen and Garden, Jennifer Davies (BBC Books, 1993)
'As the Houses, So the People; Gardeners: Their Accommodation and Remuneration 1800-1914', dissertation by Jonathan Denby (University of Buckingham, 2013)

Index

Accum, Friedrich 157
Abingdon Workhouse 167-8
Adulteration 125, 157, 159, 160
Allotments 8, 55, 98, 103, 174-82
Amateur Gardening Magazine 220, 228, 233
Apprentices 2, 4, 5, 7, 8, 14, 25, 46, 63, 217
Arts & Crafts Movement 68, 70, 78, 192
Audley End 5, 20, 24, 28
Austen, Jane 31, 49, 61, 186

Barron, James 113
Baxter, William 28
Becontree 203
Beeton, Mrs 34
Benevolent Institution for the Relief of Aged and Indigent Gardeners and their Widow 15, 29
Biddulph Grange vii, 76
Blaise Castle 50
Botanical gardens 14, 79, 92, 103, 141, 188-9, 197
Bournville 93
Bramley Apple 38
British Lawnmower Museum 147
Brockett Hall 3
Burchardt, Jeremy 179, 181, 192, 236
Burghley House 3
Burton, Mary Elizabeth 37

Cadbury 70, 92-3
Carpet bedding viii, 62, 67-8, 70-2, 90, 114, 126, 191
Carters Seeds 5, 119-20, 125
Catalogues 117-2, 124-5, 131,158, 198, 215, 221-2
Chatto, Beth 234
Chatsworth 2, 22-3, 151, 186-7, 190, 192, 228
Chelsea Flower Show 20, 33, 106, 204, 226, 233-5
Chiswick 5, 21, 28, 51, 99, 102, 116, 134-5
Christie, Ella vii, 42
Clare, John 3, 68
Cliveden 45, 72
Cochran, James 54, 112, 115-16

Coade artificial stone 159
Cobbett, William 10, 174
Commissions 27
Cockney carpet bedding 72, 90
Cook, Thomas 187
Cottage Gardener, The 32, 68, 130
Cottage gardening 67-70, 75, 100, 102, 104, 124, 130-2, 154, 174, 178, 181, 203-204, 213
Council houses 86, 201, 203, 212
Cragside 67
Cremorne Gardens 33
Cresswell, William 5
Crystal Palace 39, 104, 109, 152
Culpeper's 47-8
Culzean 28

Daily Mail, The 109, 204
Daniels Bros 105, 108, 119, 121-2, 124-5
Davison, Fiona 134, 236
Davies, Jennifer 71, 210, 219, 237
De Rothschild, Alice 36
Denby, Jonathan 26, 237
Dewstow Gardens 80, 151
Dickens, Charles 53, 75, 94, 167
Dig for Victory campaign 110, 214-15, 220, 224, 236
Duke of Devonshire 22-3, 26, 28

Earley History Group 16, 119-20, 212, 236
Edgeworth, Maria 31
Encyclopaedia of Gardening, The 4, 5, 7, 128, 205
Eyre, Jane 11

Farrer, Reginald 82
Festival of Britain 227
Fish, Margery 213, 228
First World War v, viii, 45-8, 95-6, 110, 120, 156, 160, 193-4, 196-9, 201, 207, 211, 214, 228
Florists' Association 57, 98, 100, 111
Floud, Roderick 32, 111, 236
Forrest, George 144
Friar Park 80, 86
Frogmore 28, 34, 64

Garden centres 229, 231-3
Garden City Association 94, 98
Gardeners' Chronicle, The 7, 9, 13, 15, 72, 76, 81-2, 104, 107, 115, 129, 148, 156, 157, 159, 197, 217, 220
Gardener's Magazine, The 105, 125, 127-30, 132
Gardeners' Question Time 227
Garden Museum London 20
Garden shows 74, 97-111, 163, 182, 189, 204, 208, 223-4, 233-5
Gardeners' Royal Benevolent Institution 29
Gavin, Hector 56
Glasshouses 45, 66-7, 91, 142, 151-2, 154, 172, 187, 189, 197, 211, 219
Glynde College for Lady Gardeners 41
Gnomes 82-6, 203
Gott, J. 4
Graham, Maria 141
Great Exhibition, The 23, 115, 152
Great Stove 23, 151, 187
Gressenhall Farm and Workhouse Museum 146, 167, 172
Grieve, Maud 47

Handa, Taki 43
Hampstead Garden Suburb 43, 95
Hawkstone 185
Herb Society, The 47
Hibberd, Shirley 53, 61, 130
Holkham Hall 6, 19, 38, 50, 58, 63
Hooker, Joseph Dalton Hooker 137-8
Horticultural Trades Association 27
Hothouses 3, 65, 153, 211, 218
Housing & Town Planning Act 1909 95
Howard, Ebenezer 84, 203
Howitt, William 55

Isham, Sir Charles 82, 83, 84, 85, 86
Instructions on Gardening for Ladies 31

Japanese Garden vii, 42-3, 91
Jekyll, Gertrude viii, 30, 37, 68, 74-5, 79
Johnson, George William 68
Journeymen 2, 5, 25, 63
Journal of Horticulture, The 20, 45, 71, 83, 130

Kelmscott Manor 79
Kew Gardens 40, 106, 127, 131, 137, 139-40, 142-5, 153, 189, 215-16, 218, 223, 225
Kewriosity poem 40

Lady Warwick College 41
Ladies Companion to the Flower Garden 43, 44, 71, 76, 129
Ladies' Magazine of Gardening 35
Lamport Hall 83, 86
Land Army 45, 197, 198, 201, 214
Land Girls 198
Layel, Hilda 47, 48
Lawes, John Bennet 155
Lawnmowers viii, 146-8, 212
Lawrence, Louisa 35
Lever Brothers 92
Lindsay, Norah 45
Loddiges of London 118, 127, 136, 187
London Horticultural Society 5, 7, 99, 102, 106, 128
London Labour and the London Poor 12, 126
London Season 32, 54, 88
Loudon, Jane viii, 10, 30-1, 42-3, 71, 76, 80, 129
Loudon, John Claudius 1, 4-5, 10, 14, 30, 50, 57, 89, 111, 127, 129, 132, 164, 189
Lutyens, Edwin 37

Marryat, Charlotte 35
Mass observation 217
Mavisbank 24
Mayhew, Henry 12, 128
McCulloch, William 5
Mechanic's Institute 9
Metropolitan Public Gardens Association 39
Middleton, Cecil H 214, 219, 222-3
Moggeridge, John 57
Morris, William 68, 78-9
Moser, Mary 34

Nash, John 50
National Gardens Scheme 194, 233
National Federation of Women's Institutes 220
National Trust, The 191-2, 194-5, 228
New Earswick 93, 95
Norfolk & Norwich Horticultural Society 100-102, 104, 106, 110
North, Marianne 142
Nottcutts 212, 231

Open Spaces 86, 88
Osborne House 11, 30

Parks viii, 14, 51, 72, 87-9, 91, 94, 131, 183, 188, 197, 199, 206, 212, 216, 233
Paxton, Joseph viii, 1, 15, 21-3, 26, 29, 89, 128-9, 149, 151-4, 187

Peters, William 26
Pharmacy & Medicines Bill 48
Port Sunlight 92
Potter, Beatrix 34
Pratt, Anne 44
Pre-Raphaelites 78
Prevention of Corruption Bill 27
Prince Albert 11, 19, 23, 65-6, 106, 122
Pulhamite 80, 89, 150, 151

Queen Victoria 11, 23, 28, 36, 44, 63, 65, 72, 90, 122, 142, 151, 187, 189

Reading University 41
Repton, Humphrey 49
Rivers, Thomas 112
Robinson, William 42, 68, 79, 131
Rockeries 61, 79, 80, 86, 89, 149, 150, 190, 206, 212
Rolleston Hall 3
Rose Gardens 73-4, 48
Rothamsted Experimental Station 155-6
Rowntree, Joseph 92-3
Royal Botanic Garden, Edinburgh 8, 140, 145
Royal Holloway College, Egham 34
Royal Horticultural Society 8, 38, 108, 150, 180
RHS Chelsea 20, 10, 226, 233-5
RHS Tatton Court 233-4
Royal Parks 87-8, 131, 216
Rural Life in England 55

Sackville-West, Vita viii, 47, 194, 205, 213
Sander, Frederick 'the Orchid King' 142
Sanitary Rambling 56
Scotland vii, 5, 24, 26, 28, 37, 43, 98, 113, 116, 120, 226
Second World War v, 48, 110, 214-15, 217, 219, 221, 223, 225, 228-9
Sissinghurst 48, 194-5, 213
Smallholdings and Allotment Act 182
Southwell workhouse 169-71, 236
Spencer sweet peas 25
Spry, Constance 213

Stagenhoe Park 19, 20, 24
Stewart, Edward 229-31
Stewarts 231
Stowe Landscape Gardens 150, 183
Studeley College 8
Stumperies viii, 76, 78
Suffragettes 45
Super phosphate 155
Surrey County Council 11, 205
Suttons Seeds viii, 10, 12-13, 16, 107, 114-15, 118-20, 122, 133, 159-60, 198-9, 211-12, 236
Swanley Horticultural College 8, 39-40, 46, 48, 197

Taylor, R & A 118, 169, 199, 215, 221
Thompson, Flora 177
Thrower, Percy 227, 230, 233
Times, The 32-3, 64-5, 181
Tyntesfield 73, 155

Utility Designs Act 149
Uglow, Jenny 173, 236

Victorian Flower Garden, The 71, 237

Waddesdon 36, 151
Wardian case 136-7, 140-1, 144
Whately, Thomas 184
Window Box Gardening 11, 46, 74, 76, 206, 208, 226
Windsor 19, 63-4, 118, 170, 209
Williams v Leslie 26, 27
Willes, Margaret 70, 88, 97, 202, 236
Wilmott, Ellen 30
Wolseley, Frances Garnet 41
Women's Agricultural and Horticultural Union 42, 46
Women's Farm and Garden Association 46
Workhouses 14-15, 62, 73, 116, 118, 146, 162-73, 236
Wordsworth, William 60
Wright, John 11, 132